TI

THE GRAND
CANYON

Rough Guides online
www.roughguides.com

Rough Guide Credits

Text editor: Chris Barsanti
Series editor: Mark Ellingham
Production: Andy Turner, John McKay
Cartography: Maxine Repath,
Katie Lloyd-Jones and Ed Wright

Publishing Information

This first edition published May 2003
by Rough Guides Ltd,
80 Strand, London WC2R 0RL

Distributed by the Penguin Group:

Penguin Books Ltd, 80 Strand, London WC2R 0RL
Penguin Putnam, Inc., 375 Hudson Street, New York 10014, USA
Penguin Books Australia Ltd, 487 Maroondah Highway,
PO Box 257, Ringwood, Victoria 3134, Australia
Penguin Books Canada Ltd, 10 Alcorn Avenue,
Toronto, Ontario, Canada M4V 1E4
Penguin Books (NZ) Ltd,
182–190 Wairau Road, Auckland 10, New Zealand

Typeset in Bembo and Helvetica to an original design by Henry Iles.
Printed in Spain by Graphy Cems.

© Greg Ward 2003
336pp, includes index
A catalogue record for this book is available from the British Library.

ISBN 1-84353-052-X

THE ROUGH GUIDE TO

THE GRAND CANYON

by Greg Ward

ROUGH
GUIDES

We set out to do something different when the first Rough Guide was published in 1982. Mark Ellingham, just out of university, was travelling in Greece. He brought along the popular guides of the day, but found they were all lacking in some way. They were either strong on ruins and museums but went on for pages without mentioning a beach or taverna. Or they were so conscious of the need to save money that they lost sight of Greece's cultural and historical significance. Also, none of the books told him anything about Greece's contemporary life – its politics, its culture, its people, and how they lived.

So with no job in prospect, Mark decided to write his own guidebook, one which aimed to provide practical information that was second to none, detailing the best beaches and the hottest clubs and restaurants, while also giving hard-hitting accounts of every sight, both famous and obscure, and providing up-to-the-minute information on contemporary culture. It was a guide that encouraged independent travelers to find the best of Greece, and was a great success, getting shortlisted for the Thomas Cook travel guide award, and encouraging Mark, along with three friends, to expand the series.

The Rough Guide list grew rapidly and the letters flooded in, indicating a much broader readership than had been anticipated, but one which uniformly appreciated the Rough Guide mix of practical detail and humor, irreverence and enthusiasm. Things haven't changed. The same four friends who began the series are still the caretakers of the Rough Guide mission today: to provide the most reliable, up-to-date and entertaining information to independent-minded travelers of all ages, on all budgets.

We now publish more than 200 titles and have offices in London and New York. The travel guides are written and researched by a dedicated team of more than 100 authors, based in Britain, Europe, the USA and Australia. We have also created a unique series of phrasebooks to accompany the travel series, along with an acclaimed series of music guides, and a best-selling pocket guide to the Internet and World Wide Web. We also publish comprehensive travel information on our website: www.roughguides.com

Help us update

We've gone to a lot of trouble to ensure that this Rough Guide is as up to date and accurate as possible. However, things do change. All suggestions, comments and corrections are much appreciated, and we'll send a copy of the next edition (or any other Rough Guide if you prefer) for the best letters.

Please mark letters "**Rough Guide Grand Canyon Update**" and send to:

Rough Guides, 80 Strand, London WC2R 0RL or
Rough Guides, 4th Floor, 345 Hudson St, New York NY 10014.

Or send an email to mail@roughguides.com
Have your questions answered and tell others about your trip at
www.roughguides.atinfopop.com

Acknowledgments

Thanks as ever to Sam Cook, for the fun of it all, and her sustaining love and support through a hard year back home; to my mother; and to everyone at Rough Guides, above all to Chris Barsanti for his tenacious and constructive editing, Andrew Rosenberg for his faith in the project, and Maxine Repath, Katie Lloyd-Jones and Ed Wright for the maps. I also owe a great deal of thanks to all those who helped with my research at the canyon, especially Mona Mesereau, Bruce Brossman, and Missy Ecijia at Xanterra; Mike Buchheit of the Grand Canyon Field Institute; Jerry Thull of the Grand Canyon Railway; and Don Donohue of Scenic Airlines.

Cover credits

Main front photo Colorado River ©Getty
Front small picture Cactus ©Stone
Top back picture Bald eagle ©Stone
Lower back picture North Rim ©Stone

CONTENTS

CONTENTS

MAP LIST

Map Symbols

— ·· —	State boundary	✉	Post office
50	Interstate	✚	Hospital
50	US highway	P	Parking
41	State highway	T	Toilets
··········	Unpaved/dirt road	⊠	Gate
———	Other road	♦	Point of interest
T10	Recommended hiking trail	✗	Airport
— · —	Railway	⌂	Lodge
———	River	⌂	Ranger station
▲	Peak	⚡	Ski area
⌂⌂	Mountain range	∴	Ruins
↯	Overlook	▨	Building
⚘	Waterfall	▨	Forest
⋀⋀	Spring	▨	Beach
≋	Rapids	▨	Indian reservation
⚠	Campground	▨	National monument/ park
ⓘ	Infomation office		

Introduction

Although almost five million people come to see the **Grand Canyon of the Colorado** every year, it seems to remain beyond the grasp of the human imagination. No photograph, no set of statistics, can prepare you for such overwhelming vastness. At more than one mile deep, it's an inconceivable abyss; varying in its central stretch from four to eighteen miles wide, it's an endless expanse of bewildering shapes and colors, glaring desert brightness and impenetrable shadow, stark promontories and soaring never-to-be-climbed sandstone pinnacles.

While no one is disappointed with their first stunning sight of the chasm, visitors often find themselves struggling to understand what can appear as a remote and impassive spectacle. They race frantically from viewpoint to viewpoint, constantly imagining that the next one will be the "best," the place from which the whole thing finally makes sense. This book is an attempt to guide you beyond that initial anxiety. More than anything, it's aimed at encouraging you to slow down, to appreciate whatever small portion of the canyon may be displayed in front of you at any one moment, and to allow enough time for the bigger picture to develop. You don't have to learn the names of all those buttes and mesas – dubbed Shiva Temple, Wotan's Throne and so on in a spate of late-Victorian fervor – and you may not ever be able to identify all the different rock strata or desert plants. The longer you spend at the canyon, however, the greater the chance that you will start to hear it speak.

Back in the 1920s, the average visitor would stay at the canyon for two or three weeks. These days, two or three hours is more typical, of which perhaps forty minutes are spent actually looking at the canyon. That's partly because most people now arrive by **car**. As the only part of the canyon you can reach in a car is the **rim**, seeing the canyon has thus come to mean seeing it from above, from a distance. If you really want to engage with the canyon, however, you need literally to get into it – to **hike** or ride a **mule** down the many inner-canyon trails, to sleep in the backcountry campgrounds or in the cabins at **Phantom Ranch** on the canyon floor, to **raft** through the whitewater rapids of the river itself.

Mapping and defining precisely what constitutes the "Grand Canyon" has always been controversial; **Grand Canyon National Park** covers a relatively small proportion of the greater Grand Canyon area. Only since 1975 has the park included the full 277-mile length of the Colorado River from Lees Ferry in the east to Grand Wash Cliffs near Lake Mead in the west, and even now for most of that distance it's restricted to the narrow strip of the inner gorge. Ranchers whose animals graze in the federal forests to either side, mining companies eager to exploit the mineral wealth hidden in the ancient rocks, engineers seeking to divert the river to feed the deserts of southern Arizona, and Native Americans who have lived in the canyon since long before the first Europeans reached North America, have combined to minimize the size of the park.

The vast majority of visitors arrive at the **South Rim** – it's much easier to get to, there are far more facilities (mainly at **Grand Canyon Village**, inside the park), and it's open all year round. Another lodge and campground are

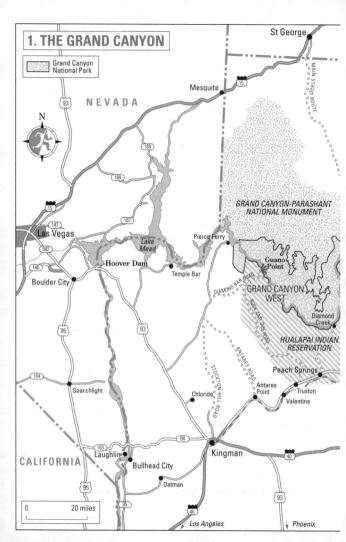

located at the **North Rim**, which by virtue of its isolation can be a lot more atmospheric, but at a thousand feet higher this entire area is usually closed by snow from mid-October until mid-May. On both rims, the main activity for most visitors consists of gazing over the gorge from **overlooks** placed at strategic intervals along the canyon-edge roads. Both also serve as the starting points for countless **hiking trails** down into the canyon, and it's even possible to hike

THINGS NOT TO MISS

With so many things to see and do in the Grand Canyon area, it's sometimes difficult to plan your day. Here's a quick list of some of the most popular and worthwhile sites in the region.

Toroweap Point The remotest major overlook within the national park, at the far west end of the North Rim, is perched above sheer 3000-foot cliffs and offers unique and extraordinary views into the Inner Gorge. See p.136

El Tovar Hotel The jewel of Grand Canyon Village, this historic hotel provides the South Rim's best food and lodging. See p.56

Condors at the South Rim The majestic silhouette of a Californian condor, soaring on its nine-foot wings above the canyon, makes an unforgettable spectacle. See p.55

Havasu Falls Hikers who make the trek down into the Havasupai reservation are rewarded with the astonishing sight of lush turquoise waterfalls buried deep within the canyon. See p.186

Desert View Watchtower Circular mock-Puebloan tower, blending into the rocks at the east end of the South Rim, that harks back to the golden years of western tourism while still providing stunning views. See p.77

all the way from one to the other, along the so-called Corridor Trails, which takes a minimum of two days from rim to rim.

Simply to drive from one rim to the other takes 215 miles, while to complete a loop around the entire national park would require you to drive almost eight hundred miles, and pass as far west as Las Vegas, Nevada. Even that long haul would miss out several of the most interesting

The North Rim Campground The most spacious, least-crowded and generally nicest of the national-park campgrounds, in a lovely wooded setting above a dramatic side canyon. See p.86

The Bright Angel Trail It's the most popular hiking trail within the park precisely because it provides such a superb introduction to life below the rim. See p.213

Flagstaff Much the liveliest and most appealing of the gateway towns, this high-desert crossroads remains redolent of the Wild West. See p.146

The South Kaibab Trail Even if you don't make the entire hair-raising descent to the bottom of the canyon, this trail offers perhaps the finest day-hikes into the canyon. See p.219

Cape Royal Thrusting south from the tip of the North Rim's Walhalla Plateau, Cape Royal is the perfect vantage point from which to appreciate the overall shape of the canyon. See p.98

Lees Ferry This atmospheric little outpost, the launching point for all Grand Canyon rafting trips, has an fascinating and romantic history of its own. See p.112

detours in the greater Grand Canyon region, into the baffling checkerboard of federal, state, Indian and private lands that lies beyond the boundaries of the park. These include several **national monuments**, including two huge ones created in 2000, **Vermilion Cliffs** and **Grand Canyon–Parashant**; a couple of **national recreation areas** at either end, **Glen Canyon** and **Lake Mead**; two sections of the **Kaibab National Forest**, north and south of the river; and four neighboring **Indian reservations**, belonging to the **Havasupai**, the **Hualapai**, the **Kaibab Paiute** and the **Navajo**. While most (though not quite all) provide recreational possibilities for visitors, detailed throughout this book, few offer any kind of accommodation or other facilities. For that, you need to call in instead at the many gateway towns on all sides of the canyon, from **Flagstaff** and **Williams** in the south, to **Kanab** in the north.

CLIMATE

The **climate** at the Grand Canyon varies with both the **season** and the **altitude**. Although most people picture the canyon as being in barren desert, in fact both the north and south rims are set in cool, high forests. The **North Rim**, the higher of the two at eight thousand feet, receives so much snow that it's completely cut off all winter, typically between late October and early May. Nights there remain distinctly chilly at the start and end of each season, and only between June and August do normal daytime temperatures rise above 70°F (21°C).

The **South Rim** is a thousand feet lower, which makes enough of a difference for the visitor facilities to remain open year-round. Temperatures still drop well below freezing at night between late October and April, however, so driving conditions can be treacherous, with occasional road

THE GRAND CANYON IN FIGURES

* The total length of the Colorado River is 1450 miles; within the Grand Canyon it measures 277 miles, from Lees Ferry to the Grand Wash Cliffs.

* The river is on average 300 feet wide and 40 feet deep, and its temperature remains at 48°F year-round.

* Grand Canyon National Park measures 1904 square miles or 1.2 million acres; that's roughly half the size of Yellowstone National Park, a third the size of Death Valley National Park, and a tenth the size of the largest US park, Wrangell-St Elias in Alaska.

* The canyon averages ten miles across and one mile deep. Its narrowest point is in Marble Canyon, at 600 feet wide, while the maximum width from rim to rim is eighteen miles.

* The highest point on the North Rim, Point Imperial, is 8803 feet high; on the South Rim it's Navajo Point, at 7498 feet. The elevation at Phantom Ranch, on the central canyon floor, is 2400 feet, while at the west end of the canyon, at Lake Mead, it's 1200 feet.

closures, and the upper portions of hiking trails may be dangerously icy. Only between May and September can you expect daytime highs above 70°F (21°C).

The **Inner Canyon** is a very different proposition. At river level, almost five thousand feet below the South Rim, thermometer readings in excess of 100°F (38°C) are recorded on most days between late May and early September, and it's unlikely to drop below 70°F (21°C) even at night. Winter temperatures are a little cooler than you might expect, because so little direct sun manages to reach the bottom of the canyon, but it very seldom freezes down there, and December highs remain well over 50°F (10°C).

CLIMATE CHART

	Jan	Feb	March	April	May	June	July	Aug	Sept	Oct	Nov	Dec
South Rim												
High (°F)	41	45	51	60	70	81	84	82	76	65	52	43
Low (°F)	18	21	25	32	39	47	54	53	47	36	27	20
Precipitation (inches)	1.32	1.55	1.38	0.93	0.66	1.81	1.81	2.25	1.56	1.10	0.94	1.64
Inner canyon												
High (°F)	56	62	71	82	92	101	106	103	97	84	68	57
Low (°F)	36	42	48	56	63	72	78	75	69	58	46	37
Precipitation (inches)	0.68	0.75	0.79	0.47	0.36	0.84	0.84	1.40	0.97	0.65	0.43	0.87
North Rim												
High (°F)	37	39	44	53	62	73	77	75	69	59	46	40
Low (°F)	16	18	21	29	34	40	46	45	39	31	24	20
Precipitation (inches)	3.17	3.22	2.65	1.73	1.17	1.93	1.93	2.85	1.99	1.38	1.48	2.83

Precipitation is seldom severe enough to spoil a visit; the greatest risk of heavy rain comes in August, when afternoon thunderstorms sweep in (and can create localized flash floods), but they're spectacular to watch and normally blow over fast. However, it has to be said that at any time of year you may turn up and find the canyon invisible beneath a layer of **cloud** or **fog**, a problem exacerbated by the sulfurous emissions pumped out by the Navajo Generating Station, seventy miles upriver at Page.

WHEN TO GO

There's no definitive answer as to which is the **best season to visit**. Summer on the South Rim can be murderously crowded and, for hikers especially, uncomfortably hot, so if you have the choice, and you plan to spend a lot of time out on the trails, spring and fall are preferable. That's less of an issue on the North Rim, which receives far fewer visitors, and stays significantly cooler. In winter, the scope for outdoor activities is greatly reduced, and the North Rim is closed altogether, but the South Rim is transformed into a haven of peace and tranquility. In terms of **aesthetics**, the canyon can look radiant, flecked with snow, on a crisp winter's day; alive with color when the cactuses and wildflowers blossom in the spring; and suffused with a golden glow in fall, as the trees close to rim level start to turn.

WHAT TO BRING

Whatever time of year you visit, you can expect to need **warm clothing**, especially for the evenings, and something **waterproof** to keep off sudden rains. Temperatures vary so much, and so rapidly, that it makes sense to dress in layers. Detailed advice on what to bring if you're **hiking** appears on p.210, and if you're **rafting** on p.253. Otherwise, if you're touring by car, and just sightseeing without strenuous physical activity, no specialist equipment is necessary. Be sure, however, that you have adequate protection from the **sun**, including a broad-brimmed hat, sunblock and sunglasses.

BASICS

Getting to the Grand Canyon

lmost all the independent travelers who visit the Grand Canyon **drive** there. Public transport to the South Rim is minimal, while to the North Rim it's virtually non-existent. You can only arrive by **plane** or **train** if you're prepared to pay an expensive excursion fare, from Las Vegas or Williams respectively, and while there is limited **bus** service up from both Flagstaff and Williams to the South Rim, it's not easy to tour the park as a whole unless you have your own vehicle.

DRIVING

Most drivers approach the Grand Canyon by means of the **I-40** interstate, which on its east–west route between New Mexico and southern California passes south of the canyon through both **Flagstaff** and **Williams**. From Flagstaff, **US-180** takes around eighty miles to wind through the San Francisco Peaks and up to the **South Rim**; **AZ-64** meets it en route, to make a total drive of sixty miles between Williams and the South Rim. Drivers from southern

Arizona can reach Flagstaff by taking I-17 north from
Phoenix.

**For a look at the routes leading to and from the
Grand Canyon, see map 1.**

It's also possible to get to the South Rim from the east,
by taking AZ-64 for fifty miles west from **US-89** at
Cameron. That's the obvious way to come if you've been
exploring southern Utah or the Four Corners region, and
it's also the most direct route from the North Rim.

The North Rim is much more isolated. The only way to
get there is via **Jacob Lake**, which stands on **US-89A** 92
miles southeast of the I-15 interstate between Las Vegas and
Salt Lake City – **St George**, Utah, is the nearest town on
the interstate – or roughly eighty miles southwest of **Page**,
Arizona. The final 44 miles south from Jacob Lake to the
North Rim are on **AZ-67**; when that's closed by snow,
which it usually is from sometime between October and
December until early May each winter, all facilities at the
North Rim shut down.

BY AIR

Grand Canyon National Park is a long drive from either of
the two closest major **airports**, in **Phoenix**, Arizona, and
Las Vegas, Nevada. Phoenix is 220 miles from the South
Rim, by way of Flagstaff, or 345 miles from the North Rim
via Flagstaff and Navajo Bridge. Las Vegas is 285 miles from
the North Rim, via St George, and 290 miles from the
South Rim, via Kingman and Williams. There is a small
airport just south of the South Rim, at **Tusayan**, but it's
served almost exclusively by sightseeing flights from Las
Vegas (see p.10). None of the national airlines provides
through service to Tusayan.

AIRLINES IN NORTH AMERICA

Air Canada ☏ 1-888/247–2262,
Ⓦ www.aircanada.ca

Aloha ☏ 1-800/367-5250,
Ⓦ www.alohaairlines.com

American Airlines ☏ 1-800/433-7300,
Ⓦ www.aa.com

American Trans Air ☏ 1-800/435-9282,
Ⓦ www.ata.com

Continental ☏ 1-800/523-3273,
Ⓦ www.continental.com

Delta ☏ 1-800/221-1212,
Ⓦ www.delta.com

Hawaiian ☏ 1-800/367-5320,
Ⓦ www.hawaiianair.com

Northwest ☏ 1-800/225-2525,
Ⓦ www.nwa.com

Scenic ☏ 1-800/634-6801,
Ⓦ www.scenic.com

Southwest ☏ 1-800/435-9792,
Ⓦ www.iflyswusa.com

TWA ☏ 1-800/221-2000,
Ⓦ www.twa.com

United ☏ 1-800/241-6522,
Ⓦ www.ual.com

BY RAIL

The nearest that **Amtrak trains** come to the South Rim are the stations at **Flagstaff** and **Williams**. In summer, westbound services, from Chicago via Albuquerque, stop at Flagstaff at 9.21pm and Williams Junction at 10.04pm daily, while eastbound trains, from Los Angeles, halt at Williams Junction at 4.35am and Flagstaff at 5.10am daily. Winter times are one hour later. Bus connections are detailed below.

From a separate station in the heart of Williams, the historic **Grand Canyon Railway** (☏ 928/773-1976 or 1-800/843-8724, Ⓦ www.thetrain.com), which is operated by **steam trains** in summer, runs a daily service up to the South Rim. Though it's more of a themed Western attraction than an efficient means of public transport – and thus charges round-trip fares that range from $55 up to $140 –

you don't have to travel both ways on the same day, so you can use it to enable a multi-night stay at the canyon. For full details, see p.31.

BY BUS

Regular Greyhound **buses** ply the I-40 corridor south of the canyon, heading east from Las Vegas, Los Angeles, and San Francisco and west from Albuquerque and beyond (℡1-800/231-2222, ⓦwww.greyhound.com). The closest stops to the canyon are also at **Williams** and **Flagstaff**.

Two daily buses in each direction, operated by Open Road Tours and Transportation (℡928/226-8060 or 1-800 /766-7117, ⓦwww.openroadtours.com), connect Flagstaff and Williams with the **South Rim**; fares and timetables are detailed on p.32. The route begins at Flagstaff's Amtrak station, and goes via the Grand Canyon Railroad Depot in Williams and the IMAX theater in Tusayan, to the Maswik Transportation Center in Grand Canyon Village. Open Road also runs four daily buses between Flagstaff and **Phoenix**, a route also served by Northern Arizona Shuttle (℡928/773-4337 or 1-866/870-8687, ⓦwww.nazshuttle .com).

The only scheduled bus service – or indeed public transportation of any kind – to the **North Rim** is the Transcanyon Shuttle, a daily van service along the 215-mile route between the North and South rims. For more details, see p.105.

TOURS

Although many national **tour companies** include the Grand Canyon on their Western-US itineraries, almost all simply stop for an hour or two on one rim or the other, with most preferring the South Rim. For anyone interested enough in exploring the canyon to have bought this book, none of these companies is worth recommending.

However, local operators based in several nearby towns run day-trips and longer excursions to different parts of the canyon. Alternatives, all detailed in the appropriate town accounts later in the book, include Canyon Country Out-Back Tours (☏1-888/783-3807, Ⓦwww.ccobtours.com), and Canyon Rim Adventures (☏1-800/897-9633, Ⓦwww.canyonrimadventures.com), both in **Kanab** (see p.130); Marvelous Marv's Tours (☏928/635-4061, Ⓦwww.marvelousmarv.com) from **Williams** (see p.164); and two independent hostels in **Flagstaff**, the *DuBeau International Hostel* (☏928/774-6731 or 1-800/398-7112; see p.150) and the *Grand Canyon International Hostel* (☏928/779-9421 or 1-888/442-2696, Ⓦwww.grandcanyonhostel.com; see p.150).

For true expert guidance, and an initiation into the canyon backcountry, by far the best option is to take a guided hiking trip with the **Grand Canyon Field Institute** (☏928/638-2485, Ⓦwww.grandcanyon.org/fieldinstitute), whose superb program of inexpensive tours is detailed on p.211.

Transport, tours and fees

The only part of the Grand Canyon that it is possible to visit using **public transport** is the **South Rim**. In fact, the park service would much prefer you not to bring your car, and **hikers** in particular can happily stay several days on the South Rim without feeling the need of one. As detailed on p.36, **free shuttle buses** link the various lodges and other facilities of **Grand Canyon Village**; run west to several viewpoints along **Hermit Road**; and also head east to **Yaki Point**, the trailhead for the South Kaibab Trail. In addition, there's a cheap bus service between **Tusayan** and Grand Canyon Village (see p.32), and commercial tour buses operate the 52-mile round trip out to **Desert View**.

However, if you're hoping to explore any of the other places covered in this book, there's little choice but to **drive**. That's the only way you're going to get to stop at the various halts on the "road between the rims," covered in Chapter Three; to admire the views from all the North Rim lookouts detailed in Chapter Two; to see the stunning overlook at Toroweap, in Chapter Four; or to reach the remote Havasupai reservation, in Chapter Six.

For those who don't live near enough to the canyon to bring their own vehicles, the best places in the Grand Canyon region to **rent a car** are major airports like those at Las Vegas and Phoenix. In addition, **Flagstaff** has several rental outlets (see p.149), and there's also a summer-only one at **Tusayan** airport, close to the South Rim (see p.33).

While the main roads up to the South Rim from I-40 are busy and well maintained, there may be times when you find yourself driving in very empty **desert**. Be sure to have two gallons of water per person in the car, and you should ideally also carry flares, matches, a first-aid kit and a compass, plus a shovel, air pump and extra gas. Take care driving at **night**; much of the country around the Grand Canyon is open range land, and livestock can wander onto unlit roads. If the car's engine **overheats**, don't turn it off; instead, try to cool it quickly by turning the air conditioning off and the heating up full blast. If you have car problems, it's best to stay with your vehicle, as you'll be harder to find wandering around alone. Note that most roads in the vicinity of the canyon are too remote for **cell phones** to pick up a signal; satellite phones are somewhat more reliable.

For a recorded message about **road conditions** and weather information in the Grand Canyon region, call ☏ 928/638-7888; for Arizona as a whole, call ☏ 1-888/411-7623.

Cycling can make an enjoyable complement to driving, especially as the South Rim roads that are closed to private vehicles remain open to cyclists, but the logistical problems of touring solely by bike in desert conditions, where it can be sixty miles between even the tiniest settlements, defeat all the but the very hardiest of adventurers. Many visitors bring bicycles as well as cars, and use them for exploring park roads, but all trails in the national park are closed to bikes.

FLIGHT-SEEING TOURS

Air tours of the Grand Canyon operate from two main bases – **Tusayan**, close to the South Rim, where, despite its small size, the airport ranks as the second busiest in Arizona, and **Las Vegas**, Nevada. A total of just under 100,000 sightseeing flights, carrying almost a million passengers, take off each year.

Controversy has long surrounded the "flight-seeing" industry. Flying conditions in the vicinity of the canyon are unusually difficult, in that light aircraft especially can struggle with a take-off altitude at Tusayan of 7000 feet, followed by fierce and unpredictable air currents over the canyon itself. The **safety record** is, to say the least, alarming. In 1956, a total of 128 people died in what was then the worst crash in US aviation history, when two commercial passenger planes collided above the confluence of the Colorado and Little Colorado rivers. Since then, a further sixty crashes have claimed around 230 more lives. As recently as November 2002, Papillon Helicopters was censured for inadequate maintenance and pilot error by a National Transportation Safety Board investigation into two crashes, one near the Hoover Dam in 2000 and another near the Grand Wash Cliffs in 2001.

Both for safety reasons, and also to diminish the barrage of **noise** within the park, strict **regulations** surround flights above the national park. Airplanes and helicopters

TRANSPORT, TOURS AND FEES

have to fly at different altitudes; no one is allowed to fly
below the level of the rim; and 75 percent of the park,
including the airspace above the South Rim lookouts and
the central rim-to-rim "Corridor," is completely off-limits.
The total number of overflights has also been restricted,
though that amounts simply to saying the number can't
increase above its current, already high level.

Only you can judge whether it's worth taking a flight.
Yes, in a sense you see more of the canyon, but it's from an
even more remote, and potentially alienating, distance than
from the rim-edge viewpoints. For many visitors, the issue
at the Grand Canyon is to find some way to engage with,
and understand, this vast, incomprehensible landscape.
Taking a scenic flight is unlikely to help. On the other
hand, it's undeniably exciting, it's an adventure, and, after
all, you are on vacation …

TOURS AND OPERATORS

Helicopter companies based at Tusayan – some of which
take off from their own landing fields rather than using the
airport proper – include **AirStar** (☎928/638-2622 or 1-
800/962-3869, ⓦwww.airstar.com); **Kenai** (☎928/638-
2764 or 1-800/541-4537, ⓦwww.flykenai.com); and
Papillon (☎928/638-2419 or 1-800/528-2418, ⓦwww
.papillon.com). Most fly three standard routes: a half-hour
western tour, straight across the canyon and back a few
miles west of the village, for around $100 per adult ($70 per
child); a forty-minute eastern tour, flying along the rim as
far as the confluence of the Colorado and Little Colorado
rivers, for roughly $145 ($100); and a fifty-minute loop trip
that combines the two by flying across the forest of the
North Rim, for perhaps $170 ($120). In addition, Papillon
also run $442 day-trips to the Havasupai reservation, as
described on p.182.

FLIGHT-SEEING TOURS

The main **airplane** or "fixed-wing" tour operators at Tusayan are **Air Grand Canyon** (☏928/638-2686 or 1-800/247-4726, ⓦwww.airgrandcanyon.com) and **Grand Canyon Airlines** (☏928/638-2359 or 1-866/235-9422, ⓦwww.grandcanyonairlines.com). Such tours can cover much greater distances than helicopter companies, but are obliged to fly at least one thousand feet above rim level, and thus tend not to offer quite such good views. Fixed-wing tour prices are lower, ranging from $75 per adult ($45 per child) for a half-hour up to around $175 ($95) for ninety minutes.

Air tours from **Las Vegas** to the South Rim typically cost $250 per person and up by helicopter, with **Air Vegas Airlines** (☏702/736-3599 or 1-800/255-7474, ⓦwww.airvegas.com) or **Maverick Helicopter Tours** (☏702/261-0007 or 1-888/261-4414, ⓦwww.maverickhelicopter.com), or around $200 in an airplane with **Scenic Airlines** (☏702/638-3300 or 1-800/634-6801, ⓦwww.scenic.com) or **Missing Link Tours** (☏1-800/209-8586, ⓦwww.tmltours.com).

Several Las Vegas-based companies also fly to the so-called **West Rim** (see p.196), which because it's on the Hualapai reservation is not governed by the same regulations as the rest of the canyon. That enables helicopters, run by both **Papillon** (☏702/736-7243 or 1-888/635-7272, ⓦwww.papillon.com) and **Sundance** (☏702/736-0606 or 1-800/653-1881, ⓦwww.helicoptour.com), to fly down from the rim and land beside the Colorado River.

ADMISSION CHARGES AND FEES

The **entrance fee** to Grand Canyon National Park is payable when you cross the park boundary, which is almost certain to be at one of the three main entry stations. Of the two South Rim stations, one is not far north of **Tusayan**

ADMISSION CHARGES AND FEES

12

on US-180 coming from Williams and Flagstaff, and the other is just east of **Desert View**, on AZ-64 west of Cameron. The North Rim equivalent is five miles south of **DeMotte Park** on AZ-67, south from Jacob Lake.

Admission is valid for seven days, and currently costs **$20** for one private, non-commercial vehicle and all its passengers, or, if you arrive on foot, bicycle, or motorcycle, **$10** for each individual.

It's also possible to buy various **passes** at the entrance stations, which supersede the need to pay the usual admission fee. The **Grand Canyon Pass**, which costs $40, entitles the purchaser and any passengers in the same vehicle, or any accompanying family members if you arrive by some other means, to unlimited admission for the next twelve months. If you plan to visit any other national parks or monuments in the course of the year, it makes more sense to buy the annual **National Parks Pass** ($50), which grants unrestricted access to the bearer, and any accompanying passengers, to all such parks and monuments for a year from the date of purchase. This has recently been introduced as a slightly cheaper alternative to the $65 **Golden Eagle** annual pass, which covers not only national parks and monuments, but also sites managed by the US Fish and Wildlife Service, the Forest Service, and the Bureau of Land Management. For most Grand Canyon visitors, who are unlikely to visit such sites, the extra $15 is not worth paying.

None of the passes or fees mentioned above covers or reduces such additional park fees as charges for **camping** in official park campgrounds (from $4 per person or $10 per group per night; see p.23); **backcountry hiking** ($10 per permit plus $5 per night; see p.207); or **rafting** ($100 per group permit plus $100 per person; see p.260).

Two additional passes grant **free access** for life to all national parks and monuments, again to the holder and any accompanying passengers, and also provide a fifty percent discount on camping fees. The **Golden Age Passport**, available at the entrance stations, is issued to any US citizen or permanent resident aged 62 or older for a one-time processing charge of $10, while the **Golden Access Passport**, available only at the visitor centers and the Tusayan Museum, is issued free to blind or permanently disabled US citizens or permanent residents.

Information, websites and maps

The best place to find **advance information** on Grand Canyon National Park is the park service **website**, at ⓦ www.nps.gov/grca. This carries full details of all park facilities, fees, activities, campgrounds, and programs. As described on p.21, however, all in-park **accommodation** is operated by Xanterra Parks & Resorts (PO Box 699, Grand Canyon, AZ 86023; ☏ 303/297-2757 or 1-888/297-2757, ⓦ www.grandcanyonlodges.com).

Once you actually arrive, the single most important source of information is the free park newspaper, **The Guide**, which is handed out at the various highway entrance stations. It is published in separate editions for the North and South rims and contains current opening hours for all park facilities, detailed hiking advice, a schedule of upcoming ranger talks, and plenty of background information on geology, natural history, and other issues. You'll also be given a glossy **park brochure** that holds some useful maps, and, if you specifically ask for them, the **Backcountry Trip Planner**, which carries full details on backpacking and camping in the park, and the **Accessibility Guide** (see p.19). All can also be obtained in advance **by mail**, by writing to PO Box 129, Grand Canyon, AZ 86023.

Although *The Guide* will probably tell you most of what you need to know, you're likely to want to call in at one of

TIME ZONES

Arizona operates on **Mountain Standard Time**, which is two hours behind Eastern Standard Time, and seven hours behind Greenwich Mean Time; 2pm at the Grand Canyon is thus 4pm in New York City, and 9pm in London. In winter, the time at the canyon is the same as in New Mexico, Utah, and Colorado, while Nevada and California, on **Pacific Standard Time**, are another hour behind.

Between the first Sunday in April and the last Sunday in October, New Mexico, Utah, Colorado and Nevada switch to **Daylight Savings Time**, and advance their clocks by one hour. Arizona, however, does not, so in summer it becomes the same as Nevada and an hour behind New Mexico and Utah. Confusingly, the **Navajo Nation** in northeast Arizona does shift to Daylight Savings Time, making it one hour later than the rest of Arizona in summer.

the **visitor centers** within the park, which are detailed
throughout this book. The main ones are at **Canyon View
Information Plaza** on the South Rim (daily: May to
mid-Oct 8am–6pm, mid-Oct to April 8am–5pm;
Ⓣ928/638-7888; see p.34) and **North Rim Visitor
Center** on the North Rim (daily May to mid-Oct
8am–6pm; Ⓣ928/638-7864; see p.81). To prevent wastage,
the rangers don't display all their leaflets, but if you have a
specific query they can often supply you with extra printed
information, for example on rafting or flight-seeing operators; the Havasupai reservation; or backcountry hiking and
driving routes. They also have up-to-date information on
current trail or road conditions, so be sure to ask if you're
planning some specific adventure.

A broad range of canyon-related books are reviewed in the
Contexts section at the back of this book (see p.293).

The official park-service information can be complemented by the much wider range of books, brochures and
maps sold in the Grand Canyon Association's **bookstores**,
which can be found across the plaza at Canyon View; at
Desert View; at *Grand Canyon Lodge*; and at several other
locations along the South Rim. A wide selection can be
ordered by mail (PO Box 399, Grand Canyon, AZ 86023;
Ⓣ928/638-0199), or online at Ⓦwww.grandcanyon.org.

USEFUL CONTACTS AND WEBSITES

Arizona Daily Sun 1751 S
Thompson Ave, Flagstaff, AZ
86001 Ⓣ928/774-4545,
Ⓦwww.azdailysun.com.
Flagstaff's daily newspaper is
the best source for up-to-the-
minute news about issues that
affect the entire Grand
Canyon region, and its
website provides a searchable
archive of past issues.

Arizona Office of Tourism PO Box 24548, Phoenix, AZ 85002 ⊤ 602/230-7733, ⓦ www.arizonaguide.com. Copious information on all aspects of visiting Arizona, available by mail or in a comprehensive website.

Grand Canyon Association PO Box 399, Grand Canyon, AZ 86023 ⊤ 928/638-2481, ⓦ www.grandcanyon.org. Non-profit organization, responsible for running the in-park bookstores, whose website is the best online source for Grand Canyon books and souvenirs.

Grand Canyon National Park PO Box 129, Grand Canyon, AZ 86023, South Rim ⊤ 928/638-7888, North Rim 928/638-7864, ⓦ www.nps.gov/grca. The park service mails out copies of its newspaper, *The Guide*, and other information, but also maintains a constantly updated online database of everything you might need to know, which includes details of park fees and closures, and features active links to rafting operators, tour companies and the like.

Grand Canyon Pioneers Society PO Box 2372, Flagstaff, AZ 86003-2372 ⓦ www.kaibab.org/gcps. This group of Grand Canyon enthusiasts publishes a monthly newsletter, *The Ol' Pioneer*, which provides details of members' latest research into canyon history, and organizes outings and activities in the region.

High Country News 119 Grand Ave, PO Box 1090, Paonia, CO 81428 ⊤ 970/527-4898, ⓦ www.hcn.org. Bi-weekly newspaper devoted to environmental issues in the West as a whole, with special reference to national parks and public lands. Its online archive offers searches for all the latest Grand Canyon news.

Xanterra Parks & Resorts PO Box 699, Grand Canyon, AZ 86023 ⊤ 303/297-2757 or 1-888/297-2757, ⓦ www .grandcanyonlodges.com or www.grandcanyonnorthrim .com. The concessionaires who operate the in-park lodges on both the South and North rims offer advance reservations by mail, phone or online.

MAPS

The best general-purpose **road map** for the total area covered by this book is the *Guide to Indian Country*, available free to members of the American Automobile Association, and sold throughout the Southwest at $3.95. It's not always reliable for dirt roads and backcountry routes, however. If you plan to do any exploring on the isolated plateaus that lie north of the Colorado, either on the North Rim or the Arizona Strip, be sure to pick up either the *North Kaibab Ranger District*, published by the Kaibab National Forest, or the BLM Arizona Strip Field Office's *Visitor Map*, both of which cost $6 from the visitor centers at Jacob Lake (see p.122) or the North Rim.

For **hiking**, it's important to have an accurate **topographical** map. The best one for the canyon as a whole is the waterproof and tearproof 1:73530 *Grand Canyon National Park*, published by National Geographic–Trails Illustrated (Ⓦ maps.nationalgeographic.com/trails; $9.95). Earthwalk Press produce a more detailed 1:24000 *Bright Angel Trail* map of the so-called Corridor Trails ($3.95). For even greater resolution, get hold of the appropriate **US Geological Survey** quadrant maps, each of which covers a square measuring seven miles by seven (Ⓣ 1-888/275-8747, Ⓦ www.usgs.gov). Orders costs $4 per map plus $5 postage.

Travelers with disabilities

For travelers with disabilities, the South Rim of the Grand Canyon makes a much more convenient destination than the North Rim; in addition to a much wider range of accommodation and other facilities, it also holds far more accessible canyon viewpoints.

The *Accessibility Guide* newspaper, available at all park visitor centers or by mail from PO Box 129, Grand Canyon, AZ 86023, includes maps and full details as to which buildings and rim-side trails are wheelchair-accessible; you can also find details online at ⓦ www.nps.gov/grca /grandcanyon/trip_planner/accessibility.htm. Broadly speaking, all the in-park accommodations on both rims, except for *Yavapai Lodge* on the South Rim, are accessible, but some of the older, "historic" structures along the South Rim, such as Hopi House and Kolb Studio, are not.

When you first arrive at the South Rim, an electric cart service is available for travel between Mather Point and Canyon View Information Plaza, on request either in the parking lot or at the visitor center. Wheelchairs are usually available for (free) loan at the visitor center.

Although most of the South Rim's free **shuttle buses** (see p.36) are not adapted for wheelchair users, by calling ☏ 928/638-0591 a day in advance you can arrange for an accessible vehicle to be made available. In addition, travelers with disabilities can obtain temporary **accessibility permits** at the entrance station, Canyon View Information Plaza, Yavapai Observation Station, or the Kolb Studio, which allow private vehicle access into shuttle-only areas. This enables you to drive the full length of Hermit Road, as outlined on p.62; the *Accessibility Guide* includes a map of "windshield views" where you can see the canyon without leaving your vehicle.

On the **North Rim**, *Grand Canyon Lodge* is accessible, and has wheelchairs for loan. The viewpoints at Point Imperial and Cape Royal can both be reached along level paved paths, but, the undulating, uneven trail to the tip of Bright Angel Point is not recommended.

Both the park **bus tours** detailed on p.38, and the **mule rides** described on p.61, can accommodate travelers with disabilities; call ☏ 928/638-2631 for full details. So too can several of the **rafting** operators listed on p.254 onwards.

Accommodation

Not surprisingly, most visitors to the Grand Canyon who stay for longer than a few hours hope to find **accommodation** within the national park. Both the South and North rims hold comfortable, atmospheric hotels, known in traditional park parlance as **lodges**. The six on the South Rim offer a total of around a thousand rooms, with the pick of them being in the venerable *El Tovar Hotel* and *Bright Angel Lodge*. There are two hundred more in the similarly appealing *Grand Canyon Lodge* that's the only North Rim option. You'll find detailed reviews of them all in the relevant chapters of this book. Note that very few rooms indeed – as in half a dozen on the South Rim, and four on the North – offer direct canyon views.

All the lodges are run by concessionaire **Xanterra**, who until recently were known as Amfac and who still use the old **Fred Harvey** name in their marketing. For all lodge **reservations**, plus those for the RV campground at Grand Canyon Village (see p.45), and Phantom Ranch down on the canyon floor (see p.229), contact Xanterra Parks & Resorts, PO Box 699, Grand Canyon, AZ 86023 (same-day ☎928/638-2631; advance ☎303/297-2757 or 1-888 /297-2757, ⓦwww.grandcanyonlodges.com). **Room rates** are set by the park service, with a typical charge for a double, en-suite room of between $70 and $130 between mid-March and mid-November, and perhaps $10–20 less in winter. Demand, especially in summer, far exceeds supply on both rims, so make your reservations as far in advance as possible.

Close to the **South Rim**, there's alternative accommodation in the gateway community of **Tusayan**, just outside the park. Several large chain motels there – reviewed on p.43 onwards – hold another thousand rooms between them. The rates tend to be much the same as in the park, but the facilities are often much more modern. Further congregations of motels can be found in the towns of **Flagstaff** (see p.149) and **Williams** (see p.164) on the I-40 interstate, though at eighty and sixty miles respectively from the canyon these are too far away to make convenient bases for multi-day stays.

At the **North Rim**, if there's no room at *Grand Canyon Lodge* your choices are very restricted. **DeMotte Park**, seventeen miles north of the canyon (see p.123), and **Jacob**

ACCOMMODATION PRICE CODES

Throughout this book, **room rates** in the park lodges, as well as in hotels, motels and B&Bs in nearby communities, are coded with the symbols below. These indicate the cost of the least expensive double rooms, **excluding taxes**, which amount to 6.38 percent inside the park, and from five to fifteen percent outside. Significant seasonal variations are indicated as appropriate, as are establishments that hold rooms at widely differing prices. The cheapest price code, ❶, is also used to indicate hostels which offer individual dorm beds, in which cases specific rates are also included.

❶ up to $30   ❹ $60–80   ❼ $130–175
❷ $30–45   ❺ $80–100   ❽ $175–250
❸ $45–60   ❻ $100–130   ❾ $250+

Lake, 44 miles north (see p.122), hold one small motel each, and there are several more in both **Fredonia**, Arizona (see p.128) and **Kanab**, Utah (see p.130), close neighbors another thirty miles north.

Finally, there are also a number of atmospheric roadside lodges and motels scattered along the 215-mile road that connects the North and South rims, for example at **Cameron** (see p.107) and **Marble Canyon** (see p.111).

CAMPING

The National Park Service maintains appealing, well-equipped **campgrounds** on both sides of the canyon, charging fees of between $10 and $15 per night per vehicle, and as little as $4 for individual backpackers. Reservations for both **Mather Campground** in Grand Canyon Village on the South Rim (see p.45), and **North Rim Campground**, a mile north of *Grand Canyon Lodge* on the North Rim (see p.83), are handled by Spherics (same-day ☏928/638-2611, advance ☏1-800/365-2267 or, from outside the US, ☏301/722-1257, ⓦwww.reservations .nps.gov), while the summer-only **Desert View Campground** on the South Rim (see p.46) is first-come, first-served. There's also **RV camping** at Grand Canyon Village in the **Trailer Village** (see p.45), run by Xanterra (☏303/297-2757 or ⓦwww.grandcanyonlodges.com).

Backcountry camping within the park, and especially down below the rim in the canyon itself, is by permit only, under tight park-service restrictions. For full details, see p.207.

Camping possibilities **outside the park** are detailed wherever appropriate in this book, including p.43 for those close to the South Rim, p.86 for the North Rim, and p.187 for the Havasupai reservation.

Health and safety

By far the most important **health and safety** issues for visitors to the Grand Canyon have to do with **hiking** and **survival** in the backcountry, and particularly down in the canyon itself. All are covered in extensive detail in Chapter Eight, including such crucial topics as **water** and **food**; **wildlife**; what to **carry** with you; and what **security precautions** to take.

If you're planning any form of backcountry adventure, whether driving, hiking, or rafting, be sure to supplement the advice in this book by asking the rangers at any of the park visitor centers for up-to-the-minute details of current road or trail conditions.

HEALTH AND SAFETY

THE GUIDE

THE GUIDE

The South Rim

When someone casually mentions visiting the "Grand Canyon," it's almost certainly the **South Rim** that they're referring to. To be more precise, it's the thirty-mile stretch of the South Rim that's served by a paved road; and most specifically of all, it's **Grand Canyon Village**, the small canyon-edge community, sandwiched between the pine forest and the rim, that holds the park's **lodges**, **restaurants**, and **visitor center**. That's why an area as vast as the Grand Canyon can find it so hard to handle the human influx. Of the almost five million visitors who come to the park each year, nine out of every ten are heading for the same tiny spot on the rim.

A map of the South Rim can be found at the
back of this book (map 3).

The reason so many people come here is not, however, because this is a uniquely wonderful spot from which to see the canyon. In terms of views, it's as good a place to start as any – every visit begins with an eager rush to catch that first breathtaking glimpse of the abyss – but really Grand Canyon Village just happens to be where the canyon's tourist facilities have come to be concentrated. Tourism to the South Rim started toward the end of the nineteenth century, when miners prospecting at various points along the rim began to put up paying guests in simple cabins and inns. Then, in 1901, a railroad was constructed north from Williams to the site that became Grand Canyon Village, and lodges, campgrounds, and other amenities swiftly sprang up around the station. Even after visitors began to arrive by car rather than by train, the convenience of having everything in one place continued to outweigh the problems of overcrowding. Things thus stayed much the same for a hundred years, until, as the millennium approached – and despite the emergence of **Tusayan**, just outside the park, as a rival accommodation center – it looked as though the village could no longer take the strain.

You arrive, therefore, at a time when, to put it charitably, the park is in limbo. An ambitious transportation scheme, under which visitors would explore the South Rim using a new **light rail** network rather than their own vehicles, has been drawn up but barely implemented – and as visitor numbers have failed to increase in line with the dire predictions of the 1990s, it seems unlikely it ever will be. All that's really happened is the construction of the large new open-air **Canyon View Information Plaza**, located well away from the village center. It looks great, but as you're supposed to drive into the village and then catch a bus back to the plaza, it's done nothing to relieve traffic congestion, and it doesn't even meet the basic requirement of making an easy first stop.

On a more positive note, the canyon is as majestic as ever, to be admired from countless differing vantage points not only within the village, but also along the eight-mile **Hermit Road** to the west and the 23-mile **Desert View Drive** to the east. The facilities in the village are of a pretty high standard – especially if you get to stay in historic properties like *El Tovar Hotel* or *Bright Angel Lodge* – and generally well priced. The village itself is also a lot more attractive than you might imagine, and once the day-trippers have gone it rarely feels as crowded as the horror stories might suggest.

The first half of this chapter covers South Rim practicalities; jump to "Exploring the South Rim," p.51, for all the sights, lookout points and scenic drives.

Getting to the South Rim

The vast majority of visitors make their way to the South Rim by way of either **Williams** (58 miles south; see p.163) or **Flagstaff** (81 miles southeast; see p.146). Both towns stand on the I-40 interstate and are served by cross-country Amtrak **trains**. In the absence of a direct Amtrak service to the canyon itself, it's possible to take a separate **excursion train** from Williams up to the South Rim, while **buses** between Flagstaff and the canyon call at Williams en route. Direct **flights** to Tusayan take off from Las Vegas and other points in the Southwest.

BY CAR

The two main roads up to the South Rim – **AZ-64** from Williams, also known as the Bushmaster Memorial Highway, and **US-180** from Flagstaff – meet at **Valle**, 25 miles south of **Tusayan**, which is itself just south of the park boundary. En route from Flagstaff, US-180 threads its way through the dramatic San Francisco Peaks, making it

BY CAR

●

the more scenic drive of the two. Both roads, however, run for most of their length over the **Coconino Plateau**, which is covered by the largest **ponderosa pine forest** in the world. Crossing this flat and undramatic landscape, you get no sense of the impending abyss until you reach the very edge of the canyon, close to Mather Point.

You can also get to Grand Canyon Village from the **east**, by driving the fifty-mile section of AZ-64 that sets off from US-89 at **Cameron** (see p.107). Coming this way, you enter the park close to Desert View, and can stop off at the East Rim overlooks before you reach the village. The obvious route to follow if you're coming in from the north, it also makes an alternative approach from Flagstaff to the south, useful if you're interested in seeing Sunset Crater and Wupatki national monuments along the way.

Parking

Parking in and around Grand Canyon Village is seldom easy. Guests staying at the various lodges – especially *Maswik* and *Yavapai* – can feel confident of leaving their cars near their rooms overnight, but finding a space in the middle of the day can be murder. Ludicrously, there's no parking at all at the visitor center – see p.34 – and very little at Mather Point nearby. Of the five free public parking lots in and near the village, the unpaved one across the railroad tracks from the station is often the best bet.

One alternative is to leave your car in **Tusayan**, even if you're not staying in one of the hotels there. In summer, hourly **shuttle buses**, known as the **Grand Canyon Eco Shuttle**, connect various points in Tusayan, including the airport, the IMAX, and the main hotels, with the Maswik Transportation Center in Grand Canyon Village (April & Oct 10.15am–4.30pm, May & Sept 10.15am–6.30pm, June–Aug 9.15am–7.30pm; $4 one way, $7 all day, $12 two

days, under-17s free; ☏ 928/638-0821, ⓦ www.grand
canyoncoaches.com). To encourage visitors to use it as a
park and ride service, park admission for shuttle users is
$6 per person.

BY TRAIN

Amtrak **trains** come no closer to the South Rim than the
stations at **Flagstaff** and **Williams**. In summer, westbound
services, originating in Chicago, arrive at Flagstaff at 9.21pm
and Williams Junction at 10.04pm daily, while eastbound
trains, which start from Los Angeles, call at Williams Junction
at 4.35am and Flagstaff at 5.10am daily. Times in winter are
one hour later. Bus connections are detailed below.

The Grand Canyon Railway

The **Grand Canyon Railway** (☏ 928/773-1976 or 1-800
/843-8724, ⓦ www.thetrain.com), which celebrated its
centenary in 2001, runs for 65 miles from **Williams** (see
p.163) to a picturesque wooden station in the heart of
Grand Canyon Village. When the line first opened, it her-
alded the start of mass tourism to the canyon, but by 1968
it had been driven out of business by the growth of private
automobile travel. Restored in 1989, the railway is now a
tourist attraction in its own right, with passengers riding in
historic cars of varying levels of comfort, and entertained
throughout the day by Wild West shoot-outs, hold-ups,
pistol-packing marshals, singing conductors, and the like.
The scenery en route – part desert scrubland, part pine forest – is far from spectacular, and you never actually see the
canyon from the train, but it's still a fun and atmospheric
way to visit the park without having to drive.

  The train operates daily all year except for Christmas Eve
and Christmas Day, leaving central Williams (not the

Amtrak station) at 10am and arriving at the Grand Canyon at 12.15pm, then setting off back again at 3.30pm and reaching Williams at 5.45pm. Sadly, it's pulled by **steam engines** only during the summer, from late May until the end of September; for the rest of year, diesels are used. Five different kinds of passenger car are in service, offering extra facilities such as larger and more comfortable seats, and complimentary food and beverages. Round-trip fares range from $55 in Coach Class ($25 for under-17s) up to $140 (under-17s $110) in the Luxury Parlor Car. Amtrak passes of any kind are not accepted, while, unless you have a national park pass, an additional fee of $8 is charged for park admission.

Most passengers use the Grand Canyon Railway as a day's excursion from Williams, but you can break your journey by staying at the canyon for as many nights as you like, and you can also make the journey in reverse, if you're staying at the canyon but you fancy visiting Williams.

BY BUS

Open Road Tours and Transportation (☏928/226-8060 or 1-800/766-7117, ⊛www.openroadtours.com) runs two **bus services** each day from the Amtrak station in **Flagstaff**, via the Grand Canyon Railroad Depot in **Williams**, to the IMAX movie theater in **Tusayan**, and the **Maswik Transportation Center** in Grand Canyon Village. The first service leaves Flagstaff at 8.30am daily, calling at Williams at 9am and reaching Maswik at 10.15am; the second leaves Flagstaff at 3pm and Williams at 3.30pm, reaching Maswik at 4.45pm. Return services leave Maswik at 11.45am and 5.45pm, arriving at Williams at 1pm and 7pm respectively, and Flagstaff at 1.30pm and 7.30pm. Tickets cost $20 each way for adults, $15 for accompanied under-12s.

HORSE RIDING

Apache Stables (☎ 928/638-2891, ⓦ www.apachestables.com), based at *Moqui Lodge* (which is itself currently closed), charges $30.50 for a one-hour trail ride through the Kaibab Forest, and $55.50 for two hours, and in the evening offers campfire rides on horseback for $40.50, or by wagon for $12.50. To see the canyon itself, you have to take the four-hour East Rim ride, costing $95.50.

BY AIR

The small **airport** at Tusayan – six miles from the South Rim, just outside the park boundary, and used primarily by "flight-seeing" tour companies (see p.10) – also welcomes scheduled services and excursions, especially from **Las Vegas**. Unlike the tours, these flights do not pass directly above the park, but they still give good views. Standard fares tend to be in the region of $135 one way and $225 round trip, but special offers can cost as little as $60 and $100, respectively. The major Vegas operators are Scenic Airlines (☎ 702/638-3300 or 1-800/634-6801, ⓦ www.scenic.com), and Air Vegas (☎ 928/638-9351, 702/736-3599 or 1-800/255-7474, ⓦ www.airvegas.com).

The only **car rental** outlet at the airport is operated by Enterprise (April–Oct only, daily 9am–5pm; ☎ 928/638-2871). In winter, when that office is closed, you can rent vehicles through their Flagstaff branch (☎ 928/774-9407), which charges an additional fee for deliveries to the canyon. Most Tusayan hotels offer courtesy pick-up for guests, and the Grand Canyon Eco Shuttle (see p.30) provides a shuttle bus service to Grand Canyon Village.

BY AIR

●

Information

While you'd think the most obvious first port of call when you arrive at the South Rim would be the **Canyon View Information Plaza**, it can be all but impossible to park anywhere near it. However, so long as you have a copy of the park's **free newspaper**, *The Guide*, it's not actually essential to call in at the visitor center. *The Guide* is handed out at the two **entrance stations** on AZ-64, when you pay the admission fees detailed on pp.12–14 – one's just north of Tusayan, the other a mile east of Desert View – and is also available in all the lodges. As well as listing current opening hours and shuttle-bus schedules, it carries a full program of **park activities** such as ranger talks and guided hikes.

In addition to the plaza, further **information desks** can be found at Kolb Studio (see p.60), Yavapai Observation Station (see p.53), Tusayan Museum (see p.74), and Desert View (see p.76). For details of the **Backcountry Office**, which issues permits for backpacking and camping in the canyon, see p.207.

CANYON VIEW INFORMATION PLAZA

Canyon View Information Plaza, unveiled in fall 2000, is located near Mather Point (daily: May to mid-Oct 8am–6pm, mid-Oct to April 8am–5pm; ☎928/638-7888, ⓦwww.nps.gov/grca), just as the spur road to the village leaves AZ-64. Its extensive, well-illustrated open-air displays and trail guides are complemented by a visitor center staffed by helpful rangers, and there's a very good separate bookstore run by the Grand Canyon Association.

Though it's all pretty impressive, the plaza was not in fact built to serve as the main park visitor center, but rather as the terminus of the proposed **light rail** system. It was envisaged that visitors would leave their cars in huge parking lots at Tusayan, be ferried up here on trains, and then change onto the park's own shuttle buses. All the outdoor information panels were erected to give passengers something to read while they were waiting at the plaza, but another new visitor center would be built in the heart of Grand Canyon Village.

As it is, however, construction of the light rail network appears to have been postponed indefinitely. At some point, a new bus system may serve the same purpose, but for now the plaza remains bizarrely inaccessible, in that it has no parking lot of its own. Although *The Guide* avoids mentioning it, suggesting instead that you should park in the village and then catch a shuttle bus back, there are a few parking spaces limited to twenty minutes per vehicle at Mather Point itself, a few hundred yards' walk away. The plaza can also be reached by walking from *Yavapai Lodge*, but, despite the impression given by the official maps, it's a mile on foot.

Getting around the South Rim

Something clearly had to be done about the traffic congestion plaguing the South Rim, but so far, the solution, the park's new "improved" **public transportation** system, is a real mess. The original idea was to ban all private vehicles from both the village and the canyon overlooks, and instead ferry visitors around on an extensive **light rail** system. However, the failure to build the rail network, and the absurd lack of parking at the information plaza, means that only a few fragments of the masterplan have been put into place. Thus new arrivals still start by driving into the centre of Grand Canyon Village, where they swiftly discover that the village **shuttle bus** is too slow and awkward to make a convenient alternative, and remain as dependent on their cars as ever. If visitors stayed long enough to get used to the shuttles, it might help, but as it is only the **Hermit's Rest Route** service, carrying sightseers to the overlooks west of the village, is an unqualified success.

DRIVING

Grand Canyon Village is always accessible to private vehicles – though as noted on p.30 **parking** can be a major problem – and so too is the road **east** from the village to **Desert View**. Both the road **west** from the village to **Hermit's Rest**, however, and the short access road to **Yaki Point**, which is the first overlook east of Mather Point and also the trailhead for the popular **South Kaibab Trail**, are only open to private vehicles during the months of December, January and February.

PARK SHUTTLE BUSES

The busiest of the park service's three shuttle bus routes, the **Village Route**, loops between Grand Canyon Village and Canyon View Information Plaza, stopping at *Maswik* and *Yavapai* lodges and Mather Campground as well as Yavapai Observation Station. Starting an hour before sunrise, buses come at half-hourly intervals until 6.30am, and then at ten-to fifteen-minute intervals until 11pm in summer (May–Sept) or 10pm otherwise.

The whole circuit takes up to an hour to complete,

which is ridiculous considering the short distances involved, and you have to suspect that it's designed as much to deter visitors from traveling around the village as it is to make their journeys easier. Quite apart from waiting for the bus in the first place, even the simplest trip from A to B seems to involve going out of your way to call at C and D as well. The shuttle is probably most useful for getting between the campground or *Yavapai Lodge* and the *Bright Angel Lodge* area, but it follows such a circuitous route in either direction that unless parking is impossible it's far quicker to drive. Wherever you're staying, you'd do better to visit the information plaza when you first drive in rather than to make your way back there by bus.

The **Kaibab Trail Route** connects Canyon View Information Plaza with **Yaki Point**, off Desert View Drive a couple of miles east of the village. Buses run at half-hourly intervals from an hour before sunrise until an hour after sunset. To use this route, you have first to catch a village bus to the information plaza, so if you're planning to hike along the **South Kaibab Trail** from the Yaki Point trailhead, as described on p.70, it's a lot quicker to catch the early-morning **Hikers Shuttle** service. This runs direct to the trailhead at Yaki Point from *Bright Angel Lodge* and the Backcountry Information Center, departing at 4am, 5am and 6am daily between June and August; 5am, 6am and 7am in May and September; 6am, 7am and 8am in April and October; and 8am, 9am and 10am from November until March. Note that you can also use a **cab** on this route; see p.39.

Finally, from March until November, buses on the **Hermit's Rest Route** follow what used to be known as the West Rim Drive, an eight-mile road west of the village that holds eight canyon overlooks. The whole point of the trip is to take your time and enjoy the views; allow at least

PARK SHUTTLE BUSES

37

two hours. All the overlooks are described, together with advice on how to make the best use of the shuttle, from p.62 onwards. Buses operate from an hour before sunrise until an hour after sunset, at ten-minute intervals between 7.30am and sunset and at half-hourly intervals otherwise.

PARK BUS TOURS

As well as managing the park lodges, Xanterra also operates guided **bus tours** along the South Rim. For current schedules, which vary according to the times of sunrise and sunset, or to make a reservation, contact the "transportation desk" in any lodge, or call ☎928/638-2631. Adults can take any two tours, not necessarily on the same day, for $32.50, while accompanied children under the age of 17 travel free on all the in-park tours.

The **Desert View Tour** heads along Desert View Drive on the East Rim – a route that's open to private vehicles but not served by park shuttle buses – with stops at Yavapai Observation Station and Lipan Point, as well as at Desert View at the far end. It's a 52-mile round trip that takes just under four hours, and costs $27.50. The evening run is timed to coincide with sunset at Desert View.

West of the village, the **Hermit's Rest Tour** is a two-hour jaunt along Hermit's Road that costs $15.50. As it follows exactly the same route, with some but not all of the same stops, as the free Hermit's Rest shuttle bus – see p.62 – you're basically paying for the generally rather banal commentary.

Shorter **Sunrise** and **Sunset** tours head east and west of the village respectively, with an adult fare of $12. Finally, it's also possible to take a tour down to Williams, traveling one way by bus and the other on the **Grand Canyon Railway** (see p.31), for $49 for adults or $29 for under-17s.

TAXIS

If you're at all pressed for time during your visit, it can be well worth taking advantage of the local 24-hour **taxi** service, reached on ☎ 928/638-2822. In particular, a taxi can spare you a lengthy wait for a shuttle bus by taking you direct to the South Kaibab trailhead at Yaki Point.

CYCLING

The park's transportation masterplan calls for the opening of a bicycle-rental facility at the information plaza, and the construction of a 73-mile **Grand Canyon Greenway** to enable cyclists to follow the rim in both directions and get around Grand Canyon Village. However, bike rental so far remains unavailable, and only a few segments of the Greenway are ready, including the trail that links the information plaza with the heart of the village, and the Rim Trail to either side of Mather Point. Cyclists are, however, permitted on all the public highways, and on Hermit Road (see p.64).

Accommodation

Roughly two thousand guest **rooms** are available in the immediate vicinity of the South Rim: half of them in and around **Grand Canyon Village** within the park, of which under three hundred are close to the rim, and a further thousand seven miles south, just outside the park in the dull gateway community of **Tusayan**. Given the choice – and with demand far exceeding supply in high season, you probably won't be – the best place to stay has to be on the very lip of the canyon, though surprisingly few rooms have canyon views. While the more basic in-park lodges, away from the rim, still make more convenient bases than Tusayan, the hotels in Tusayan, however, tend to be much more modern and better equipped, and are significantly more price-sensitive in low season.

GRAND CANYON VILLAGE

As detailed on p.21, all **accommodation** options within Grand Canyon National Park are run by **Xanterra**. For all **reservations** for lodges or RV camping at Grand Canyon Village, and for Phantom Ranch, contact Xanterra Parks & Resorts, PO Box 699, Grand Canyon, AZ 86023 (same-day ☎928/638-2631, advance 303/297-2757 or 1-888 /297-2757, ⓦwww.grandcanyonlodges.com).

Most of the nicest lodgings are available in two venerable Fred Harvey properties right on the edge of Grand Canyon Village, the magnificent **El Tovar Hotel**, as described below, and the almost as attractive **Bright Angel Lodge** (see also below). As rates are set by the National Park Service, and depend on hotel facilities rather than whether there's a canyon view, it's no more expensive to stay in a characterful rim-side cabin than in a room in an anonymous motel block a mile from the edge. There are, however, far more of the latter than the former; in fact the number of rooms with significant canyon views barely reaches double figures. In any case, during busy periods – pretty much from early May until late September – the best rooms are likely to be booked as much as two years in advance, and by June it would be very unusual for any same-day bookings to be available at all. The rates shown here apply during high season; in the depths of winter, prices along the rim drop by around $20 per night, while *Maswik* and *Yavapai* lodges can be as much as $40 cheaper.

Bright Angel Lodge

Designed by Mary Jane Colter (see box on pp.58–59) in 1935, the *Bright Angel* complex consists of an imposing central lodge plus a westward sprawl of "rustic" but comfortable detached log cabins. Staying in a cabin makes for a delightfully atmospheric experience, whether you're in a "Rim Cabin" with a tremendous view or in one of the cheaper so-called "Historic Cabins," set a little further back. Most of the rooms in the lodge itself are very basic and plain, and share bathrooms, though a few do have their own showers. Best of all is the Bucky O'Neill Suite, which has two front doors opening right onto the rim plus its own large living room with working fireplace. Lodge rooms and Historic Cabins ❹, Rim Cabins ❻, Bucky O'Neill Suite ❾

El Tovar Hotel

This log-built canyon-edge hotel, named for an early Spanish explorer, remains the centerpiece of Grand Canyon Village, and continues to exude the same combination of rough-hewn charm and elegant sophistication that made it the very peak of fashion when it opened in 1905. Only three suites enjoy extensive canyon views; the rest of the 78 tastefully furnished guest rooms come in two different sizes, but are otherwise very similar, with no extra charge for those that offer partial glimpses of the abyss. Almost all hold only one bed. Standard ❻, larger ❼, suites ❽

Kachina Lodge

Anonymous but perfectly adequate motel-style rooms, each with two queen-size beds, set in a low two-story block separated by twenty yards of grass from the rim. None claims to offer canyon views, but you should see at least a little of it if you're on the rim side, especially on the upper floor. Registration is via the lobby of the adjoining *El Tovar Hotel*. Standard ❺, canyonside ❻

GRAND CANYON VILLAGE ACCOMMODATION

Maswik Lodge

The large *Maswik* complex, a few hundred yards back from the rim at the southwest end of the village, holds a cluster of basic summer-only cabins – each of which contains two double beds, and, if let to a group of four travelers, is the closest the village comes to budget accommodation – plus two distinct blocks of motel-style rooms, which tend to be heavily booked by tour groups. Rooms in the *Maswik North* building are considerably nicer than those in the small, cramped *Maswik South*. Cabins and Maswik South ❹, Maswik North ❻

Thunderbird Lodge

Both the *Thunderbird* and the identical *Kachina Lodge* next door – see above – were built of gray brick in the 1960s and intended to last only ten years. Both are still going strong without being in any way distinctive. The *Thunderbird* is run from the front desk of *Bright Angel Lodge*, and 37 of its 55 twin-bedded rooms are located on the canyon side of the

building. Standard ❺, canyonside ❻

For details of staying at **Phantom Ranch** – the only option at the bottom of the canyon – see p.228.

Yavapai Lodge

With 358 rooms, *Yavapai* is the largest of the in-park lodges, but it's also the lowest in the pecking order, in that it's the last to fill up, and thus the most likely to be available if you try to book at short notice. The main drawback is it's half a mile from the rim, and twice that – further than you'd want to walk, especially at night – from central Grand Canyon Village, which can leave you all too dependent on the slow shuttle buses. In late fall and early spring, one or other of the lodge's two similar sections, *Yavapai East* or *Yavapai West*, is liable to shut down, while the whole lodge closes in the depths of winter. The rooms themselves offer perfectly decent motel-style accommodation, mostly with twin beds, and as they're set back in the woods in relatively small blocks they're pretty quiet too. **5**

OUTSIDE THE PARK: TUSAYAN

Sprawling along the highway just over a mile south of the park entrance, and thus seven miles from Grand Canyon Village, **TUSAYAN** is an unattractive strip-mall of a town that holds nothing beyond an IMAX cinema (reviewed on p.50), one or two stores and restaurants, and half a dozen large **hotel/motels**. Its basic function has traditionally been as an overspill when all the in-park accommodations are full, though large tour operators have in recent years come to prefer its hotels as offering a higher standard of amenities and a greater ease in feeding, entertaining and generally managing their groups. Note that the prices below are for high season; all are liable to drop significantly in low season.

The closest **youth hostels** to the park are in Flagstaff (see p.150) and outside Williams (see p.166).

Park concessionaires Xanterra also own the right to operate the sizeable **Moqui Lodge**, just outside the park on the north edge of Tusayan, but in the face of competition from its newer neighbors the lodge has remained closed since 2001.

Best Western Grand Canyon Squire Inn
PO Box 130, Grand Canyon, AZ 86023 ⓣ 928/638-2681 or 1-800/622-6966, ⓦ www .grandcanyonsquire.com.

Tusayan's most lavish option, billing itself as the canyon's "only resort hotel," with outdoor pool, indoor spa, and even its own four-lane bowling alley. The accommodation is spacious and very comfortable, if in no way particularly characterful, while paying a little extra gets you an enormous deluxe room, with oval bath. **6**

The Grand Hotel

PO Box 3319, Grand Canyon, AZ 86023 ⊤ 928/638-3333, Ⓦ www.gcanyon.com. Smart new hotel, built in a modern style with nods to traditional park-lodge design. Once you get past the very smart public spaces – designed with tour groups in mind – the rooms themselves are no better than in its cheaper neighbors or the lesser in-park options, but there's a nice figure-of-eight indoor pool, and it's also home to the *Canyon Star* restaurant (see p.49). **4**–**6**

Holiday Inn Express

PO Box 3245, Grand Canyon, AZ 86023 ⊤ 928/638-3000 or 1-888/473-2269, Ⓦ www.grandcanyon.com/HI. Unenthralling but perfectly acceptable chain motel, right on the highway, with no pool or restaurant. **5**

Quality Inn Grand Canyon

PO Box 520, Grand Canyon, AZ 86023 ⊤ 928/638-2673 or 1-800/221-2222, Ⓦ www .grandcanyonqualityinn.com. Though it's not very conspicuous from the highway, tucked away behind the IMAX cinema and the *Rodeway Inn*, the *Quality Inn* is actually huge, with 176 rooms and 56 suites, plus an outdoor pool and indoor spa, and a large but uninspiring restaurant in its central atrium. **5**

Rodeway Inn Red Feather Lodge

PO Box 1460, Grand Canyon, AZ 86023 ⊤ 928/638-2414 or 1-800/538-2345, Ⓦ www.redfeatherlodge.com. The former *Red Feather* motel has been joined by a new hotel block to form the large *Rodeway Inn*; they share a pool, the rates aren't bad, and the newer rooms especially are of a reasonably high standard. Motel **4**, hotel **5**

Seven Mile Lodge

PO Box 56, Grand Canyon, AZ 86023 ⊤ 928/638-2291.

The last little roadside motel left in Tusayan, this tiny twenty-room place is very plain and unadorned, but it's the least expensive option around. **❸**

FURTHER AFIELD

If even Tusayan is booked up, it's worth considering the large new *Grand Canyon Inn*, alongside the Chevron station at the intersection of AZ-64 and US-180 in **VALLE**, another twenty miles south (☎928/635-9203 or 1-800/635-9203; ⊛www.grandcanyoninn.com; **❹**). This may be a bit of a godforsaken spot, with only the Flintstones for company (see below), but the inn has modern rooms at reasonable prices, a heated outdoor pool, and a standard restaurant that's open for all meals. The *Grand Canyon Motel*, across the highway, is booked through the same office.

CAMPING

Tent and RV camping (without hookups) is available at the park service's year-round **Mather Campground**, south of the main road through Grand Canyon Village not far from Market Plaza. Sites for up to two vehicles and six people cost $15 per night between April and November, when reservations, which are strongly recommended, can be made up to five months in advance through Spherics (same-day ☎928/638-2611; advance 1-800/365-2267 or, from outside the US, ☎301/722-1257), or online at ⊛www.reservations.nps.gov. No reservations are accepted between December and March, when sites are first-come, first-served, and the fee drops to $10 per night. The adjacent **Trailer Village** consists exclusively of RV sites with hookups, costing $24 per site per night for two people, plus $2 extra for each additional adult; reservations on ☎303/297-2757 or ⊛www.grandcanyonlodges.com.

In summer, additional first-come, first-served camping sites, without hookups, are on offer 25 miles east of Grand Canyon Village at the *Desert View Campground* (mid-May to mid-Oct; no reservations; $10).

For details of **backcountry camping** in the park, see p.207.

Outside the park, there's a commercial campground, *Camper Village* (☏ 928/638-2887; some RV hookups; $15–23), in **Tusayan**, while the Kaibab National Forest runs the minimally equipped, first-come, first-served *Ten-X Campground* (mid-April to Sept; no hookups or showers; $10 per night), two miles south. Twenty miles further south, in Valle, *Flintstone's Bedrock City* (mid-March to Oct; ☏ 928/635-2600; $12 tents, $16 RV hookups) is a family-oriented commercial campground with its own prehistoric theme park as well as a simple store and snack bar.

Eating and drinking

Although only the gorgeous canyon-rim dining room at *El Tovar* is noteworthy, there's a reasonable selection of places to **eat** in Grand Canyon Village, and you certainly don't gain anything by opting for Tusayan instead. However, summer crowding can lead to endless queueing, so it's worth bringing at least some food with you. It's also possible to buy basic **groceries** at the Canyon Village Marketplace near *Yavapai Lodge*, or in Tusayan, while if you're out exploring you'll find **snack bars** at Hermit's Rest (summer daily 9am–sunset, otherwise daily 9am–4pm) and Desert View (summer daily 8am–7pm, otherwise daily 9am–5pm).

GRAND CANYON VILLAGE

Both *El Tovar* and *Bright Angel Lodge* hold proper **restaurants**, but with capacity far too low to meet the demand, you'll probably end up eating in the large *Maswik* or *Yavapai* **cafeterias**. For an even quicker meal, the Canyon Village Marketplace holds a pretty good **deli counter** (summer daily 7am–6pm, otherwise daily 8am–5pm).

As for **drinking**, *El Tovar* has a cozy wood-paneled **cocktail lounge** (daily 11am–11pm) which also features an outdoor terrace, on the lawn within a few feet of the rim, and serves a small menu of appetizers and desserts, while the *Bright Angel* has a traditional Western-style **saloon** (daily 11am–11pm) that often features live country and western music. Over at *Maswik Lodge*, beside the cafeteria, there's a **sports lounge** (daily 5–11pm) with big-screen TV.

Arizona Room
Bright Angel Lodge.
Informal, plain but good-quality restaurant, just a few yards from the rim; there are no views to speak of, but you do get a great sense of space. The open kitchen at the far end serves conventional meat and seafood entrees, such as a slab of baby back ribs for $20, a 12oz steak for $18, or a roasted half-chicken for $15. No reservations are accepted; your best bet is to nip in a little before sunset, otherwise you may have to wait in the bar by the entrance for up to two hours. Dinner only, daily 4.30–10pm. Closed early Jan to mid-Feb.

Bright Angel Restaurant
Bright Angel Lodge.
Straightforward, windowless diner open for every meal of the day, and serving pretty much anything you might want, from snacks and salads for under $10 to steaks at over $20. No reservations, daily 6.30am–10pm.

El Tovar
El Tovar Hotel ☎ 928/638-2631 ext 6432.
Very grand, very classy dark-wood dining room, with

subdued lighting and lovely big windows that focus all attention outwards, especially at sunset – though only the front tier of tables have actual canyon views. Reservations are accepted for dinner only, and tend to be grabbed days in advance. The food itself is rich and expensive, especially at dinner, when almost all entrees, such as braised lamb shank, peppercorn filet mignon, or salmon tostada, cost well over $20. Appetizers are a bit more imaginative, with barbecued sea scallops at $11 and even *Clesan-du-Klish*, or Navajo blue-corn tamales, at $9. Daily 6.30am–11am, 11.30am–2pm & 5–10pm.

Maswik Cafeteria
Maswik Lodge.
Self-service fast food, aimed especially at tour groups, with separate Mexican and Italian sections as well as burgers and standard plate lunches. Breakfast can come in under $5, but lunch and dinner entrees are closer to $10. Two spacious seating areas and a bar alongside. Daily 6am–10pm.

Yavapai Cafeteria
Yavapai Lodge.
This large cafeteria is preferable to the *Maswik*'s for its salad bar and fried chicken, and slightly lower prices for burgers and daily specials; visitors are unlikely to spot the difference, and if you're not staying here it's not worth a special trip. The central dining area has a dull canteen-like feel, but there's a nicer glassed-in annex. Summer daily 6am–9pm, spring and fall daily 7am–8pm; shorter hours and probable closures in low season.

TUSAYAN

Tusayan's two finest restaurants are, not surprisingly, located in its two fanciest hotels. All the other sizeable hotels have their own run-of-the-mill dining rooms, however, while the town also holds the self-explanatory *We Cook Pizza and*

TUSAYAN EATING AND DRINKING

Pasta (☏ 928/638-2278) plus a *McDonald's*, a *Pizza Hut*, a *Taco Bell* and a *Wendy's*.

Canyon Star
The Grand Hotel ☏ 928/638-3333.

Large, attractive hotel restaurant, where dinner is a choice between "hardy ranch fare," like $20 steaks or barbecue ribs, and strongly Mexican-tinged Southwestern dishes, like fajitas, enchiladas or burritos, at more like $12–15. Lunchtime salads, sandwiches and Mexican staples mostly cost under $10. The food's not at all bad, but the real *raison d'être* is the central dance floor, scene of "Native American Experience" dances for tour groups at 6.30pm and 8pm nightly. Daily 7–10am, 11am–2pm & 5–9pm.

Coronado Room
Best Western Grand Canyon Squire Inn ☏ 928/638-2681.
Much like the *Canyon Star*, the *Squire Inn's* smart dinner-only dining room serves both all-American entrees such as prime rib or filet mignon for around $20, and "Southwest Favorites" like fajitas and chimichangas for $15. Its trademark dessert is a white chocolate piano filled with chocolate mousse. Daily 5–10pm.

Listings

BANK The bank in Market Plaza is open Mon–Thurs 10am–3pm, Fri 10am–5pm, and has a 24hr ATM machine.

CAMPING EQUIPMENT Can be bought or rented at the Canyon Village Marketplace in Market Plaza; summer daily 7am–8.30pm, otherwise daily 8am–7pm.

DISABLED TRAVELERS The park's very comprehensive *Accessibility Guide*, available at all visitor centers and lodges,

LISTINGS

provides full accessibility details for all park facilities, from lodges and stores to overlooks and trails; for further information, call ⓣ 928/638-2631 or look online at ⓦ www.nps.gov/grca. Note that park admission is free for all permanently disabled US citizens, using the Golden Access passport. At either park entrance station, you can request a permit to be allowed to park at the Canyon View Information Plaza. Once there, you can obtain a further permit enabling you to drive on the otherwise restricted Hermit Road. While most shuttle buses cannot accommodate wheelchairs, you can ask for an accessible bus by calling ⓣ 928/638-0591 a day in advance; the Xanterra tours detailed on p.38 can also accommodate wheelchairs by prior arrangement.

GARAGE SERVICE The auto repair garage in the heart of Grand Canyon Village is open daily 8am–noon & 1–5pm; 24hr emergency service also available ⓣ 928/638-2631.

GAS The closest gas stations to the South Rim are in Tusayan and at Desert View.

IMAX THEATER Tusayan's one sightseeing attraction features hourly shows, on the half-hour, of *Hidden Secrets of the Grand Canyon*, a 35min big-screen movie that dates from 1984 and centers on a reconstruction of John Wesley Powell's pioneering canyon voyages; while mildly entertaining, it's far from essential viewing (daily: March–Oct 8.30am–9.30pm, Nov–Feb 10.30am–6.30pm; $10, $7 under-12s).

INTERNET ACCESS Public machines at *Bright Angel Lodge*, *Kachina Lodge*, *Maswik Lodge*, *Yavapai Lodge* and Camper Services.

LAUNDROMAT There's a large and very inexpensive laundromat just outside the entrance to *Mather Campground*. Summer daily 6am–11pm, last load 9.45pm; spring and fall daily 7am–9pm, last load 7.45pm; winter daily 8am–6pm, last load 4.45pm.

MEDICAL HELP Call ⓣ 911 for emergencies; ⓣ 928/638-2551

for the village clinic (mid-June to mid-Sept Mon–Fri 8am–8pm, Sat 9am–1pm; mid-Sept to mid-June Mon–Fri 9am–6pm, Sat 10am–2pm; emergencies only at other times); ⊤ 928/638-2460 for the pharmacy; and ⊤ 928/638-2395 for dentist.

POST OFFICE In the Market Plaza, near *Yavapai Lodge*. Mon–Fri 9am–4.30pm, Sat 11am–3pm; lobby, with stamp machines, daily 5am–10pm.

SHOWERS Coin-operated showers, starting at $1 and available to all visitors, are located in the laundromat building at the entrance to *Mather Campground*. Summer daily 6am–11pm; spring and fall daily 7am–9pm; winter daily 8am–6pm.

WEDDINGS The park service allows visitors to rent the lovely isolated viewpoint at Shoshone Point – see p.71 – for marriages and other special occasions, between mid-May and mid-October only. Call ⊤ 928/638-7761 for details.

Exploring the South Rim

Naturally enough, the first thing every visitor wants to do is to see the canyon. Where you see it first doesn't actually matter all that much; there are twenty or so major, named viewpoints along the South Rim, plus any number of others in between, and no one of them can be said to be the "best." In any case, you don't have to move from place to place to obtain radically different views of the canyon; staying in one spot, and watching the colors and shadows change as the day progresses, achieves much the same end.

However, contrary to what you might expect, the views from **Grand Canyon Village** itself are not exceptionally good. To enjoy long-range panoramas, you have to head at least as far from the central village as **Maricopa** or **Yavapai** points. Both of those, as well as the majority of the overlooks along the two rim-edge sightseeing routes – **Hermit Road** to the west, and **Desert View Drive** to the east – make ideal vantage points from which to see an unforgettable canyon **sunrise** or **sunset**.

GRAND CANYON VILLAGE AND AROUND

For almost a century after the *El Tovar Hotel* opened in 1905, at the center of what was to become **Grand Canyon Village**, most South Rim visitors got their first glimpse of the canyon from the rim-edge footpath alongside the hotel. These days, however, thanks to the construction of the new information plaza two miles east, your initiation may well come at nearby **Mather Point** instead. That's no cause for regret; the sweeping canyonscape visible from there is far more comprehensive than any obtainable from the village.

All the **hiking trails** that lead into the inner canyon from the South Rim are described in Chapter Eight.

Mather Point

Mather Point, which has its own (woefully inadequate) parking lot and stands just a couple of hundred yards' walk from the information plaza, centers on a rocky outcrop, jutting just below the rim, that can get very crowded indeed. There's always space somewhere along the railed rim trail here, however, and strolling around is in any case rewarded with subtly changing views at every step.

For prospective hikers in particular, Mather Point makes a perfect introduction to the canyon. Its basic orientation being northeastwards, you find yourself looking straight up

Bright Angel Canyon on the far side, as it skewers its way to the North Rim. This is the route followed by the **North Kaibab Trail**, down from the *Grand Canyon Lodge* area (see p.83); a glint of metal halfway along betrays the presence of the footbridge that spans Bright Angel Creek. Two other rim-to-river trails can be spotted closer at hand. To the east, the **South Kaibab Trail** zigzags down from Yaki Point, while the further west of the two visible stretches of the Colorado River marks the point where it's reached by the **Bright Angel Trail**. And you can even see what all the trails are heading for: nestling close to the other tiny patch of river are the cabins of **Phantom Ranch**.

Yavapai Point

If you walk west for around ten minutes from Mather Point – that is, turn left along the rim as you come from the information plaza – you'll come to **Yavapai Point**, which is also the easternmost point served by shuttle buses on the Village Route. Long-range views from here are similar to those from Mather, meaning that the full range of pyramid-shaped buttes known as "temples" line up in front of the North Rim. From left to right, the sequence runs Osiris, Shiva, Isis, Buddha, Manu, Deva, Brahma, Zoroaster, and Vishnu. Two different segments of the river are now on view, one of which happens to include both the Kaibab Suspension Bridge, or "Black Bridge," across the Colorado, and Phantom Ranch.

- -
Temples and other rock formations within the canyon
are described in more detail in "The geology of the
Grand Canyon," p.277.
- -

Nearby, if you can tear your eyes away from the view through its tinted bay windows, the **Yavapai Observation Station** (daily: hours vary from 8am–8pm in summer down to 8am–5pm in winter; free) holds illuminating displays on how the canyon may have been formed. It takes another ten minutes' walk west along the rim before rounding the corner of Grandeur Point brings you within sight of the village proper.

The view from El Tovar

Grand Canyon Village ranges along the inner curve of a recess that cuts well back into the South Rim. Such features are known to geologists as "**arenas**"; this one is also a "**swale**," in that the middle is significantly lower than the two sides. As a result, from the paved, railed terrace that follows the rim for the length of the village you can only see straight across the canyon – though by any standards that's still a stupendous prospect. The long promontories to either side end at **Maricopa Point** to the west, the ridge beneath which stretches into a sturdy sandstone mesa known picturesquely as the Battleship, and **Grandeur Point** to the east. Straight down below, the **Bright Angel Trail** threads through the oasis of **Indian Gardens** before disappearing into a deep crevice, while another long trail leads across the flat, pale-green Tonto Platform to its dead end at **Plateau Point**.

The defining absence in the view from *El Tovar* is the Colorado itself. Although the mighty walls of the Inner Gorge – the granite chasm in the center of the canyon that holds the actual river – are visible on the far side, you can't see their full 1300-foot depth, and the river remains out of sight at the bottom. Thanks to the Bright Angel geological fault, however, there is a gap in the gorge, where Bright Angel Canyon heads up to the **North Rim**. Just to the left at the top is *Grand Canyon Lodge*, though you're only likely to spot it after dark, when the lights come on.

THE RETURN OF THE CONDOR

Of all the awesome spectacles on display along the South Rim, few can match the sight of a fully grown California condor soaring on the canyon updrafts. These magnificent birds, whose wingspan measures over nine feet, and which live for up to sixty years, were reintroduced to Arizona in 1996. They can now frequently be seen hovering above Grand Canyon Village, or perching just below the rim.

The birds were native to the canyon, and indeed to most of North America, for thousands of years, but their population was dwindling long before the first Europeans arrived. During the 1980s, by which time no condor had been seen in Arizona for a hundred years, the last remaining 22 individuals were trapped in California. A captive breeding program was instigated, with birds being reintroduced first in California, and subsequently in northern Arizona.

At the Arizona release site, located on the Vermilion Cliffs fifty miles northeast of the South Rim – see p.119 – scientists take great pains to keep contact between condors and humans to a minimum, so the birds don't learn to associate humans with food. Condors are very inquisitive creatures, however, and to the delight of tourists almost all the Arizona birds spend much of their time in the vicinity of the village. Project workers and park rangers are on hand to discourage them from approaching too close, and leave animal carcasses out for them in remote places. These natural scavengers also manage to find carrion by themselves.

Although around thirty free-flying condors now live in the Grand Canyon area, and they're known to have started laying eggs, no baby condor has yet been raised in the wild. Nonetheless, hopes are high that a viable population will soon be established. For the latest news, call in at park visitor centers, or contact the Peregrine Fund (☎ 928/355-2270, ⓦ www.peregrinefund.org).

A WALKING TOUR OF THE VILLAGE

Grand Canyon Village stretches a lot further back into the woods than you might imagine, and includes a well-hidden residential district used by park employees. While those parts hold no interest for sightseers, the rim itself is lined by a surprisingly attractive assortment of historic buildings.

El Tovar Hotel

Designed by Charles F Whittlesey, the *El Tovar Hotel* opened in 1905, two years after the *Old Faithful Inn* in Yellowstone National Park had established a taste for this kind of overgrown log cabin. The name was taken from Pedro El Tovar, a member of Coronado's expedition who was the first European to hear about the canyon, but was not among the party who actually came here in 1540 (see p.268).

According to the hotel's original brochure, it "combined in admirable proportions the Swiss châlet and the Norway villa," and guests were invited to come in search of "freedom from ultra-fashionable restrictions." At that time, each of its four floors held one single bathroom to serve 25 rooms. The hotel today holds no exhibits or displays for tourists, but you can get the old-time, unhurried flavor of the place by wandering through the lobby, and both its dining room and cocktail lounge are highly recommended (see p.47). Accommodation at *El Tovar* is reviewed on p.41.

Hopi House

Grand Canyon Village's most distinctive structure, the triple-tiered **Hopi House**, opened on January 1, 1905, just two weeks before its close neighbor the *El Tovar Hotel*. Modeled on an actual Hopi dwelling in the village of

Oraibi, a hundred miles to the east, it was designed – by Mary Jane Colter (see box p.58) – as a place where "the most primitive Indians in America" could both live and display their skills. Early residents included the now venerated Pueblo potter Nampeyo. These days it's neither so overtly educational nor so patronizing; instead it's a high-class gift store of native American crafts such as silver jewelry, Navajo rugs, and ceramics. The main store on the ground floor is open daily from 8am until 8pm (9am–5pm in winter), while the more exclusive upstairs gallery is always open between 9am and 5pm only.

Verkamp's Curios

The easternmost building on the rim is a small two-story gift store, **Verkamp's Curios** (summer daily 9am–8pm, fall and spring daily 9am–7.30pm, winter daily 9am–5pm), that clashes with the log-cabin style prevailing in most of the village. Trader John G Verkamp first appeared on the South Rim selling souvenirs from a tent in 1898. He returned to erect this store in 1905, and it's remained here ever since, centering on a large fireplace and selling both cheap tat and ultra-expensive Native American crafts.

Bright Angel Lodge

Bright Angel Lodge, a few hundred yards west of *El Tovar* beyond the nondescript *Thunderbird* and *Kachina* lodges, was Mary Jane Colter's last major work at the canyon. Completed in 1935, as tourist numbers began to pick up after the worst of the Depression, it replaced *Bright Angel Camp*, a ramshackle assortment of cabins and tents. The idea was to provide several cheaper grades of accommodation in a complex that looked more like a genuine village, consisting of several differing but homogenous

MARY JANE COLTER

No one has done more to shape and enhance visitors' experiences of the Grand Canyon than the remarkable architect Mary Jane Colter (1869–1958). Not only was she largely responsible for crafting the look of Grand Canyon Village, but her hand can be seen along the full length of the South Rim, from Hermit's Rest in the west to the Desert View Watchtower in the east, and down by the river at Phantom Ranch. Indeed her influence extended all the way from Chicago to LA; she designed the interiors of Union Station in the former and La Grande Station in the latter, as well as numerous hotels and restaurants in between.

Colter spent fifty years working for both the Santa Fe Railroad and the Fred Harvey Company, in an era when women architects were few and far between. That Fred Harvey, the concessionaire responsible for lodging, dining, and entertaining tourists on the transcontinental railroad, is often said to have "invented the Southwest" is due in large part to her vision.

Born in Pittsburgh in 1869, Mary Colter was raised in St Paul, Minnesota. She was trained at the California School of Design in San Francisco, where she was heavily influenced by the nascent Arts and Crafts movement. Proponents of Arts and Crafts argued that American architects should seek their inspiration at home, using local materials and looking to indigenous examples, rather than feeling obliged to work in traditional European styles. Colter herself, above all, had a lifelong passion for Native American design.

Colter's first Grand Canyon commission produced the Pueblo-influenced Hopi House, a showcase for Hopi craft workers, in 1905. Both Hermit's Rest and Lookout Studio followed in 1914, with Phantom Ranch appearing in 1922. Her best-loved masterpiece, the **Desert View Watchtower**, was completed in 1932, and **Bright Angel Lodge** came along three years later. Meanwhile she also created such signature Harvey hotels as **El Navajo** in Gallup and **La Posada** in Wilmslow.

Her role went far beyond producing the overall design. She'd supervise every step of construction, choosing individual rocks and timbers for both authenticity and inherent beauty, and tearing apart anything that failed to meet her exacting standards. Her attention to detail was legendary, with the interior design seen as every bit as important as the overall edifice. For example, she was responsible for the *Super Chief* train's china service, which incorporated motifs taken from ancient Mimbres pottery.

Even as Colter was completing her final job in 1949, a cocktail lounge at *La Fonda* hotel in Santa Fe, her various Route 66 landmarks were starting to close down. Having sadly observed "there's such a thing as living too long," she died in January 1958, bequeathing her extensive collection of Native American jewelry and ceramics to the museum at Mesa Verde National Park. Since her death, however, her unique contribution to the American West has been increasingly recognized, and much of her finest work has been lovingly restored.

Author Frank Waters conjured up a beautifully romantic portrait of Colter in his 1950 book, *Masked Gods*: "For years an incomprehensible woman in pants, she rode horseback through the Four Corners making sketches of prehistoric pueblo ruins, studying details of construction ... She could teach masons how to lay adobe bricks, plasterers how to mix washes, carpenters how to fix *viga* joints."

MARY JANE COLTER

buildings. Two historic structures were incorporated in their entirety: the gable-roofed pioneer **Buckey O'Neill Cabin**, attached to the main lodge, and the separate **Cameron Hotel**, also known as Red Horse Station, which has at various times been a stagecoach station, a hotel, and a US post office.

To the left of the lobby, the lodge's **History Room** features a ten-foot-tall fireplace which displays all the principal types of rock found in the Grand Canyon, in the correct chronological sequence. It also hosts displays on varying aspects of the canyon's past, focussing especially on the heyday of the Fred Harvey company. Lodging at *Bright Angel Lodge* is reviewed on p.41, and its restaurant on p.47.

Lookout Studio

Lookout Studio, which appears to grow organically from a narrow rocky protuberance just west of *Bright Angel Lodge*, was built by Mary Jane Colter for the Fred Harvey company in 1914 as a "tiny rustic club." The idea was that tourists would shelter here rather than the rival Kolb Studio during bad weather, or simply while away their afternoons in solitude. Both the building itself, with its Pueblo stylings, and the view from its open-air terrace are as appealing as ever, but it now holds just another hectic gift store (summer daily 8am–sunset, otherwise daily 9am–5pm).

Kolb Studio

At the head of the Bright Angel Trail, the **Kolb Studio** spills over the edge of the canyon, with its entrance at rim level and another story down below. This was originally the home and workplace of Emery and Ellsworth Kolb, two brothers who set it up as their photographic studio in 1902. They'd take pictures of each day's contingent of departing

MULE RIDES

Joining a **mule train** to ride down the Bright Angel Trail from Grand Canyon Village is a fine old canyon tradition. Places are limited, so it's best to make a reservation, on ☎ 928/638-2631, as far in advance as possible; they're accepted up to a year ahead of time. If you arrive without a reservation, put yourself on the waiting list that's maintained at the Transportation Desk at *Bright Angel Lodge*, and turn up there at 6am on the morning you want to ride; there are normally a few last-minute cancellations each day. Riders must be at least four feet seven inches tall (1.38m), speak fluent English, and weigh not more than 200 pounds (91kg); it's not unusual to see would-be mule riders jogging in a desperate attempt to sweat off those last few pounds. You don't have to have any experience, but it's worth taking seriously the warnings that you should be afraid neither of large animals nor of great heights.

All rides set off early in the morning, with precise schedules varying through the year. **One-day**, seven-hour round trips as far as Plateau Point cost $120, including lunch, and get you back to the village in mid-afternoon. **Overnight** trips take the morning to descend the full length of the Bright Angel Trail to **Phantom Ranch**, where you spend the rest of the day beside the river, and sleep in two-person cabins. Soon after sunrise the next morning, the mules set off up along the South Kaibab Trail; you're met by bus at the top, and should be back at *Bright Angel Lodge* in time for lunch. Including cabin accommodation and all meals, they cost $338 for one person, $604 for two. **Two-night** rides, available between mid-November and March only, follow the same route but stay another night down at the ranch, at a cost of $461 for one, $781 for two.

The Bright Angel Trail is described in detail on p.213, and the South Kaibab Trail on p.219, while there's more on Phantom Ranch on p.228.

mule riders, run down the trail to do their developing using the water at Indian Gardens, and then run back to have the prints ready when the riders returned. During 1911 and 1912, they shot the first-ever film of a boating expedition along the entire canyon. This became the longest-running movie of all time; Emery presented it here daily from 1915 until soon before his death, aged 95, in 1976.

No longer an active studio, it's now divided between a well-stocked bookstore upstairs, and a gallery that hosts changing exhibitions downstairs, where there's also a nice little bay window offering superb views (daily: summer 8am–8pm, fall and spring 8am–7pm, winter 8am–5pm).

HERMIT ROAD

The eight-mile, dead-end scenic drive officially known as **Hermit Road**, but also familiar to many visitors as the **West Rim Drive**, starts a hundred yards west of *Bright Angel Lodge*, just as Grand Canyon Village peters out. Offering a succession of very different but consistently impressive canyon panoramas, it's the most obvious, and most enjoyable, half-day sightseeing trip from the village. As the only vehicles allowed access in summer are the free Hermit's Rest Route **shuttle buses**, detailed on p.37, the Xanterra bus tours, and those displaying disabled permits – private cars without disabled permits are only permitted between December and February – it also makes a welcome escape from the crowds and traffic elsewhere along the rim.

What was then called the **Hermit Rim Road** was constructed by the Santa Fe Railroad between 1910 and 1912 so they could provide stagecoach excursions for their rail passengers. At that time, the Bright Angel Trail was privately owned, so the Santa Fe laid out their own Hermit Trail, at the far end of the road, which they used for mule rides and overnight trips. It's still there; see p.69. The "**Hermit**"

name, incidentally, was a piece of harmless myth-making centered around one Louis Boucher, a white-bearded old prospector who made his home for twenty years at Dripping Springs, near the head of trail.

While for most of its length the road runs within a few yards of the canyon, it's paralleled, as ever, by the **Rim Trail**, even closer to the edge. No one ever bothers to walk the entire eight miles, but the ideal way to explore is to combine judicious use of the shuttle buses with stretches of **walking**. Paved for the first 1.4 miles, as far as Maricopa Point, the trail later becomes an unmarked, and not always very conspicuous, dirt path. It's not an utterly straightforward hike, as it can be very uneven underfoot, and occasionally teeters along alarming drop-offs – in which case you can always retreat to the road – but it's not nearly as tiring as the inner canyon trails. So long as you bring a bottle of water, you should have no problems.

It's important to realize that although the buses make eight stops, they do so only on their **outward** journey. You can only pick up a bus heading back to the village from three places: Hermit's Rest, Mohave Point, or Hopi Point. That means you can't simply walk or take a bus to any of the first three overlooks and then ride straight back again. You can ride to one of those overlooks and hike back, but if you want to catch a bus home you must first get at least as far as Hopi Point. Possible permutations are endless, but **recommended hikes** include the twenty-minute walks between Hopi and Mohave points, and between Pima Point and Hermit's Rest.

Traveling the full length of Hermit Road without ever getting off the bus takes about ninety minutes. To allow time for a couple of short hikes, and a stop at Hermit's Rest, give yourself perhaps three hours. Alternatively, you need never get on a bus at all; the four-mile round-trip hike from the village to Hopi Point, for example, takes under two hours. And finally, **cycling** is permitted on Hermit Road year-round, though you're expected to dismount every time a shuttle bus goes past.

Trailview Overlook

The first stop on the shuttle bus, **Trailview Overlook**, is in fact a large parking lot that serves two distinct viewpoints, known as **Trailview I** and **II**. Still well within the "arena" that centers upon the village – although the road makes an extravagant loop inland as it first sets off, this spot is less than three-quarters of a mile along the Rim Trail – these offer similar views to those obtained from the village, albeit from a slightly higher elevation. In addition, they offer a sweeping prospect of the village itself, straggled along the lip of the canyon.

As their name suggests, however, the viewpoints also provide a fine overview of the **Bright Angel Trail**. Prospective hikers can see exactly what they're in for, with every cruel red-dirt switchback clearly etched against the canyon walls below.

Maricopa Point

A little over a mile along, the Rim Trail rounds a corner and passes out of sight of Grand Canyon Village. Views now finally open up to the west as well as to the east, so the railed, rocky overlook at **Maricopa Point**, the second shuttle stop, commands a sweeping canyon panorama. This is a prime spot for identifying the majestic buttes on the far side of the river, such as the Brahma and Zoroaster "temples," each with its capping layer of hard red sandstone.

The monumental parade stretches from Vishnu Temple in the east, isolated beyond Cape Royal – the last point visible on the North Rim – to Isis Temple far to the west.

HERMIT ROAD

Lower in the foreground stands Cheops Pyramid, with beneath it what geologists call the "Grand Canyon Series" of tilted silt, shale and sandstone, and below that the harsh twisted schist of the Inner Gorge. To the south of the unseen river, the Battleship promontory, so stark and conspicuous from the village, can now be seen, if not as readily recognized, from above.

Powell Point

West of Maricopa, both the road and the trail (now unpaved) detour inland around a high fence, festooned with solemn radiation warnings. In the heart of this enclosure lurks the hulking headframe of the **Orphan Mine**. Having started out mining copper a thousand feet below the rim in 1893, it became America's largest uranium producer in the 1950s. Amazingly, the company that owned it also ran an on-site hotel, the *Grand Canyon Inn*, which it threatened to expand in terraces far beneath the rim. Both hotel and mine went out of business in the late 1960s, however, and the land here was acquired by the park in 1988. Nonetheless, there are still significant uranium deposits in the vicinity, located by no coincidence at all in areas that remain outside the protection of the park.

The next headland west of the mine is **Powell Point**, where a short walk from the shuttle bus leads to the spot where the park was officially dedicated on April 30, 1920. This was known as Sentinel Point until 1916, when a Maya-style stepped pyramid was erected as a memorial to John Wesley Powell, who had recently died, and the crews of his two Colorado expeditions. From the paved but railless viewing area on its far side, you can look across the river to the curious semicircular cliff wall of the "temple" known as the **Tower of Set**; shaped like an opening bracket, it's mirrored by a similar wall on **Isis Temple** to the east.

HERMIT ROAD

Hopi Point

Two miles out from Grand Canyon Village, **Hopi Point** is the busiest of the western viewpoints, as both an ideal destination for hikers and the closest stop served by buses returning to the village. Its reputation as the perfect place from which to admire the **sunset** rests on the fact that this promontory thrusts further north than any of its neighbors, with the vast panoply that spreads to the west forming just part of what's virtually a 360-degree canyon prospect.

The shuttle buses don't go right to the tip of the large parking lot here, so you can take a short loop stroll around its tiered perimeter, catching assorted glimpses of the Colorado along the way. The most dramatic segment lies immediately below Plateau Point (see p.216). It's hard to believe that the river is 350 feet wide down there, lying at the foot of gnarled and impossibly ancient walls of black schist streaked through with vertical pink faults. To the west, the Colorado threads its tortuous way toward the ocean between interleaved spurs of red rock, and a maze of lesser canyons twists among the mighty buttes.

A plaque at Hopi Point commemorates the Civilian Conservation Corps, a Depression-era labor force, nicknamed "The President's Tree Army," that did much valuable work in the park between 1933 and 1942. Another directs your attention to Birdseye Point on the North Rim, and honors Colonel Claude Hale Birdseye, the Chief Topographic Engineer of the US Geological Survey, who headed a survey expedition through the canyon in 1923.

Mohave Point

Road and trail curve gracefully west of Hopi Point for three-quarters of a mile, tracing the lip of a lesser basin

HERMIT ROAD

sometimes known as **The Inferno**, to reach **Mohave Point**. The long-range prospect from this large railed promontory (pronounced *mo-harvey*) remains substantially unchanged, though for once there are no placards to tell you what you're seeing.

Views back to the east are comprehensively blocked by the sheer cliffs below Hopi Point – at least now you can appreciate quite how steep it is. These stark sandstone walls glow spectacular shades of red toward dusk, while the equally impressive cliffs to the west acquire creeping impenetrable shadows. Two more stretches of the Colorado can now be seen, including the foaming white turmoil of **Granite Rapid**.

The Abyss

Another huge recess indents the line of the South Rim west of Mohave Point, named **The Abyss** in tribute to its immensely steep sides. Shuttle buses make their next stop a mile along, at the far end of the **Great Mohave Wall**, which plummets over three thousand feet straight down.

Though the casual observer might well assume that the peaks now visible on the western horizon lie further along the South Rim, they are in fact across on the far side of the river. They belong to the **Uinkarets** range, and include the 8026-foot **Mount Trumbull**, which is almost 60 miles distant. Closer at hand, four successive parallel sandstone ridges stand like stage scenery in front of Pima Point.

The main reason anyone gets off the bus at the Abyss is to hike in either direction along the vertiginous Rim Trail. There's no real danger to the trail, but as ever, if the drop starts to bother you, you can always walk along the road instead.

HERMIT ROAD

Pima Point

Pima Point lies four miles beyond Mohave Point, along a spur road off Hermit Road, and at the tip of a promontory that separates the basins cut by Monument Creek to the east – responsible for the Abyss – and Hermit Creek to the west. By now, this side of the canyon is so abrupt that the Colorado is less than two horizontal miles distant, and you can look straight down into the maw of the three-quarter-mile **Granite Rapid**. From the far bank, however, it's another twelve labyrinthine miles to the North Rim. Looking west, a significant stretch of **Boucher Rapid**, named for the "Hermit," is also visible. This whole west-ward prospect is especially stunning in the early morning, with the last headland visible on the South Rim, **Havasupai Point**, separated by only the tiniest notch in the horizon from **Powell Plateau** on the other side. Helpful park-service displays near the bus stop illustrate the canyon's geological structure using photos of nearby forma-tions, and explain how the canyon starts to change further to the west, beyond the areas visible from Hermit Road.

In the days when Santa Fe mule rides headed down the Hermit Trail – also conspicuous down on the Tonto Platform – tourists would stay overnight at **Hermit Camp**. Few traces survive of the camp itself, and none of the aerial tramway that supplied it, from the west side of Pima Point.

Hermit's Rest

Hermit Road ends slightly over a mile past Pima Point, at the **Hermit's Rest** waystation, laid out by Mary Jane Colter in 1914 as an artful evocation of the dwelling of some imaginary canyon prospector. The path from the parking lot leads through a deliberately crude archway of stone slabs, decked with a hanging bell found by Colter in an antique store, and then along the canyon rim to what at first glance appears to be no more than a ramshackle pile of rocks stacked against the hillside. Closer inspection reveals a rambling but very inviting structure, centering on a massive domed fireplace, and holding a large gift store (summer daily 8am–7.30pm, otherwise daily 9am–sunset). The soot that blackens the fireplace is all fake; as Colter put it, "You can't imagine what it cost to make this place look old." Simple snacks are also available.

As Hermit's Rest is oriented toward the side canyon shaped by Hermit Creek, it doesn't offer quite the same extensive views as Pima or Maricopa points. Only a tiny patch of Colorado is now visible, but you can at least look up the creek towards its source, **Dripping Spring**, where hermit Louis Boucher really did make his home. **Hermit Trail**, abandoned by the Santa Fe in 1931 but still popular with inner-canyon hikers (see p.236), starts a little way past the store.

DESERT VIEW DRIVE

Desert View Drive runs for 23 miles east from Mather Point to Desert View itself, just inside the park's eastern entrance station. It was constructed in 1931, as East Rim Drive; more visitors were now arriving by car than by rail, and they wanted to be able to follow the full length of the South Rim. These days it counts as a continuation of Hwy-64 up from Williams, which extends all the way east to Cameron, but there are no further canyon overlooks beyond Desert View.

Despite threats to restrict all the Desert View Drive parking lots to shuttle and tour buses, only Yaki Point has so far been closed to private vehicles. Free shuttle buses only run that far, although the Xanterra bus tours make the entire round trip to the end and back; for details on both options, see p.37. For the moment, however, this is the one part of the South Rim open year-round for self-guided driving tours. Allow two hours at the very least to get to the end and back. In addition to the formal viewpoints described below, the road occasionally runs very close to the rim; you're not supposed to stop for picnics and sightseeing, but plenty of people do.

Yaki Point

The first of the Desert View Drive lookouts, **Yaki Point** – located a mile along a spur road that begins a short way east of the start of the drive – is only accessible in your own vehicle in December, January and February, though as detailed on p.37 it's served year-round by free shuttle buses.

A mere two miles east of Yavapai Point as the condor flies, Yaki Point commands much the same trans-canyon views as its neighbor. Straight across the river stands Zoroaster Temple with its fluted sides, while thanks to the curve of the Colorado, Vishnu Temple to the right is silhouetted against the eastern horizon. The stark finger of the Watchtower at Desert View can also be seen to the east, almost fifteen miles distant.

Although five different **inner-canyon trails** are visible from Yaki Point – including the Bright Angel, Plateau Point, and Tonto trails this side of the river, and the Clear Creek Trail on the far side – the Colorado itself remains stubbornly out of view. The fifth of those trails, the **South Kaibab Trail**, is the main reason people come to Yaki Point; it starts its quickfire descent to Phantom Ranch from its own separate parking lot, just 0.3 miles off Desert View Drive (see p.219). From the main overlook, you can spot it far below, switchbacking down an exposed scree slope of red rock between two buttes, while scrambling out onto the rocks beyond the viewpoint offers clearer views down to its principal staging post, O'Neill Butte. Unless you're actually hiking the trail, there's no reason to call in at the trailhead parking lot, which stands alongside the mule corral used by pack trips returning from Phantom Ranch (see p.61).

Shoshone Point

Located a couple of miles east of Yaki Point, **Shoshone Point** is the least-known and least-visited of the South Rim viewpoints, for the simple reason that it's only accessible on **foot**, along an easy one-mile trail from Desert View Drive. In addition, the park service deliberately does not publicize it to casual visitors, preferring instead to make it available, between mid-May and mid-October, for weddings and other private gatherings; as mentioned on p.51, it can be reserved by calling ☏ 928/638-7761. During the winter, and at other times when it hasn't been reserved (ask at the information plaza), Shoshone Point is open to ordinary hikers – and it's an absolute gem, offering an unparalleled sense of peace and privacy. An hour's round-trip hike from the road may well offer your only chance to be alone with the canyon on the South Rim.

The trail to Shoshone Point begins from an unpaved parking lot in the woods on the canyon side of Desert View Drive, located 1.4 miles east of the turn-off to Yaki Point. You'll know you're at the right place if you see a yellow metal gate barring a dirt road, and a brown park notice reading "Site Use by Permit Only." Walking at a fairly brisk pace, it takes around fifteen minutes to follow the meandering trail, with minimal elevation change, through first ponderosa pines and then pinyon and juniper – the shade is welcome in summer – as far as the canyon rim.

Beyond a clearing that holds picnic tables, barbecue grills, and a couple of portable toilets, the point itself is

DESERT VIEW DRIVE

truly spectacular, standing in splendid isolation far from the clamor of the crowds and the noise of traffic on the roads. A solitary pale hoodoo (a Southwestern term denoting a bizarrely balanced rock) marks the tip of its slender neck, which can feel a little precarious in the absence of the usual railings. The sublime views range along the full panoply of the North Rim, culminating to the east with the end of the Walhalla Plateau at Cape Royal, and the crest of Vishnu Temple out in the canyon. All but straight ahead, Zoroaster and Brahma temples stand in line.

Grandview Point

Eight miles east of Yaki Point along Desert View Drive, or 6.4 miles beyond the Shoshone Point parking lot – making a total of twelve miles out from the village – you reach the first year-round parking lot at **Grandview Point**. Among the most dramatic and all-embracing of all canyon view-points, Grandview is thought to mark the general vicinity from which Spanish adventurers first saw the Grand Canyon, in 1540 (see p.269). It's suggested that their Hopi guides deliberately led them to a spot from which no trails were visible, so the canyon would appear an even more impassable obstacle.

- -
All the **hiking trails** that lead into the inner canyon
from the South Rim are described in Chapter Eight.
- -

Grandview Point was also the place where **tourism** first took off at the Grand Canyon. Prospector Peter Berry discovered rich deposits of copper three thousand feet below the rim in 1890, and constructed the Grandview Trail down to his **Last Chance** mine in 1892. Five years later, with visitors now gravitating to the site, Berry opened the *Grandview Hotel*. It thrived at first, but within ten years the coming of the railroad, over to the west, drove Berry out of business. A few traces of the hotel now remain, a mile or so back from the edge.

In terms of **views**, however, Grandview is unarguably superior to Grand Canyon Village. There's no need to set foot on the precarious Grandview Trail (see p.234) in order to plot the sinuous course of the Colorado, which makes its broad and langorous entrance off to the east before disappearing into the stunning sandstone labyrinth. Down below, the twin prongs of **Horseshoe Mesa**, home to Berry's copper mine, reach out toward the North Rim. The left points to the mesa of **Wotan's Throne**, detached from the rim but still towering a couple of hundred feet taller than Grandview itself; in the center is **Cape Royal**, at the tip of the Walhalla Plateau (see p.93); and more obvious to the right, **Cape Final** juts out at the far eastern end of the North Rim, above and behind Vishnu Temple.

Grandview Point is also an attractive spot in its own right, located in one of the very few stands of pure ponderosa pine to be found on the South Rim, and frequented by roaming elk at both sunset and sunrise.

Grandview Monocline

Starting three miles beyond Grandview, Desert View Drive abruptly descends the three-hundred-foot incline of **Buggeln Hill**, the most visible evidence of the **Grandview Monocline**. In a land of such wonders this inconspicuous geological feature – a small fold in the rock manifesting itself as an unremarkable little hill – hardly merits a second glance, but it may well be responsible for the greatest wonder of all. Up till this point, the course of the Colorado has been southwards, slicing through softer Moenkopi Formation rock as it skirts the edge of the Kaibab Plateau. Now, however, the Grandview Monocline thrusts into its path, presenting an equally difficult wall of hard Kaibab limestone. With no easy way out, the river is finally forced to turn west, and cut down into the Kaibab, creating the Grand Canyon as we know it.

Moran Point

Moran Point, not far beyond Buggeln Hill and named for the nineteenth-century artist Thomas Moran, faces west toward the heart of the maelstrom. Close at hand, but higher than the lookout, the isolated fin of rock known as the **Sinking Ship** juts out into the canyon from the top of the hill. Its stratified layers of sandstone perfectly reveal the Grandview Monocline's angle of tilt.

Tusayan Ruin and Museum

The next parking lot, four miles on from Moran Point, is unexpectedly located south rather than north of the highway. Set back in the forest a quarter of a mile from the rim, **Tusayan Ruin** – not to be confused with the modern town of Tusayan – is an open-air archeological site that centers on the remains of a typical twelfth-century **pueblo**. Consisting of fifteen separate "rooms," including a circular ceremonial chamber or *kiva*, this was built in approximately 1185 AD. It was occupied for perhaps 25 years by a community of around thirty people, whose clear cultural connection with modern Pueblo Indians means that these days they're referred to as **Ancestral Puebloans**, in preference to the older and more familiar term **Anasazi**.

Although at that time the Ancestral Puebloans were gradually withdrawing from the Grand Canyon area, the inhabitants of Tusayan, as well as farming the wash close to their homes, trekked regularly into the canyon, using what's now called the Tanner Trail. They seem to have felt some sense of menace or apprehension, as fort-like structures found at various points along the rim nearby date from the same era.

Only low stone walls now survive of the original Tusayan complex, so – much like the other two thousand or so Ancestral Puebloan sites so far identified in and around the Grand Canyon – it's nothing like as spectacular as the relics to be found in such places as the Canyon de Chelly and Mesa Verde. Its very existence, however, enabled President Teddy Roosevelt to accord National Monument status to the entire Grand Canyon (see p.273). A small **museum** on site (daily 9am–5pm; free) holds displays on the contemporary Navajo and Hopi peoples, as well as 4000-year-old twig figurines and Ancestral Puebloan pottery found nearby. Park rangers lead **tours** of the ruins daily at 11am and 1.30pm.

Lipan Point

Another couple of miles on from Tusayan Ruin, **Lipan Point** ranks in the very top tier of South Rim overlooks. While the overall prospect is not very different to that from Desert View, less than three miles east, and there are no comparable facilities, Lipan tends to be a lot quieter, and it's even more perfectly poised to appreciate several pivotal events in the life of the Colorado.

Emerging from Marble Canyon to the north, the Colorado becomes visible just after it meets the Little Colorado, which cuts in from the east through the endless flat Marble Platform. The vertical canyon walls marking the edge of the platform are known as the **Palisades of the Desert**. Immediately below Lipan, at the mouth of Tanner Canyon – a spot accessible via the **Tanner Trail** (see p.231), which starts beside the parking lot – the river makes its dramatic change of direction, to flow westwards rather than southwards. At first it meanders through the gently

DESERT VIEW DRIVE

sloping eroded formations of the Grand Canyon Series, making an extravagant double curve at the mouth of **Unkar Creek**. The Unkar Delta here once held an extensive Ancestral Puebloan population, who farmed both down by the river and up on the Walhalla Plateau of the North Rim (see p.93). It's a beautiful spot, with distinct sandstone strata that strike maroon, ruby and raspberry notes at sunset. To the west, river runners face their first major whitewater challenge, as the Colorado gouges its way into the Inner Gorge and enters the ferocious mile-long **Hance Rapid**.

Desert View

Desert View, 25 miles east of Grand Canyon Village, is the last canyon viewpoint along Desert View Drive. As AZ-64, however, the road continues another 34 miles to meet US-89 at Cameron (see p.107), so Desert View also provides visitors approaching from the east with their *first* opportunity to see what all the fuss is about. Few will be disappointed: like Lipan Point, Desert View offers two staggering panoramas in one.

To the north, four miles distant, the Colorado River can be seen approaching its sudden westward turn. The stark Palisades of the Desert delineate the South Rim, while above them the pallid plains of the Marble Plateau stretch to the horizon, beneath an overwhelming sky. Ninety miles northeast, beyond the Vermilion and Echo Cliffs, lies the gray bulk of Navajo Mountain. During the Mesozoic era, until 65 million years ago, the entire vast landscape was buried beneath an additional four or five thousand feet of sedimentary sandstone. Thanks to subsequent erosion, all that remains are a few tiny vestiges, such as the reddish mesa of **Cedar Mountain** a mile or two back from the rim.

Over to the west, by contrast, the river disappears deep

into the Inner Gorge, engulfed on all sides by buttes and mesas, temples, shrines and tabernacles. During the morning they present an extraordinary panoply of colors and shapes; the rich golds and reds are the first to go, leached out by the midday sun, while as dusk draws on they seem to lose all form as well, turning into mysterious interleaving shadowy screens, devoid of all three-dimensional quality.

Rather than the canyon itself, however, what immediately draws the eye is the remarkable structure perched at its very lip – the **Desert View Watchtower**. Melded almost imperceptibly into the sandstone blocks of the rim, this circular tower counts as the greatest *tour de force* of architect **Mary Jane Colter** (see pp.58–59). Based on her study of Ancestral Puebloan remains throughout the Four Corners region, it was completed in 1932, with its design modeled on the Round Tower in southwest Colorado's Mesa Verde National Park, and the style of its masonry construction on the various towers at Hovenweep National Monument in southeast Utah. Some of the stone used was taken from nearby ruins, while it also incorporated genuine petroglyphs found near Ash Fork, and even timbers from the much more recent, abandoned *Grandview Hotel* (see p.72). Colter's aim was not to create a replica of an actual Indian building; she simply wanted to provide a fitting but not too intrusive landmark at journey's end for Fred Harvey's sightseeing tours, and to educate tourists about native American culture ancient and modern.

It's no longer obvious that the ground floor of the Watchtower, which is open daily between 8am and sunset, was laid out as a ceremonial *kiva* – it's too cluttered with gifts and souvenirs – but it's still well worth paying 25¢ at the turnstile to climb through its three upper stories. A mural by Hopi artist Fred Kabotie in the first circular chamber depicts the snake legend of the Hopis, while the second holds reproduction pictographs and petroglyphs painted by a Fred Harvey employee. The uppermost floor, or "Eagle's Nest," is all but bare, but holds large panoramic windows. There's no access to the roof.

Over the years, the Watchtower has acquired a plethora of much less distinguished neighbors, including an **information center** and bookstore (summer daily 9am–7pm; spring and fall daily 9am–6pm; winter daily 9am–5pm); the Desert View Marketplace **general store** (daily 9am–5pm); a **gas station** (daily 9am–6pm); and the Trading Post gift store and **snack bar** (7.30am–6pm), where the ultra-basic menu features a hamburger for $2.75, a cold sandwich for $3.25, and a slice of pie for $1.95, The **Desert View Campground** (see p.46) is located at the end of a short spur road from the gas station.

Few visitors make a beeline for **Navajo Point**, served by a separate parking lot a few hundred yards west of Desert View, even though it's the highest spot along the whole South Rim. At 7498 feet, it's still 500 feet lower than **Cape Final**, eight miles away on the North Rim, but at least you get a real sense of the forested plateau on the far side.

The North Rim

Higher, bleaker, and much more remote than the South Rim, the **North Rim** of the Grand Canyon is accessible to travelers for less than half the year. Once the only road in, **AZ-67**, has been blocked by the first major snowfall of each winter, the entire North Rim section of the national park remains closed until the following spring. Although traditionally that first snow has arrived toward the end of October, these days locals report that the area is receiving only a fraction of its official average annual snowfall of 140 inches, and in 2002, for example, the road did not close until December 9. In any case, the one accommodation option on the North Rim, *Grand Canyon Lodge*, continues to operate to a more rigid schedule, opening during the second week of May and closing on October 15. After it closes, there's a hiatus until the snow comes, during which the park itself remains open, but no food, gas, or lodging other than camping is available, and visitors must be prepared to leave at a moment's notice.

A map of the North Rim can be found at
the back of this book (map 4).

Even in peak season, the North Rim offers a sense of splendid isolation, and its annual quota of between 350,000

CHAPTER 2 • THE NORTH RIM

and 450,000 visitors is less than a tenth of the South Rim's. While that doesn't mean you'll have the place to yourself, it can still make you feel as though you're venturing into unexplored wilderness. The basic principle, however, is the same as at the South Rim, with a cluster of venerable park-service buildings at **Bright Angel Point**, where the main highway reaches the canyon, and another rim-edge road where drivers can take their pick from additional lookouts.

Driving to the North Rim, much like the South, entails a long haul through ponderosa forests, albeit here interspersed with appealing, often flower-filled meadows. The canyon itself, however, is significantly different on this side of the Colorado. Erosion is much more active; twice as much rain falls, and it freezes more often. As the Kaibab Plateau slopes south, the water flows toward the rim, which it has cut twice as far back from the river. Thus the North Rim is far more indented with massive side canyons, the largest of which, the little-known **Kanab Canyon**, effectively splits it in two. The area known as the "North Rim," and covered in this chapter, is strictly speaking just the eastern portion of the Grand Canyon's northern rim. Its western half, and most notably the superb **Toroweap** viewpoint, can only be reached from the Arizona Strip, and is therefore covered in Chapter Four.

Human occupation of the North Rim has always been minimal, with Native Americans merely passing through in summer. Mormons and prospectors seldom ventured this way, so apart from the odd trapper and adventurer, the North Rim was hardly explored until geologists, hunters and even a few tourists began turning up at the start of the twentieth century. The first dirt road arrived from Kanab, Utah in 1919, while driving from the South Rim only became practicable with the opening of Navajo Bridge in 1929.

Arrival and information

The only access to the North Rim is via **AZ-67**, which, as described on p.122, runs south for 44 miles from **Jacob Lake** to Bright Angel Point. En route, it climbs one thousand feet, reaching the highest portion of the Kaibab Plateau five miles south of DeMotte Park. That barely perceptible nine-thousand-foot ridge, around twelve miles short of the North Rim, roughly corresponds to the boundary of the national park. Rangers at the park **entrance station**, on the highway just beyond, collect the fees detailed on p.13, and hand out the park newspaper, *The Guide*, which is published in a separate edition for the North Rim.

The road then drops gradually south for another nine miles, passing Fuller Canyon Road – the access road to the Walhalla Plateau overlooks, described on p.93 onwards – three miles from the end, and then the North Kaibab Trailhead and the turn-off for the campground. You never quite see the canyon from the highway, which comes to a halt at a turnaround in front of *Grand Canyon Lodge*, with several large parking lots off to the left.

INFORMATION

The **North Rim Visitor Center**, the first building on the left in the lodge complex, is the main source of information for visitors (daily May to mid-Oct 8am–6pm; ☎ 928/638-7864). Staff drawn from several different public-lands agencies can advise on routes and current conditions for hiking and backcountry road trips. They also have details of the day's free program of **ranger talks** – held at both the lodge and the campground – and **guided walks**. A ninety-minute nature walk starts here daily at 9.30am. Sharing the

ARRIVAL AND INFORMATION

same space, the small Grand Canyon Association **book-store** stocks maps and trail guides.

The **North Rim Backcountry Office**, which issues the backcountry permits required by anyone going on an overnight backpacking trip is housed in a different ranger station, just over a mile back up the highway a quarter-mile north of the campground (daily 8am–noon & 1–5pm; ☏928/638-7868). Day-hikers do not need permits.

For more information about trails from the North Rim, and backcountry permits, go to the Hiking chapter (p.201).

TRANSPORTATION AND TOURS

No organized sightseeing tours are currently available at the North Rim, and there's no equivalent to the buses that operate along the South Rim. The only long-distance public transportation is provided by the Transcanyon Shuttle (☏602/638-2820), whose van service to the **South Rim** leaves from outside *Grand Canyon Lodge* at 7am daily. Having reached the South Rim at 11.30am, it departs again at 1.30pm, and arrives back at the North Rim at 6pm. A one-way trip costs $65, and the round trip $110; no credit cards are accepted.

There's also a hiker shuttle to the North Kaibab Trailhead, which leaves *Grand Canyon Lodge* at 5.20am and 7.20am daily. It costs $5 for the first person in your group, and $2 for each additional passenger.

A desk in the lobby of the lodge handles reservation for North Rim **mule rides** (☏435/679-8665, ⓦ www.onpages .com/canyonrides). A one-hour rim-edge ride costs $20, while both the alternative half-day options – either along the rim to Uncle Jim Point, or down the North Kaibab Trail as far as the Supai Tunnel – cost $45. A full-day canyon ride, down to Roaring Springs and back, is $95, and there are no overnight trips. The minimum age limit is 7 for the one-hour rides, 8 for the two half-day rides, and 12 for the full-day trip.

Grand Canyon Lodge and around

The rambling, atmospheric **Grand Canyon Lodge**, a glorified log cabin in the finest national-park tradition, is poised majestically near the tip of the promontory that ends at **Bright Angel Point**. Designed by Gilbert Stanley Underwood, it was built in 1928 for the Union Pacific Railroad. Not that their trains passed anywhere nearby; instead they'd bring excursionists here as part of bus tours that also took in Zion and Bryce. After the lodge burned down in 1932, it was rebuilt in 1936 using a bit more stone and a bit less timber. The park service took it over in 1971, when Union Pacific closed down.

The lodge's lovely dining room, reviewed on p.85, is just to the left of the entrance lobby. Straight ahead, however, steps down lead to the building's best feature, a spacious viewing lounge known as the **Sun Room**, where rows of comfortable armchairs face huge picture windows. The foreground view here is of the side canyon known as **The Transept**; the Grand Canyon proper lies beyond, though you don't so much see it as sense its vast empty presence. Open patios to either side of the lounge encourage you to relax and enjoy the spectacle. The one to the left, often used for ranger talks, holds ranks of long benches, while the smaller one to the right is equipped with individual reading chairs. Short footpaths lead to railed rim-edge overlooks just below, quite as dramatic as those at the point itself, and invariably packed at sunset.

Accommodation

The **guest rooms** at *Grand Canyon Lodge* are located not in the main building, but in a complex of individual cabins and larger motel-style blocks. Almost all are ranged in tiers over the well-wooded hillside beside the approach road; as they're across the road from the parking lot, they're usually remarkably quiet. Little paved footways thread between them, dimly lit at night beneath a sky filled with stars.

There are three different kinds of cabin. Each of the 51 well-appointed **Western Cabins** (❼) holds two queen beds, with a full-size bathroom and a porch, and can sleep up to four people. A mere four of them stand close enough to the rim to offer **canyon views**, the only North Rim accommodation options to do so; they cost $10 extra per night (still ❼), and tend to be booked as much as two years in advance.

The 83 more spartan **Frontier Cabins** (❻) can accommodate three guests each, with one double bed and one single, and have smaller bathrooms, while the 22 similar **Pioneer Cabins** (❼), capable of sleeping five people, consist of two separate bedrooms – one with a double bed and a single bed, and the other with two single beds – and a small bathroom.

In addition, a couple of two-story blocks located furthest from the lodge hold twenty **motel rooms** each (❻), with a queen bed and private bathroom. Only the Frontier cabins and the motel rooms have telephones.

As the whole place tends to be booked up months in advance, **reservations** are essential. They're handled by the same agents as for the South Rim, Xanterra Parks & Resorts (same-day reservations, or to contact guest, ☎928/638-2611; advance 303/297-2757 or 1-888/297-2757, ⓦwww.grandcanyonnorthrim.com).

Eating and drinking

Eating in the main **Dining Room** at *Grand Canyon Lodge* – open daily for all meals, 6.30–10am, 11.30am–2.30pm, and 4.45–9.30pm – is a truly memorable experience. The setting is magnificent: the room itself, with its soaring timber ceiling, is elegant and impressive, and if you're lucky enough to have a window table (assigned at random, not by reservation) you get awesome canyon views. The food, a robust but relatively modern interpretation of American resort cuisine, is of a very high standard as well. For dinner, pasta entrees, such as shrimp with feta and pine nuts, range $14–19; steaks are more like $24; and specials like Four Corners Lime Chicken or the substantial roasted pork rancheros cost $16. All include soup or salad. Lunch options, at around $10, center on sandwiches, light grilled specials, and salads, while breakfast can either be a full buffet for around $9 or à la carte. Service is friendly rather than formal; the staff seems impressively keen to answer the same old canyon queries from every table.

Reservations (☎ 928/638-2612 ext 160) are accepted only for dinner, when they're essential. In fact, you should book your table as early in the season as possible; trying to do so when you first arrive at the North Rim is liable to be way too late. Turn up without a reservation, and you'll eat at 9pm at the very best, or more likely not at all.

Two alternative options stand to either side of the lodge driveway, neither within sight of the canyon. The **Café On The Rim**, a little cafeteria with no windows, is open daily from 7am until 9pm, serving very ordinary breakfasts, and then later on deli sandwiches or salads for around $6, and pizzas either by the slice or at $12–17.50 for a whole pie. Across the way, the **Rough Rider Saloon** (daily 5–9am & 11am–10pm) is a suitably rough-hewn **bar**, stocked with a wide range of beers and liquor, that has a separate early-

GRAND CANYON LODGE

morning incarnation as an **espresso bar** doling out coffee and pastries. **Groceries** are available at the store by the campground.

CAMPING

Approached via a spur road that leaves AZ-67 a little over a mile north of the lodge, the very pleasant *North Rim Campground* holds 87 car-camping sites, spaced out through the forest. RV hookups are not available. All sites cost $15 per night, except for the four ranged along the rim of the Transept, which charge $20. Although all are often reserved in advance, through Spherics (same-day ☎ 928/638-2611, advance ☎ 1-800/365-2267 or, from outside the US, ☎ 301/722-1257, ⓦ www.reservations.nps.gov), additional room is always available for backpackers, bicyclists, and others traveling without their own vehicles, who pay $4 per person.

The campground reopens each year at the same time as the lodge, but depending on the weather often stays open a little longer at the end of the season, until perhaps late October. A general store, a gas station, and a laundromat with coin-operated showers are located just outside the gates.

For details of backcountry camping within the park, for which permits are required, see Chapter Eight. It's also possible to camp outside the park boundaries in the Kaibab National Forest – contact the North Rim or Kaibab Plateau visitor centers for details – or at the campgrounds at Jacob Lake (see p.122) and DeMotte Park (see p.123)

LISTINGS

CAMPING EQUIPMENT AND GROCERIES Can be bought at the General Store, opposite

North Rim Campground. Hours vary throughout the season, never longer than 7am–8pm.

GAS Chevron station near *North Rim Campground*. Open daily 7am–7pm, so if you're planning to leave the rim outside those hours, be sure to plan ahead.

LAUNDROMAT AND SHOWERS Near *North Rim Campground*. Daily 7am–9pm. Showers $1.25.

MEDICAL HELP There is no health clinic on the North Rim. Call ☎ 911 for emergencies.

POST OFFICE In *Grand Canyon Lodge*. Mon–Fri 8–11am & 11.30am–4pm, Sat 8am–1pm.

WEATHER For the latest North Rim weather information, call ☎ 928/638-7888.

Bright Angel Point

A short paved trail, starting to the left of *Grand Canyon Lodge*, leads to the very tip of **Bright Angel Point**. It's an easy walk, but the path does rise and fall a little, and in places it fills the full width of the slender spit of land, with sheer drops to either side. You're poised here between two relatively minor tributary canyons, with the deep **Transept** to your right and the mighty red wall of **Roaring Springs Canyon** to your left.

After four hundred yards, you reach the sanctuary of a railed viewing area, backed by massive boulders that dare-devils climb in search of solitude. Everyone understandably regards the prospect ahead as one of the great Grand Canyon panoramas, but strictly speaking the canyon itself is all but obscured by the long straight gorge of **Bright Angel Canyon**, cutting at an oblique angle across your entire field of vision.

Bright Angel Canyon is so unusually straight because it was formed at least in part by seismic action. It therefore follows the line of the **Bright Angel Fault**, earthquakes along which were responsible for creating both this and corresponding canyons south of the river (see p.282).

Away to the right, you can just about see where it joins the Grand Canyon proper, but none of the Inner Gorge, let alone the Colorado River, is visible. You may hear the sound of rushing water, but it's coming from **Roaring Springs**, much closer to hand almost 3500 feet below, which supplies all the water used by the park on both rims (see p.224).

Mentally extending the line of Bright Angel Canyon across to the far side reveals the fault continuing up to the South Rim, though it's hard to spot a sign of life at Grand Canyon Village, eleven miles away, until the sun goes down and the lights start to flicker. That simple turn of the head also traces the easiest trans-canyon hiking route – the **North Kaibab Trail**, which drops down to the Colorado on this side via Roaring Springs and Bright Angel canyons, and climbs up via the matching **Bright Angel Trail** across the river. On foot, that's a 24-mile one-way hike.

On a clear day, looking directly ahead from Bright Angel Point, you can see far beyond the South Rim to the **San Francisco Peaks** near Flagstaff. The highest point on the horizon, **Mount Humphreys**, is 62 miles distant and 12,633 feet high. A few major inner-canyon buttes can be identified immediately below it, sandwiched between the far wall of Bright Angel Canyon and the South Rim beyond. The most prominent is the neat-capped **Brahma Temple**, framed between the lesser Deva and Zoroaster temples.

Kaibab Plateau trails

All **inner-canyon** hiking trails, including those that start from the North Rim, are described in Chapter Eight, where you'll also find detailed advice on necessary precautions and preparations. Assuming that you're reasonably fit, and that you're not here on a scorching midsummer's day, then at least a brief foray down the **North Kaibab Trail** – see p.222 – has to be the most satisfying dayhike for North Rim visitors. However, a number of much less demanding trails remain on top of the **Kaibab Plateau**, offering the chance to experience the silence of the ponderosa forest as well as lesser-known canyon perspectives. No **permits** are necessary for dayhikes on any of the trails described below.

THE TRANSEPT TRAIL

The short **Transept Trail**, measuring 1.5 miles one way, is a backwoods route between **Grand Canyon Lodge** and the **campground**. Rather than walking along the highway, you hike beside the tributary canyon known as **The Transept** instead. Though dwarfed by the Grand Canyon proper, it still plummets an awesome half-mile below the cliff-edge path. Starting from the west side of the lodge, the trail follows the contours of the rim, circling the campground to arrive beside the general store. While it's an enjoyable enough walk, it's more of a convenient route from A to B than a hiking trail in its own right, and no one takes it for pleasure alone.

UNCLE JIM TRAIL

If you're looking for a medium-length dayhike on the Kaibab Plateau, the four-mile loop of the **Uncle Jim Trail** is your best option. It sets off from the same parking lot as the North Kaibab Trail, beside the highway 1.5 miles north of *Grand Canyon Lodge*; see p.83.

From the mule corral at the east end of the lot, the trail heads up into the woods. At first, you get some inspiring views down the full length of **Roaring Springs Canyon**, but before long the path loses touch with the canyon rim. Half a mile along, the Ken Patrick Trail, described below, forks to the left while the Uncle Jim veers right. Another half-mile after that, another junction marks the start of its loop segment. Whichever route you choose will take you in the course of the next two miles to two stunning overlooks. One, the closest to **Uncle Jim Point**, faces east across the head of Bright Angel Canyon toward the Walhalla Plateau. The other looks south, to the South Rim and beyond, and also back west toward the trailhead, offering a superb view of the switchbacks via which the North Kaibab Trail insinuates itself into Roaring Springs Canyon.

The "Uncle Jim" in all this, incidentally, was James T. Owens, a forest service warden credited with shooting 532 mountain lions on the North Rim between 1906 and 1918. Theodore Roosevelt wrote approvingly of Owens that "he early hailed with delight the growth of the movement among our people to put a stop to the senseless and wanton destruction of our wild life." The destruction Roosevelt and Owens deplored was of "good" animals, such as deer, by "bad" predators such as lions; their solution, to eliminate the lions, had the bonus of leaving plenty of deer for hunters to kill, which was of course neither senseless nor wanton. That early attempt at wildlife management resulted in an explosion of the deer population, followed by mass starvation, and led to a change in the policy of the park service, which no longer attempts to wipe out predators.

KEN PATRICK TRAIL

A much longer plateau dayhike can be had by following the **Ken Patrick Trail**, which as mentioned above branches off the Uncle Jim Trail half a mile along. It's a total of ten miles long, meeting **Cape Royal Road** seven miles out from the trailhead, and then continuing to **Point Imperial** (see p.94) three miles after that. Not all that many hikers pass this way, which means route-finding can be hard, with the occasional fallen tree and large patches of blackened wastelands still charred from the ferocious **Outlet Fire** of May 2000, a "prescribed burn," set by the forest service, that rapidly blew out of control.

In terms of views, the best stretch is the final rim-edge segment up to Point Imperial, which provides some wonderful prospects over to the Marble Plateau in the east. If you can arrange to be dropped off and/or picked up, that makes a great three-mile hike. It's also possible to continue north from Point Imperial on the **Point Imperial Trail**, which takes you three more miles along the rim, again through a heavily burned area, as far as Saddle Mountain, where it meets the **Nankoweap Trail** down into the inner canyon (see p.243).

THE WIDFORSS TRAIL

The only trail to offer access to the North Rim west of the lodge area, the **Widforss Trail** is a five-mile trek to the tip of the next headland along from Bright Angel Point. While it's a relatively easy walk, the only way home is to double back on yourself, entailing a ten-mile round trip that's likely to take around five hours. Making it all the way to the end is rewarded with tremendous views, but the second half of the trail runs through dense forest, so most visitors choose instead to hike just a short distance, and settle for enjoying the views close to the start.

To reach the Widforss trailhead, follow a gravel road that heads west from AZ-67 a quarter-mile south of its junction with Fuller Canyon Road, roughly three miles north of *Grand Canyon Lodge*. Just over half a mile along, you come to the natural clearing of **Harvey Meadow**; with luck, a dispenser here should hold copies of a park-service brochure detailing fourteen numbered points along the first two miles of the trail. (Note that the gravel road continues for seventeen miles to **Point Sublime**, as described on p.101, but deteriorates enough to be only recommended for 4WD vehicles.)

Having skirted Harvey Meadow, the trail climbs gently to crest some forested rocky outcrops before serving up its first glimpse of the yawning chasm of **The Transept**. Thereafter, as it meanders and undulates up to the rim and then back into the woods, you get repeated variations on the same theme. The longest-range panorama comes just under two miles along, at the very head of the Transept. By now your trusty brochure will have identified especially fine specimens of ponderosa pine, oak, aspen and maple, as well as a droning sewage treatment facility concealed beneath the lodge.

Pressing on further takes you into the depths of the forest for something over two miles. You finally re-emerge at a stunning overlook that faces due south. Bright Angel Point is now hidden from view, but by way of compensation the core of the Grand Canyon lies right there in front of you. Lift your eyes from the Buddha and Isis temples straight ahead, and the whole of the Grand Canyon Village area of the South Rim, and the Coconino Plateau beyond, spreads out for your delectation.

Strictly speaking, you're not quite at **Widforss Point**, which is the stark headland a few hundred yards to your

THE WIDFORSS TRAIL

left, but in the absence of a permanent trail there you'd do best to settle for what you've got. Both trail and point were named for Gunnar Mauritz Widforss, the so-called "Painter of the National Parks," who was born in Sweden in 1879.

The Walhalla Plateau

Except for those around *Grand Canyon Lodge*, all the North Rim **canyon overlooks** accessible by paved road are ranged along the eastern edge of the **Walhalla Plateau**. This fifteen-mile headland, east of Bright Angel Point, juts far out toward the Colorado as the river makes a colossal sweeping curve, and stops flowing southwards to head northwest instead. As a result, the plateau makes a superb vantage point, affording some of the finest views available anywhere in the national park, and revealing how the Grand Canyon fits into the larger context of the northern Arizona desertscape.

Once you've driven as far as the lodge, it's a real mistake to turn back without exploring the Walhalla Plateau as well. Be warned, however, that barring a few chemical toilets it holds no facilities of any kind. That includes gas stations; make sure your tank is full enough for a round trip of at least fifty miles.

Access is provided by the **Cape Royal Scenic Drive**, reached by turning east from AZ-67 onto **Fuller Canyon Road** three miles north of the lodge. Five miles along, you come to a junction where **Point Imperial Road** branches off to the left, while **Cape Royal Road** turns right to cross the neck of the plateau itself and winds its way into the cool dense woods. The area around the junction still visibly bears the scars of the Outlet Fire of May 2000.

POINT IMPERIAL

Before or after your exploration of the Walhalla Plateau, it's well worth making the short detour to **Point Imperial**, a gradual three-mile climb from the intersection described above. At 8803 feet, this is the highest spot along either rim of the entire canyon, though to reach the actual overlook you have to descend a short distance from the parking lot.

A long, red sandy ridge pokes out just below the viewing area, with a stark butte at the end. Looking down into the dry-as-dust labyrinth below, it's virtually impossible to guess which is the main gorge of the Colorado. In fact, the canyon here is just over nine miles wide, but the river is under a mile from the sheer wall of the **Desert Façade** on the far side. Almost everything you can see within the canyon is on the same side of the river as you.

Nonetheless, the horizon stretches for a phenomenal distance beyond the canyon. The vast spreading **Marble Platform** is almost three thousand feet lower than Point Imperial, so a huge swathe of the Navajo reservation lies flat and bare before you. Almost the only breaks in the monotony are the slight hump of Navajo Mountain in the far distance, and the crack cut by the Little Colorado River as it meets its elder sibling.

An even better propsect of the Marble Platform can be enjoyed from an overlook closer to the parking lot, labeled "**Northeast View**." Through a notch between two minor peaks, you can see Marble Canyon snaking its way through the rock. It's framed by the Vermilion Cliffs to the left and the Echo Cliffs to the right, so the dot where the two seem to meet can only mark Lees Ferry.

POINT IMPERIAL

VISTA ENCANTADA

Walhalla Plateau is narrowest at its northern end, where it clings to the rest of the North Rim by a slender thread. At some point, it will presumably become a mighty detached mesa; for the moment, however, Cape Royal Road manages to wriggle onto the level plateau top. The first stop comes after just over four miles, where the **Vista Encantada** overlook faces northeast across the canyon.

Views are much the same as from Point Imperial; both look down into the basin of **Nankoweap Creek**, which was responsible for the curving rim between the two. Once again, the Colorado is nowhere to be seen, but the pale green flatlands of the Navajo reservation spread away endlessly into the haze. Picnic tables make this a popular spot for midday breaks.

ROOSEVELT POINT

Until it was renamed during the 1990s in honor of Theodore Roosevelt – an early champion of the Grand Canyon – **Roosevelt Point** was known as the Painted Desert Overlook. It's only two miles on from Vista Encantada, so the short-range views are naturally similar, but that's enough to open up additional Navajo Nation panoramas. Navajo Mountain is still there on the northeast horizon, eighty miles distant, but you can now see southeast as well, to catch at least a hint of the **Painted Desert** badlands that extend from around Cameron almost to New Mexico. That said, the name change was probably for the best, in that the most spectacular parts of the Painted Desert are much too far away to be seen from here.

Closer at hand, Roosevelt Point provides a unique chance to gaze head-on at the **confluence** of the Colorado and the Little Colorado. Unusually, the rivers meet at right angles, with the Little Colorado emerging from a sheer-sided, half-mile-deep gorge of its own. Geologists puzzle over how that came about, with some suggesting that the Colorado itself once flowed through the Little Colorado gorge in the opposite direction, before being somehow "captured" to follow its present course west.

CAPE FINAL

For the next six miles beyond Roosevelt Point, Cape Royal Road stays within the forest. Your one chance to get a glimpse of the canyon comes toward the end of that stretch, when a **hike** of two miles each way leads to the remote viewpoint of **Cape Final**. By now, you're near enough to Cape Royal that there's no great need to add yet another overlook to your itinerary. The reason to pause here is if you just plain like the idea of spending a couple of hours on an easy trail through the woods, away from the crowds and with the bonus of a couple of little-known perspectives on the inner canyon.

The **Cape Final Trail** leads uphill from a little forest clearing, exactly 11.8 miles south of the intersection with Point Imperial Road. Though you'd never know to look at it, this rudimentary dirt track, meandering between the pines, was once a full-fledged park road. It soon levels off, then drops gently down until after half an hour it suddenly confronts the lip of the canyon at a big northeastward view. Nearby to the left, colossal monoliths such as **Poston Butte** and **Siegfried Pyre** soar almost to the height of the rim, but the **Chuar Valley** below slopes evenly down toward the river.

Turning right, away from the rim, the trail becomes even more scanty. As the ponderosas dwindle, to be replaced by oak and pinon, it crosses to the south side of this minor headland, and comes to an end after another half-hour at a south-facing eminence. The Colorado is now very clearly visible, at the point where it's joined by Unkar Creek to create the **Unkar Delta Rapid**, as described below.

WALHALLA OVERLOOK

A mile on from the Cape Final trailhead, the **Walhalla Overlook** is a canyon-edge parking lot that offers another fine view down to the confluence of Unkar Creek and the Colorado, almost exactly a mile below. The **Unkar Delta** there holds some of the most fertile farming land in the canyon, and around a thousand years ago was home to a thriving **Ancestral Puebloan** community. They grew corn, squash and beans on irrigated fields close to the river, and terraces at higher, drier elevations.

As population pressure increased, the group adopted a sophisticated strategy to exploit resources along the North Rim as well as down in the inner canyon. With its heavy annual snowfall, most of the North Rim is simply too cold to support agriculture, but the Walhalla Plateau is a unique case. It's effectively a peninsula, all but surrounded by the Grand Canyon, and thus warmed by the air that rises from the canyon depths.

Over one hundred ancient farming sites have been identified near the southern tip of the plateau, in the so-called **Walhalla Glades**. After wintering at the bottom of the canyon, the Ancestral Puebloans would climb out in early spring along the line of Unkar Creek – there's no trail now, but it was a fast and direct route back then – and plant their crops where they'd be fed by snowmelt. They'd also pack snow into storage jars, to water the seedlings as they grew. Harvest season, in the fall, would coincide with the best time to hunt deer and other forest mammals.

A very short trail, across the road from the overlook, ends at the foundation walls of a small **pueblo**. The main six-room structure is thought to have been occupied for roughly a century, from 1050 onwards, by a family group of around twenty members. In truth, these scanty stone piles do not make a spectacular sight – certainly not for anyone familiar with ancient ruins elsewhere in the Southwest – but they do provide an emotive reminder of the canyon's long human history.

CLIFF SPRING TRAIL

A quarter-mile past **Walhalla Overlook**, another minor overlook offers views toward Cape Royal, and in particular the Angels Window described below. The same parking lot serves as the start of the short **Cliff Spring Trail**, which crosses the road and then descends a dry, gravelly streambed towards the west. Having passed a remarkably complete Ancestral Puebloan granary, tucked under a boulder, you soon reach a damp, mossy alcove hidden beneath the canyon rim. Seepage through the Kaibab limestone above collects in small pools, but the water is not safe to drink. The round-trip hike this far is about a mile, and takes less than half an hour. Continuing as far again, on what becomes a difficult trail that requires a certain amount of scrambling, leads to impressive westward views. Eventually the ledge you're on dwindles to nothing, above a thousand-foot drop, and you're forced to turn back.

CAPE ROYAL

By the time you reach **Cape Royal**, where the Walhalla Plateau finally peters out, the promontory extends so far out above the canyon that it's constantly bathed by warm air currents. As a result, the ponderosa disappears, and pinon-juniper woodland predominates.

There's nothing to see from the unremarkable loop parking lot where the highway turns back, 14.3 miles from the junction. Instead, an even, paved footpath, laid out as a nature trail identifying the trees and plants along the way, leads to the two principal overlooks. A round-trip **hike** of roughly half a mile, it's just long enough to make it worth wearing real shoes and carrying water.

The trail leads first of all to the **Angels Window**, a wedge-shaped natural archway pierced just below the top of a rocky spur. As you approach, it perfectly frames a small segment of the Colorado River. If you're feeling adventurous, a brief detour to the left of the main trail leads you along a safe but extremely narrow railed pathway across the top of the "window" to the precarious slab at the far end, for views over to the Navajo flatlands. Two broad, green-trimmed stretches of the river are now on show, including once again the foaming Unkar Creek Rapid.

Views from **Cape Royal** itself, a couple of hundred yards further along the main trail, extend much farther west. For that matter, they're virtually the full 360 degrees, though the intervening ridge immediately west obscures Bright Angel Point. This is the only Walhalla viewpoint from which you can see the central portion of the Grand Canyon, with major landmarks like **Wotan's Throne** and **Vishnu Temple** straight ahead, and **Brahma** and **Zoroaster** temples off to the right.

As the crow flies, the canyon is now roughly eight miles wide. In theory, most of the best-known **South Rim viewpoints** are visible, including Desert View – with the flat-topped little mesa known as Cedar Mountain just behind it – and Yaki, Yavapai, Hopi and Pima points, but it's hard to distinguish one from the next. It's tempting to leave the path and ledge-hop even closer to the rim, but bear in mind that with its crumbling stone slabs this spot is notorious for fatal falls.

The Western Kaibab Plateau

Many North Rim visitors are frustrated that this vast area seems to hold so few roads. You can't help feeling that there must be a whole lot more spectacular scenery nearby that you'll never get to see. In fact, get hold of a good map – ideally the *North Kaibab Ranger District*, published by the Kaibab National Forest, or the BLM Arizona Strip Field Office's *Visitor Map*, both of which cost $6, and *not* the otherwise reliable AAA *Indian Country* one – and you'll soon realize there are plenty of minor roads out there. The trouble is, none is paved. All are gravel, dirt or worse, and most are only recommended for **high-clearance 4WD vehicles**.

The most rewarding area to explore lies to the **west** of Bright Angel Point and AZ-67. Most of this belongs to the **Kaibab National Forest**, where the roads tend to be passable in ordinary vehicles – this is after all a "land of many uses," so they're maintained for logging trucks and the like. However, the canyon rim itself remains inside the national park boundaries, and it's usually the final section of the drive to any viewpoint, on park-service roads, that requires 4WD.

The routes described below are the pick of literally dozens of possibilities, leading to exceptional viewpoints and also hiking trailheads. Before taking any of them, it's absolutely **essential to ask for advice** either at the Forest Service information center in Jacob Lake (see p.122) or at the Grand Canyon visitor center. As well as selling the best maps, rangers will be able to tell you which roads are clear, which may well entail following a highly convoluted route rather than what looks the shortest. Don't follow your own whims, and don't underestimate how much time it will all take; you can't reckon on driving more than twenty miles per hour at the very most.

Note that although the magnificent **Toroweap Overlook** is technically on the North Rim, it's only accessible from the Arizona Strip, and is therefore covered in Chapter Four.

POINT SUBLIME

In the estimation of Clarence Dutton, the pioneer surveyor who named it in 1882, **Point Sublime** is perhaps the finest Grand Canyon viewpoint of them all. Sadly for less hardy modern visitors, however, it stands at the end of a seventeen-mile dirt road that's usually restricted to 4WD vehicles. If you have one, drive three miles north of *Grand Canyon Lodge*, then take the gravel road west of AZ-67 that leads to the Widforss Trail, as detailed on p.91. Assuming you follow the curve of the road by turning left half a mile after the trailhead, you can't go wrong.

The views at the far end are absolutely colossal, extending both east and west and incorporating a fifty-mile stretch of the full glory of the inner canyon. Point Sublime is closer to the Colorado than any other North Rim viewpoint, so you even get a glimpse of the river itself, at **Boucher Rapid**. Rhapsodizing that "the infinity of sharply defined detail is amazing," Dutton was especially struck by the isolated butte he called **Shiva Temple**. The American Museum of Natural History sent an expedition to this "lost world" in 1937, hoping that its flat 275-acre summit might hold species unknown to science. All they found was evidence that large mammals somehow manage to visit the mesa-top regularly – and that the Ancestral Puebloans did so too.

Tuna Creek, immediately below Point Sublime to the

POINT SUBLIME

101

east, was the scene of a dramatic rescue in June 1944. Three airmen who parachuted from a bomber whose engines had failed during a training run were stranded down there for ten days, before park rangers were able to plot a route to reach them on foot.

SWAMP POINT

Both the Colorado, and the canyon rim with it, curve northwards to the west of Point Sublime. The next major promontory along, the **Powell Plateau**, comes even closer to the river, to within just two miles. However, despite being higher than the rest of the North Rim at this point, it has become detached from it, so there's no accessible over-look at its far end. The closest viewpoint, **Swamp Point**, is located just above the **Muav Saddle**, the short "neck" of land, dropping a thousand feet below the rim, that leads to the plateau.

As well as providing a view of the plateau itself – which although it holds no permanent water sustained a sizeable Ancestral Puebloan population – Swamp Point commands a fine prospect northwest, centering on the **Tapeats Amphitheater**. Even so, almost no one drives here just to enjoy the view. They come because it's also the trailhead for the grueling, experts-only **North Bass Trail**, as described on p.244, and the shorter **Powell Saddle Trail**, a five-mile dead-end hike onto the Powell Plateau.

Once again, 4WD is essential, and even that won't help you before early June each year, when the winter's fallen trees still block the way. Once it's clear, take Forest Service road 22, which climbs away enticingly due west from AZ-67 just under a mile south of DeMotte Park. Turn south onto 270 after 2.1 miles, then west again on 223 (signed for Fire Point) 2.3 miles beyond that. Another 5.8 miles on, turn left onto 268, and follow the signs, which should point you along another turn, onto 268B, after 0.3 miles. Once you cross the park boundary, 1.2 miles along, the road seriously deteriorates; it's 7.8 more miles to the end.

FIRE POINT

Little more than a mile north of Swamp Point, but much more likely to be accessible in an ordinary vehicle, **Fire Point** is another spectacular overlook that provides a dramatic side-on prospect of the striated Powell Plateau, and also gazes right across the canyon to **Great Thumb Mesa** on the far side. To reach it, start by following the directions for Swamp Point above, but simply keep going on 223 rather than turning left onto 268. Six miles after that junction – a total of sixteen miles from the highway – you're there. The whole route is normally passable in summer, though the last mile, the only section within the national park, is sometimes closed.

CRAZY JUG POINT

Of the many other western Kaibab Plateau viewpoints, the best, and the most readily accessible in a standard car, is probably **Crazy Jug Point**. It stands, however, a full 27 miles of gravel- and dirt-road driving from the highway, so be sure to allow plenty of time. Your reward if you make it is a dramatic glimpse of the Colorado snaking its way between Powell Plateau and Great Thumb Mesa, with the **Tapeats Amphitheater** spread out below you, and volcanic peaks such as Mount Trumbull away to the west.

As before, take Forest Service road 22 from DeMotte Park – it actually runs all the way to Fredonia, so you could approach from that direction – but this time stick with it for sventeen north-trending miles before turning left (west) onto 425 and then left again (south) on 292.

The road between the rims

Although the South and North rims stand just eleven miles apart, in the absence of a road across the Grand Canyon, the shortest possible driving route between the two takes 215 miles, or at least four hours. Starting from Grand Canyon Village, you have to follow first Desert View Drive and then AZ-64 east until you meet US-89 at **Cameron**, then head north to cross **Marble Canyon** on Navajo Bridge, before doubling back west to **Jacob Lake** to join the 44-mile AZ-67 south to the North Rim.

A map of the entire Grand Canyon National Park can be found at the back of this book (map 2).

Although there are very few towns along the way, the scenery is seldom less than spectacular. Highlights include the twin escarpments that blaze to either side of the Colorado as it emerges from Glen Canyon only to plunge into the Grand Canyon – **Echo Cliffs** on the east bank, and the **Vermilion Cliffs** to the west – and the fascinating

historical site of **Lees Ferry**, the official start of the Grand
Canyon. Several lodges and motels, dotted in splendid isolation, make for atmospheric overnight stays en route.

While the first explorers to attempt a Colorado crossing
in this region were two Spanish friars, padres **Domínguez
and Escalante**, who did so back in 1776, the route only
began to see regular traffic a century later, with the establish-
ment of the **Mormon Trail**. Linking Mormon settlements
in Utah with new (and for the most part unsuccessful)
"colonies" in Arizona, the trail was kept busy in part by
Mormon newlyweds, who, having married in civil cere-
monies in Arizona, would head at the next opportunity to
have their vows sealed at the nearest Temple, in St George,
Utah. Hence its alternative name – the **Honeymoon Trail**.

Transcanyon Shuttle (☎ 602/638-2820) runs daily vans
along the route described in this chapter, leaving the
North Rim at 7am to reach the South Rim at 11.30am, and
the South Rim at 1.30pm, arriving back at the North Rim
at 6pm. A one-way trip costs $65, and the round trip $110;
no credit cards are accepted.

LITTLE COLORADO RIVER GORGE

In its thirty-mile run between Desert View on the South
Rim (described on p.76) and its junction with US-89 just
south of Cameron, AZ-64 descends more than three thousand feet. Once past the first dozen miles, which lie within
the pine forests of the Coconino Plateau, vast views open
up across the Painted Desert to the northeast. Closer at
hand, a crack in the flatlands betrays the presence of the
Little Colorado River, snaking northwards at the bottom
of its own deep canyon to meet its bigger brother.

Ten miles out of Cameron, between mile markers 285

and 286 – by which time both road and river are running parallel east to west – the **Little Colorado River Gorge Navajo Tribal Park** gives visitors their best chance to catch a glimpse of the river. Though there's no admission charge, per se, you can only reach the end of the promontory that offers the finest views by running the gauntlet of several dozen **Navajo crafts stalls**, mostly selling good-quality jewelry and trinkets.

The drop down into the chasm here measures around 1200 feet; the cliffs are so sheer that it's hard to lean out far enough to see the river itself. In any case, for several months of the year – especially in spring and early summer – the Little Colorado is liable to dry up altogether. At other times, however, it's capable of powerful flash floods. The fact that the river remains undammed, despite repeated early Mormon attempts, has acquired an added significance since the completion of the **Glen Canyon Dam** in 1963. Now that the Colorado itself carries almost no sediment into the Grand Canyon, certain river species, such as the humpback chub, can only breed in the muddy waters of the Little Colorado.

The Little Colorado continues to play a crucial role in **Hopi** cosmology. Modern Hopi still follow in the steps of their ancestors along the ancient **Salt Trail** which leads from their mesas, sixty miles east, beside the Little Colorado into the Grand Canyon. Not far up the Little Colorado from its confluence with the Colorado proper lies the legendary *sipapu*, the hole through which the Hopi believe that human beings first entered this, the Third World. You won't find this natural dome-shaped hot spring marked on any map; only the Hopi are allowed access, or even know where it is.

Back on the highway, further crafts stalls, some at lesser overlooks, are dotted along the roadside for the rest of the way down to Cameron.

CAMERON

Tiny **CAMERON**, which amounts to little more than a handful of buildings, lies a mile or so north of the intersection of AZ-64 and US-89. The Mormon Trail originally crossed the Little Colorado River at a rocky ford six miles upstream. That became known as **Tanner's Crossing**, in honor of Seth Tanner, a Mormon prospector from Tuba City who built a house nearby in the 1870s. He later expanded his operations into the Grand Canyon area, where he also gave his name to the Tanner Trail.

After the danger from quicksand and flooding at Tanner's Crossing led to the construction of the first **suspension bridge** across the gorge in 1911, Cameron – named for another legendary canyon prospector, Ralph Cameron – sprang into being on the south side of the span. That old one-lane bridge is still there, but now it only carries an oil pipeline, having been superseded by a broader modern highway bridge.

Cameron Trading Post

The ever-expanding **Cameron Trading Post**, clustered beside the two bridges, remains at heart what it started out as in 1916 – a trading center for the Navajo Nation. Reservation residents still flock in to stock up on wool, flour and other supplies, catch up with friends, fill up their gas tanks, and pick up their mail, and much of the trading post's business is still conducted by barter.

That Old West tradition is now complemented by a brisk **tourist** trade, however. Beautifully landscaped gardens sloping down toward the river surround a large **motel** complex, where all the rooms are smartly presented, and those on the upper floors have large balconies that look out across the Little Colorado to the open desert (PO Box 339,

CAMERON

Cameron, AZ 86020 ⊤602/679-2231 or 1-800/338-7385,
ⓦwww.camerontradingpost.com; Feb ❸, March–May &
mid-Oct to Jan ❹; June to mid-Oct ❺). There's also **RV**
parking for $15.

In the complex's main building, an atmospheric tin-
roofed **dining room**, centering on a massive fireplace,
serves all meals (summer daily 6am–10pm, otherwise daily
7am–9.30pm). The food's OK, but with the principal customers being tour groups in a hurry to be somewhere else,
it's nothing special, and here on the reservation **no alcohol**
is served. The adjoining **souvenir store** stocks a huge array
of Southwest arts and crafts, both authentic and mass-pro-
duced, but for a real treat it's worth crossing to the nearby
Gallery, which stocks Native American pieces such as genuine Hopi *kachinas* and museum-quality Navajo rugs. Even
a small rug from the 1890s can cost up to $20,000.

Gray Mountain

When there's no room at Cameron, the nearest alternative
accommodation is nine miles south on US-89, in the even
smaller community of **GRAY MOUNTAIN** (population
68). Located just outside the reservation, it's a lonely desert
outpost, atmospheric in its own desolate way, consisting
almost entirely of the *Anasazi Inn* complex (PO Box 29100,
Gray Mountain, AZ 86020 ⊤928/679-2214 or 1-800
/678-2214, ⓦwww.anasaziinn.com; ❷–❺). This boasts
three separate **motel** blocks – all the rooms are of reasonable standard, with prices varying according to how close
you are to the pool – plus the *Gray Mountain Restaurant*
across the highway, which serves Mexican specialties and
Navajo tacos as well as steaks.

Aerial view of the Grand Canyon

A juniper tree on the South Rim

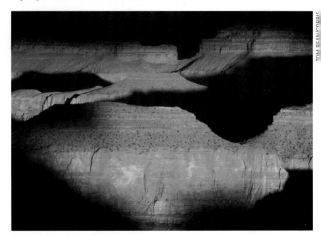

Sunrise from Lipan Point

Hikers on Bright Angel Trail

Havasu Falls

Mules on South Kaibab Trail

View from Toroweap Point

THE ECHO CLIFFS

Driving north from Cameron on US-89 is a delight, with the unfolding views of the unearthly, multicolored Painted Desert marred only by rows of mighty electricity pylons marching across the plateau from the Navajo Generating Station at Page. Though it's far from fertile country, much of this is open ranching land, so watch out for cattle if you're driving at night.

Fifteen miles north of Cameron, US-160 climbs away northeast via **Tuba City** towards Monument Valley and Colorado. Continuing north, US-89 passes through **Hidden Springs** in another five miles, the home of a small group of **San Juan Southern Paiute**, who were recognized as a separate tribe in 1990.

By now, the rich orange **Echo Cliffs** – the visible face of the Echo Cliffs Monocline – have started to climb to the east of the road. Over the next fifty miles, they reach well over two thousand feet above the Colorado. Their name was given by members of John Wesley Powell's second expedition in 1871, who fired a shot at the river from the top of the ridge, and heard the echo come back 24 seconds later.

The one natural break in the cliffs, ten miles on from Hidden Springs, is a small trading post logically enough called **The Gap** (daily 7am–9pm). A dirt road climbs up through the notch, leading to a defunct copper mine and, eventually, Page, but it's not recommended for ordinary vehicles.

If it's **Page** you're heading for – and it's not covered in this book partly because it's just outside the Grand Canyon area, but mainly because it's a really, really dull and unattractive little town – just stay on US-89. The highway eventually veers to the right twenty empty miles beyond The Gap at **Antelope Pass**, where a route was blasted through the cliffs to provide access to the Glen Canyon Dam construction site. Page lies 25 miles along the top of the mesa. **US-89A**, on the other hand, forks left at Antelope Pass, then presses on at the foot of the Echo Cliffs before dropping down to reach Navajo Bridge after a further fifteen miles.

MARBLE CANYON

Although the spot where US-89A finally crosses the Colorado is often loosely referred to as being **Lees Ferry**, the highway bridge actually stands six miles downstream from the ferry crossing it superseded. By this point, the Grand Canyon has officially begun, and is already almost five hundred feet deep. John Wesley Powell named this segment of the gorge **Marble Canyon**, on account of its highly polished walls, indented with caverns and carvings that appeared almost architectural. Marble Canyon stretches a total of 61.5 miles from Lees Ferry to the Colorado's confluence with the Little Colorado, and it's another fifty miles from the bridge before the chasm reaches a mile deep. Here, near its starting point, it's such a narrow interruption in the vast flat plains – which have become known in turn as the **Marble Platform** – that you can barely tell it's there until you're right on top of it.

Navajo Bridge

Even though Prohibition meant that the newly built **Navajo Bridge** could only be baptized in ginger ale and not champagne, its opening in 1929 marked a turning point in Arizona history. Until then, no bridge spanned the Colorado between Searchlight, Nevada, and northern Utah, while the ferry crossing nearby was so dangerous that it had been abandoned altogether. When a crucial piece of

THE ROAD BETWEEN THE RIMS

equipment needed to finish Navajo Bridge was stranded on the wrong side of the river, the only way to get it across was to take it eight hundred miles by road, via Las Vegas.

Nowadays, the nearest bridge to Navajo Bridge is a mere fifty yards away. The original span was joined by a modern replica – all but identical, but at 44 feet more than twice as wide – in 1995. The old bridge is reserved for pedestrians, so you can walk out to the middle and gaze 470 feet down to the Colorado, green with algae, at the bottom of Marble Canyon. Just to add to the spectacle, this spot is popular with **condors** too.

Land ownership here is extraordinarily convoluted, by the way. The top of the west bank belongs to the Glen Canyon National Recreation Area, though Bureau of Land Management holdings start not far beyond; the top of the east bank belongs to the Navajo Reservation; and both bridge and river are in Grand Canyon National Park.

On the west bank, the **Navajo Bridge Interpretive Center** (daily April–Sept 8am–5pm, closed Oct–March; restrooms always open; ☎928/608-6404, Ⓦwww.nps.gov/glca) holds some hair-raising photos of Navajo steel workers at work on the 1995 bridge, plus displays and literature about the Glen Canyon region. The large viewing area outside is festooned with all sorts of plaques, including the one honoring John Doyle Lee that's mentioned on p.114.

Marble Canyon Lodge

Not far beyond the west end of Navajo Bridge, just past the turn-off for Lees Ferry, the **Marble Canyon Lodge** (☎928/355-2225 or 1-800/726-1789; ④) has over fifty conventional motel-style rooms, with TVs but no phones, in low-slung buildings at the foot of the cliffs. The central *lodge* itself holds a small gift store and an adequate but unexciting **restaurant** that's open for all meals daily, with dinner entrees priced at $8–14. While the lodge as a whole can be a little slapdash, it's a romantic enough overnight halt, what with its spectacular desert setting and roadrunners scurrying through the sands.

Marble Canyon Lodge has always catered especially to adventurers planning rafting and fishing trips on the Colorado, and makes a 6am start each day to meet the needs of these river rats. An array of plaques and monuments across the highway honors river pioneers from the 1776 Domínguez and Escalante expedition (see pp.120–121) onwards. Back in the 1940s, lodge owner Art Greene used to run boat trips upriver as far as Rainbow Bridge (the world's largest natural bridge, forty miles northeast). When he got wind of the proposal to dam Glen Canyon in the early 1950s he shrewdly leased the land at the mouth of nearby Wahweap Creek at a knockdown rate. Knowing it would make the perfect site for a marina, Greene refused to yield to the fury of the federal authorities, and wound up making a killing as official concessionaire for what became the major tourist center on Lake Powell.

LEES FERRY

Reached via a gently sloping six-mile spur road that branches right from US-89A shortly after Navajo Bridge, **LEES FERRY** is little more than a dot on the map; it's not a town, and has a population of zero. Nonetheless, it can boast the geographical distinction of being the official starting point of the Grand Canyon, and even greater hydrological significance as marking the boundary between the upper and lower basins of the Colorado River. That's actually a political rather than a geographical concept; broadly speaking, under the Colorado River Compact of 1922, half the water in the river "belongs" to the states upstream from Lees Ferry, and the other half to those downstream. The complications and contradictions concealed within that simple formula are far too convoluted to go into here, though you'll notice that none of the river is thereby left in peace to flow into the ocean.

The practical importance of Lees Ferry stems from the fact that it's the only place within hundreds of miles that offers easy land access to both banks of the Colorado. That's because it stands at the confluence of the **Paria River**, flowing southeastwards from southern Utah, with the Colorado.

Mormon elder Jacob Hamblin was guided to this remote spot by Naraguts, a Paiute, in 1858, while John Doyle Lee's eponymous **ferry** service – see box below – was instigated in 1871. After Lee's death, his wife Emma remained in the vicinity, but sold the ferry back to the Mormon Church for $3000 worth of cattle. Always a hazardous operation, with the boats in constant danger of being swept downstream, the ferry was finally abandoned after an accident in June 1928, in which three lives, plus a Model T Ford, were lost.

Four miles down from Marble Canyon, the road passes the fairly basic **Lees Ferry Campground**, which belongs to the Glen Canyon National Recreation Area and offers water and toilets but not showers ($10 per night; ☎928 /355-2334). A few hundred yards further on, it crosses the Paria River, then swiftly reaches the Colorado at a large parking lot and launching ramp. It's the concrete gauging station visible on the far bank that counts as the exact start – **Mile 0** – of the Grand Canyon. This is where **whitewater rafting** expeditions set off into the canyon; passengers can get out at Phantom Ranch, five or six days downriver, but the first point where the boats can be taken out again is at Diamond Creek, around twelve days away by muscle power.

For more information on rafting the Grand Canyon, see our chapter devoted to the subject, p.246.

LEES FERRY

JOHN DOYLE LEE (1812–77)

Travelers who read the plaque at Navajo Bridge that hails John Doyle Lee as "a man of good faith, sound judgment and indomitable courage" might never realize that the man who put the Lee in Lees Ferry was also a prime mover in one of the most notorious episodes in Western history.

While the precise truth remains in dispute, the generally accepted story runs something like this. In 1847, Mormons fleeing persecution in Illinois ventured west beyond the United States, and established Salt Lake City. Almost immediately, however, the US extended its boundaries to the Pacific, and California-bound pioneers began to stream through Mormon territory. By 1857, tensions were such that a "Mormon War" was seen as inevitable.

That August, finding that no one would sell them supplies, a wagon train of settlers from Arkansas and Missouri resorted to raiding Mormon farms. Camping at Mountain Meadows in southern Utah, the settlers were ambushed, and then besieged, by warriors dressed as Native Americans. Whether the attackers were genuine Utes, or white Mormons in disguise – as Mark Twain reported in *Roughing It* – is still open to question. Clearly, however, local Mormons saw the wagon train as a threat to be eliminated. Their commander, John Lee, rode up to the beleaguered Gentiles on September 11, claiming to have negotiated a truce with the "Indians," and stated that if they laid down their guns they would be allowed to proceed west in peace.

Desperately short of ammunition, the migrants agreed. Each was assigned a Mormon escort, and together they set off west. Within a mile, Lee called the order "Halt! Do your duty!," whereupon the Mormon militiamen, possibly with assistance from Native Americans, killed the entire group, amounting to 120 unarmed men, women and children.

When reports of the massacre reached the rest of the country, it was widely believed to have been carried out on the orders of Mormon President Brigham Young. No serious legal investigation ever took place, however, and most of the perpetrators lay low in remote desert outposts. In due course, Young bowed to national pressure; Lee was excommunicated in 1870, arrested in 1874, and executed by firing squad in Mountain Meadows on March 23, 1877.

Lee's version of events was quite different. He claimed to have acted as a loyal servant of the Church; not to have actually killed anyone; to have given Brigham Young the names of all involved; and to have been made a scapegoat.

It was during his years on the run, albeit in answer to a request from Brigham Young, that Lee set up the first ferry service across the Colorado. He arrived here in 1871, with just two of his eighteen wives still standing by him. Lee utilized three boats abondoned by John Wesley Powell before building his own boat *Colorado*, big enough to carry four wagons. The boat was swept across the river in both directions by the current, and then towed back upstream to its starting point; the fare was $3 per wagon, 75¢ per animal.

Many legends surround Lee's years in the Grand Canyon. Tales that he planted the peach orchards of the Havasupai are untrue – though he did visit them in his wanderings – while persistent stories of lost gold mines have never been proved. He's said to have been in the habit of disappearing for days at a time and returning with cans filled with gold nuggets. His wife Emma believed he'd struck lucky, but none of the prospectors who followed her suggestions ever found a thing.

Haunting photos of Lee on the day he died show a gaunt old man sitting on his coffin, waiting for the firing squad – hidden beneath a blanket to prevent reprisals – to do its work. He suffered one final indignity: the US Congress, determined not to honor a convicted murderer, formally stripped Lee's Ferry of its apostrophe.

JOHN DOYLE LEE (1812–77)

Some boats do, however, leave the water at Lees Ferry. Commercial operators based in Page run half-day **smooth-water** trips that float here from just below Glen Canyon Dam. That 15.8-mile stretch, fed by the cold, clear water released from the dam – and soon to be muddied by the influx from the Paria – has became famous for its **trout fishing**. All the local lodges, together with operators such as Lees Ferry Anglers (☎928/355-2261 or 1-800/962-9755, Ⓦwww.leesferry.com), organize guided fishing expeditions at varying prices. There's an official daily catch limit of two trout per person.

Lees Ferry trails

Rudimentary trails from the far end of the parking lot lead within a couple of hundred yards to an assortment of buildings left over from the ferry era. Most were constructed, not surprisingly, using slabs of red sandstone. They include a small post office, and the sturdy **Lees Ferry Fort**, erected in 1874 as defense against Navajo attacks that never materialized.

The most prominent remains, however, date from an abortive experiment by **Charles H. Spencer**, who set out in 1910 to mine **gold** from the Chinle shale exposed on the slopes above Lees Ferry. Spencer's elaborate scheme, under which he'd sluice the shale down the hillside using pressurized hoses, required him to haul coal to the site, which he attempted both by **mule train** over the Echo Cliffs, and by **steamboat** along the river. His precipitous **Spencer Trail** is still there, switchbacking up the cliffs – though its poor condition means that it's closed to hikers – while the boiler of his abandoned boat lies rusting in the Colorado. What ultimately stymied Spencer's endeavor was that something kept clogging his amalgamators, making them unable to extract gold. Only fifty years later did he find out that the problem was caused by **rhenium**, a metal unknown to science back in 1912. Amazingly enough, he returned to Lees Ferry, now aged over 90, and embarked on another unsuccessful mining venture, this time in pursuit of rhenium itself.

Keep walking beyond Spencer's employees' bunkhouse, and more derelict machinery, and after about a mile you'll come to the actual launch point of Lee's famous ferry. It's a hard, thirsty hike, however, with little concrete reward at the far end.

Lonely Dell Ranch

John Lee lived not at the ferry site, but in the much more congenial surroundings of the **Lonely Dell Ranch**, nestled in a fertile curve of the Paria River around half a mile up from the confluence. Having crossed the river on your way back from the modern boat ramp, head right on the unpaved road and you'll swiftly reach the Park Service's replanted approximation of Lee's **orchards**, rich with apple, pear, plum, and peach trees.

His original **log cabin** stands not far beyond, constructed largely of driftwood and chinked with thick, red river mud. The smaller **blacksmith shop** alongside it was also Lee's, and is shaded by a large mulberry tree planted to help raise silkworms. Various other structures were added by Lee's successors, who were also responsible for the green farm machinery left to rust in the fields, and some of whom now themselves lie in the tranquil little **cemetery** at the end of the road. Uninhabited since the 1940s, the ranch now has the feel of a desert oasis, and is a popular halt for migratory birds.

For serious backpackers, Lonely Dell Ranch marks the end of an epic four- to six-day hike that traces the full length of the Paria Canyon, starting at the White House trailhead off AZ-89 between Kanab and Page. The canyon forms part of the Paria Canyon-Vermilion Cliffs Wilderness, which is itself subsumed within Vermilion Cliffs National Monument (see below).

THE VERMILION CLIFFS

For the first thirty miles west of Marble Canyon, US-89A curves at the foot of the **Vermilion Cliffs**. In November 2000, in one of his final acts as president, Bill Clinton designated a vast 294,000-acre expanse that includes the cliffs, the Paria Plateau above, and Paria Canyon, as **Vermilion Cliffs National Monument**. Administered by the Bureau of Land Management from its office in St George, Utah (☎435/688-3200, ⓦ www.az.blm.gov), it's not expected to change significantly, or to open up for tourism, in the foreseeable future.

Although the road itself is all but featureless, and the desert almost entirely devoid of vegetation, it's a superbly dramatic drive, with the soaring sandstone walls glowing a magnificent red at sunrise and sunset. However, you'd never know the Grand Canyon was out there to the east, slicing through the Marble Platform. Only a couple of small **motels** offer any incentive to get out of your car.

Lees Ferry Lodge

Enjoying great views from a very pretty location three miles west of *Marble Canyon Lodge*, the smaller **Lees Ferry Lodge** complex dates from 1929 (☎928/355-2231 or 1-800/451-2231, ⓦ www.leesferrylodge.com; ❸). Besides offering appealingly rustic guest cabins of varying sizes, the lodge is centered on the friendly little *Vermilion Cliffs Bar & Grille*, which serves good food washed down with an extraordinary range of bottled beers, and also holds its own fly shop for anglers.

Cliff Dweller's Lodge

Originally built in 1890 as a mocked-up "ancient ruin," the **Cliff Dweller's Lodge**, in another dramatic spot amid the jumbled rocks a half-dozen miles beyond *Lees Ferry Lodge*, is these days a standard-issue Western motel (℡928/355-2228; ❹). Like its neighbors, it's geared primarily towards river runners, so its restaurant – which has an attractive shady patio – makes a very early start (Mon–Thurs 5–10am & 4–10pm, Fri–Sun 5am–10pm).

House Rock Valley

AZ-89A rounds the southernmost promontory of the Vermilion Cliffs a little under twenty miles out from Navajo Bridge. Not far beyond, as the highway begins its straight-as-an-arrow run across the desert toward the Kaibab Mountains, a dirt road sets off south between mile markers 559 and 560. It's heading for the **House Rock Buffalo Ranch**, headquarters for a hundred-strong herd of buffalo that roams at will throughout the **House Rock Valley**. In recent years the buffalo have also tended to wander up onto the Kaibab Plateau and along the North Rim, so your chances of spotting them are pretty minimal; you'd have to be very keen indeed to think it worth driving the slow fifty-mile roundtrip to the end of the road and back.

Another five miles up the highway, taking a gravel road to the north shortly after mile marker 565 – signed to Vermilion Cliffs National Monument, it closely parallels House Rock Wash – brings you within three miles to the **Condor Release Site**. This is mission control for the Peregrine Fund's attempt to repopulate Arizona with wild condors. A roadside pavilion points out the precise spot, high on the Vermilion Cliffs, where the first six birds were

THE VERMILION CLIFFS

released from a glorified coop on December 12, 1996. As the abundant guano stains prove, they and their siblings regularly return "home." With powerful binoculars, you may well see them perched on the clifftops, or flying far overhead, but you're actually more likely to get close-up views at Grand Canyon Village on the South Rim.

DOMÍNGUEZ AND ESCALANTE

On July 29, 1776 – three weeks after Congress endorsed the Declaration of Independence – a party of twenty explorers set off from Santa Fe, the capital of the Spanish province of New Mexico. Led by two Franciscan friars, **Atanasio Domínguez** and **Silvestre Vélez de Escalante**, they hoped to establish a route to the Spanish mission at Monterey, California. Knowing that the Grand Canyon blocked their path, but not knowing how far it stretched, they headed north, planning to turn west once they felt confident the canyon had petered out. They eventually crossed the Colorado River somewhere east of modern Grand Junction, Colorado, then continued north and west as far as what's now Provo, Utah, which they named San Antonio de Padua. By October, they were in southern Utah, at what they calculated was the same latitude as Monterey. However, the distant western horizon was lined by snow-capped mountains, and winter blizzards were setting in.

By casting lots, the expedition made the difficult decision to head home, and attempt to blaze a more direct trail back to Santa Fe. Their Indian guides steered them across the Kaibab Plateau, and down through House Rock Valley to the Vermilion Cliffs. A roadside plaque, eighteen miles southwest of Navajo Bridge near mile marker 557, commemorates the **San Bartolome Campsite** where they halted on October 25.

The following day, they approached the Colorado at Marble Canyon, a spot they described as "a corner all hemmed in by

---

The last 22 California condors in existence were trapped in
the 1980s. See p.55 for more about attempts to reintroduce
them to the Grand Canyon region.

Shortly after the release-site turn-off, AZ-89A finally hits
the **Kaibab Mountains**, and begins to climb the final

very lofty bluffs and big hogbacks of red earth which ... present a pleasingly jumbled scene." Crossing the mouth of the
Paria River, they then made their camp amid the more difficult
terrain of what's now Lees Ferry, roughly a hundred yards
downstream from the present-day boat-launch site. Two members of the party managed to swim across the Colorado – at
the cost of losing all their clothes – but returned having been
too exhausted to climb the cliffs on the far side. Next they built
a raft, but three times failed to pole it all the way across. After
eleven days, convinced of the impossibility of coaxing their
horses (some of which they were in any case by now having to
eat) through quicksand and onto makeshift rafts, they gave up.

They headed north instead, managing to climb out of Paria
Canyon a few miles along, and eventually forded the Colorado
on horseback on November 7 at what became known as the
Crossing of the Fathers in Glen Canyon. That uniquely shallow ford was dynamited by Mormon settlers in the 1870s to
thwart its use by Navajo cattle raiders, and now lies drowned
beneath the waters of Lake Powell.

The Franciscans eventually returned to Santa Fe on January
2, 1777, having promised to return to Utah to set up a mission
among the Laguna. Thanks to general cutbacks by the
government in Spain, however, they never did so, meaning that
the vast new lands explored by the expedition remained virgin
territory until the arrival of the Mormons seventy years later.

THE VERMILION CLIFFS

eleven miles to Jacob Lake. A panoramic viewpoint after the first few switchbacks, before the road plunges for good into the thick forests of the Kaibab Plateau, commands a superb prospect of the cliffs, the Marble Platform, and the slender crack of Marble Canyon.

JACOB LAKE

Set deep in the pine forest forty miles up from Navajo Bridge, the crossroads community of **JACOB LAKE** looks more like a Canadian logging camp than anything you'd expect to find in Arizona. Named for Jacob Hamblin, a Mormon missionary to the Paiutes and Navajo, it guards the sole access route to the North Rim of the Grand Canyon: **AZ-67**, whose 44-mile run down to *Grand Canyon Lodge* is closed to all traffic between the first serious snowfall of each winter and the following spring's thaw. Jacob Lake thus goes into a state of quasi-hibernation in the winter, emerging in summer to make its living from the constant stream of tourists.

The *Jacob Lake Inn*, a sprawling complex of timber-frame buildings at the road junction, stays open all year round (T 928/643-7232, W www.jacoblake.com). As well as its simple **motel** rooms (❻) and log cabins (❺), it incorporates some pricier family units capable of sleeping up to six (❻), plus a gas station, a general store, an old-fashioned diner counter and a restaurant. Alongside it, the Forest Service's **Kaibab Plateau Visitor Center** contains displays and information on the surrounding area (daily 8am–5pm; T 928/643-7298, W www.fs.fed.us/r3/kai), and can also issue the **backcountry permits** necessary for overnight expeditions into remote areas of the national park, as detailed on p.13.

The Forest Service is responsible for the lovely *Jacob Lake Campground*, on US-89A just west of the intersection, which has facilities for **tent campers** only (mid-May to Oct; ☎928/643-7395). **RVs** can stay instead at the equally attractive *Kaibab Camper Village*, well off AZ-67 a mile southwest of the inn, near the eponymous lake itself, which is actually a collapsed limestone sinkhole (mid-May to mid-Oct; ☎928/643-7804).

DEMOTTE PARK

Mormon settlers made little use of the forests that lie to the south of Jacob Lake, other than grazing their cattle in the large meadow-like clearings that punctuate the road to the canyon. No one knows quite how these came into being; the theory that some natural mechanism deters trees from encroaching is undermined by the observable fact that the trees are in fact doing just that, year upon year.

One especially idyllic such meadow, **DEMOTTE PARK**, 27 miles down AZ-67 from Jacob Lake, is now the site of the *Kaibab Lodge* (mid-May to mid-Oct only; ☎928/638-2389 in summer, 928/526-0924 in winter, or 1-800/525-0924, ⓦwww.canyoneers.com). This offers two different kinds of cabin – characterful older ones with bare wooden floors, and a few slightly more expensive ones with motel-style trimmings – plus a simple restaurant open for breakfast and dinner daily. Immediately south, there's another Forestry Service, tent-only campground, *DeMotte Park Campground* (mid-May to Oct; ☎928/643-7298). The **gas station** nearby is the last before the canyon; the park entrance is another five miles down the road, with visitor facilities nine miles beyond that.

With a good map – ideally the Forest Service's *North Kaibab Ranger District* map of the Kaibab National Forest, and *not* the otherwise reliable AAA *Indian Country* one – it's possible to drive the dirt roads that branch both east and west from AZ-67 near DeMotte Park to all sorts of

DEMOTTE PARK

●

dramatic viewpoints. These include Crazy Jug Point, above the Grand Canyon to the west, as detailed on p.103, and a number of eminences that overlook the Marble Platform to the east.

The Arizona Strip

hanks to its sheer remoteness, the **Arizona Strip** –
the anomalous area of northern Arizona that's
sandwiched between the North Rim and the Utah
state line – remains one of the least-visited parts of the
Southwest. Writer Wallace Stegner described it as "sceni-
cally the most spectacular and humanly the least usable of
all our regions … as terrible and beautiful wasteland as the
world can show," and much of it remains absolute wilderness. Almost no one ever sees the colossal canyon formed
by **Kanab Creek**, which splits this entire region in two,
while the new million-acre **Grand Canyon–Parashant
National Monument**, created in 2000, makes no
provision to tourism whatsoever.

Map 1 at the front of the book includes the Arizona Strip.

Virtually no roads cross the Strip, and those that do hold
just a few tiny, secretive and often semi-derelict hamlets.
Although you have to pass this way in order to complete a
full tour around the Grand Canyon, the majority of visitors
tend rather to be racing between the Grand Canyon and
the national parks of southern Utah. Few are aware that
they're missing perhaps the most spectacular section of
Grand Canyon National Park: the **Tuweep** district, home

to two stunning overlooks at **Toroweap Point** that provide a rare opportunity to see the canyon's innermost core.

The Arizona Strip has never held more than five thousand inhabitants. Roughly that many **Kaibab Paiute** were living here – mostly as nomads, but also farming what little arable land exists – when **Mormon** explorers arrived in the 1850s, and set up ranches wherever they found water. By 1909, decimated by diseases and the inevitable conflicts, the Paiute population had dwindled to just 89. However, the ranchers in turn largely gave up by the mid-twentieth century, and only a couple of their settlements, **Fredonia** and **Colorado City**, ever grew to any significant size.

By any logic, you'd expect the Strip to belong to Utah rather than Arizona. In 1864, Mormon leader Brigham Young called on Congress to grant the Mormons all territory that lay within two degrees of latitude of either side of the Colorado; the boundary was drawn instead along the 37th Parallel, and that remains the Utah–Arizona border. At least four attempts to incorporate the Strip into Utah failed, largely because many of those Mormons who chose to remain in this remote region were renegades who didn't accept their church's reversal of doctrine on multiple marriage. Effective isolation from the state authorities of both Utah and Arizona continues to suit these die-hard **polygamists** just fine.

Other than plenty of time, and a reliable vehicle, the principal requirement needed to explore the Arizona Strip is a good **map** – ideally, the BLM Arizona Strip Field Office's $6 *Visitor Map*.

THE LE FEVRE OVERLOOK

The Kaibab Plateau extends for a good fifty miles north of the Grand Canyon's North Rim. Only once you've driven the full length of AZ-67, and then continued northwest on

US-89A from the intersection at **Jacob Lake** (see p.122), does the ground finally begin to slope downwards.

Ten miles along, between mile markers 590 and 591, the roadside **Le Fevre Overlook** presents a jaw-dropping panorama across the Arizona Strip and into southern Utah. Tier upon tier of cliffs rise one behind the other into the distance, making it abundantly clear why the entire region is known to geologists as the **Grand Staircase**. First comes the red sandstone of the Vermilion Cliffs, the formation pierced by **Zion Canyon**; next are the White Cliffs, which form the **Kolob Canyons** district of Zion National Park; and beyond them, forty miles away, stand the softer Pink Cliffs, sculpted into the hoodoos of **Bryce Canyon**. Apart from the occasional jewelry seller, the lookout holds no facilities of any kind.

FREDONIA

US-89A eventually levels out at the foot of the Grand Staircase on **Muggins Flat**, reaching the very hot – in terms of temperature, not nightlife – little community of **FREDONIA** just over thirty miles from, and three thousand feet lower than, Jacob Lake. While a population of around 1300 makes this the largest town on the Arizona Strip, the presence of the bigger and more interesting **Kanab** a mere seven miles north, across the Utah border, means that few visitors spend the night here.

Fredonia was originally founded alongside Kanab Creek by Mormon farmers in 1885, under the more down-to-earth name of Hardscrabble, and remains a dusty and unadorned desert outpost. Sadly there's no Marx Brothers connection; the Republic of Fredonia lampooned in *Duck Soup* probably took its name from a Fredonia in New York State.

The new and very helpful **welcome center**, on the east side of US-89A close to the state line at the north end of

FREDONIA

town (☎ 928/643-7241; Mon–Sat 9am–5pm), is the best place to get advice on the Strip's backcountry routes, and to buy the necessary maps.

Practicalities

Fredonia holds a few small but adequate **motels**. Driving south to north on US-89A, you pass the very plain log-built *Crazy Jug*, 465 S Main St (☎ 928/643-7752; ❶); the slightly run-down *Blue Sage*, 330 S Main St (☎ 928/643-7125; ❶), which also has space for RVs; and the ivy-covered *Grand Canyon*, 175 S Main St (☎ 928/643-7646; ❶), which boasts a red British telephone box in the garden. The *Crazy Jug* has its own on-site diner, while *Nedra's Café*, 165 N Main St (☎ 928/643-7591), is a surprisingly good **Mexican restaurant**, where if you're a newcomer to this neck of the woods you might want to sample the first Navajo taco of your life.

KANAB

Until new roads were pushed through the region in the 1950s, **KANAB**, Utah, just two miles north of the Arizona state line, was renowned as perhaps the most inaccessible town in the US. Now it's a significant tourist halt, thanks to a position halfway between the Grand Canyon, 80 miles southeast, and Bryce Canyon, 83 miles northeast.

Kanab started life as **Fort Kanab**, a frontier outpost so prone to Indian attacks that it only survived from 1864 until 1866. The town itself was founded by Jacob Hamblin in 1870 as a God-fearing ranching community with a sideline in harboring Mormons who fell foul of the federal government, among them several perpetrators of the Mountain Meadows Massacre (see p.114). That lawless image was later cultivated by pulp novelist Zane Grey, who set many of his

Westerns nearby, while Kanab's rugged surroundings made it a focus for Western movie-makers from Tom Mix, who filmed *Deadwood Coach* here in 1924, to Clint Eastwood with *The Outlaw Josey Wales* in 1976.

Ranching in southern Utah has long been in decline, but the citizens of Kanab would still much prefer to wrest their living from the earth. Their biggest payday came in the late 1950s, when this was the original base for the construction of **Glen Canyon Dam**. During the eighteen months it took to upgrade the 72-mile dirt road to the dam site, and build the new town of Page, Arizona, locals scurried to grab their share of the 200 million federal dollars that were pumped into the project. In November 1958, the workers decamped for Page, and the boom was over.

For many years thereafter, Kanab pinned its hopes on the prospect of large-scale coal-mining on the **Kaiparowits Plateau** to the northeast. The politicians and environmentalists, such as Robert Redford, who thwarted such plans in the 1970s were burned in effigy on the streets of Kanab, while the town closed down in protest for an hour in October 1996 when President Clinton's proclamation of Grand Staircase–Escalante National Monument precluded that possibility forever.

Kanab has thus been left to survive by catering for tourists, which it does with reasonably good grace. US-89 is lined with an above-par assortment of motels and restaurants, with the greatest concentration where the highway briefly doglegs to run east–west along **Center Street**. A few blocks south, US-89 proper branches off east toward Page, while US-89A continues south into Arizona.

Apart from some large Western-themed souvenir stores, such as Denny's Wigwam, opposite *Parry Lodge* at 78 E Center St (☎ 435/644-2452), there's almost nothing to do in Kanab.

KANAB

Information and tours

Kanab's large **visitor center** – slogan: "The Greatest Earth on Show" – is just south of Center Street at 78 South 100 East (Nov–Feb Mon–Fri 9am–5pm; March, April & Oct Mon–Fri 8am–8pm, Sat 8am–5pm, Sun 1–5pm; May–Sept Mon–Fri 9am–8pm, Sat 9am–5pm, Sun 9am–1pm; ☎435/644-5033 or 1-800/733-5263, ⓦwww.kaneutah.com). Interesting displays tell the story of the town's movie-making past. The local **BLM** office, 318 North 100 East (Mon–Fri 7.45am–5pm, Sat 9am–5pm; ☎435/644-4600, ⓦwww.ut.blm.gov), carries full information on nearby public lands, including Grand Canyon-Parashant National Monument, and up-to-date details on driving conditions.

Several local companies offer one-day or multi-day **tours** of the surrounding backcountry. Operators include Canyon Country Out-Back Tours (☎1-888/783-3807, ⓦwww.ccobtours.com), who run 4WD tours for $22.50 per person per hour, to nearby slot canyons as well as all the way to Toroweap (a six-hour roundtrip that costs $135), and Canyon Rim Adventures (☎1-800/897-9633, ⓦwww.canyonrimadventures.com), whose camping, biking and/or backpacking trips cost $495 and up for three days.

Accommodation

Kanab holds a number of good-value budget **motels**, so don't feel compelled to pay extra for a fancier name. All are within easy walking distance of downtown, but since there's nowhere very much to walk to that makes little difference.

Aiken's Lodge – National 9 Inn
74 W Center St ☎435/644-2625 or 1-800/524-999,

🖷644-8827, ⓦwww.geocities.com/aikenslodge1.
The ideal budget motel: crisp and clean, right in the heart

KANAB

of town, and with its own pool. ❷

Best Western Red Hills

125 W Center St ⓣ 435/644-2675 or 1-800/830-2675, ⓕ 644-5915, ⓦ www.kanabbestwestern.com.
Strangely ugly, somewhat overpriced, but very central motel. Large modern rooms plus a pool and whirlpool. Winter ❸, summer ❹

Canyonlands International Hostel

143 East 100 South ⓣ 435/644-555, ⓦ www.grandcanyonhostel.net.
Friendly private hostel, in a converted motel a block east of the highway near the visitor center. Each of its five dorm rooms holds five or six beds – priced at $10 per night – plus a shower; there's also a kitchen, library and laundry. ❶

Holiday Inn Express

815 E AZ-99 ⓣ 435/644-8888 or 1-800/574-4061, ⓕ 644-8880, ⓦ www.hikanabutah.com.
Large new motel, perched on a bluff at the eastern edge of

town, that's a little isolated but offers the highest standard of rooms in Kanab. ❸

Parry Lodge

89 E Center St ⓣ 435/644-2601 or 1-800/748-4104, ⓕ 644-2605, ⓦ www.infowest.com/parry.
Opened in 1931, Kanab's oldest motel has an undeniable air of romance, with its lobby and restaurant festooned with photos of movie-star guests and name-plates to tell you which rooms they (officially) slept in. You can even bathe in John Wayne's extra-large bathtub. *Parry's* isn't *that* great, though, even if you can get room service from the restaurant, and some of the newer rooms are both dingy and noisy. Winter ❷, summer ❹

Shilo Inn

296 West 100 North
ⓣ 435/644-2562 or 1-800/222-2244, ⓕ 644-5333, ⓦ www.shiloinns.com/utah/kanab.
Large and very presentable motel, at the north end of town. Some rooms have kitchens, and there's a pool and spa. Winter ❷, summer ❹

KANAB

131

Super 8
70 South 200 West ⓣ 435/644-5500 or 1-800/800-8000, ⓕ 644-5576.
Dependable budget motel, in a quiet location a block south of Center Street, with large pool and hot tub. Winter ❷, summer ❸

Eating

Around twenty largely formulaic **restaurants** cling to the edge of the highway as it passes through Kanab. One or two make the effort to be distinctive, while the others rest safe in the knowledge that however bad they may be, there's precious little choice for a hundred miles in any direction.

Four Seasons Fifties-Style Restaurant
36 North 300 West ⓣ 435/644-2415.
Fun mock-Fifties diner, with a 10¢ jukebox and a menu of burgers, sandwiches and fried meats, to be washed down with (nothing stronger than) copious malts and shakes. Closes 7pm in winter.

Houston's Trails End
32 E Center St ⓣ 435/644-2488.
Western-themed family diner, serving chicken-fried steaks, ribs, fish and fried breakfasts. Open daily for all meals, but closed mid-Nov to mid-March.

Nedra's Too
310 South 100 East ⓣ 435/644-2030.
Informal local place on the south side of town at the junction of US-89 and US-89A, which has another branch in Fredonia (see p.128). The unifying factor of the Mexican/American menu is the frier; even the ice cream comes deep-fried. Open daily for all meals.

Parry Lodge
89 E Center St ⓣ 435/644-2601.
Atmospheric dining room where the menu occasionally hints at the healthy, in the form of dishes like poached

salmon, and they're unusual for Kanab in having a license to sell alcohol. Open for all meals in summer, breakfast and dinner only in spring and fall, and closed Nov–March.

Rocking V Café
97 W Center St ☎ 435/644-8001.

This valiant bid at improving Kanab's culinary reputation is housed in one of the town's oldest buildings, a former bank. Classic French and Italian dishes for dinner at around $15 per entree, and cheaper, lighter lunches. Open daily for lunch and dinner.

PIPE SPRING NATIONAL MONUMENT

Thirteen miles west of Fredonia, just off AZ-389, **PIPE SPRING NATIONAL MONUMENT** (daily 8am–5pm; $3, under-16s free; ☎ 928/643-7105, ⓦ www.nps.gov/pisp) marks the site of one of the very few water sources on the Arizona Strip. Not surprisingly, ownership of this precious spring has been much contested: it has spent time in both Utah and Arizona, and belonged to three different counties. In 1863, a Mormon rancher, Dr James Whitmore, appropriated it from the Paiutes, who knew it as *Mu-tum-wa-va*, or Dripping Rock. After Whitmore was killed three years later by Paiute and Navajo raiders, Brigham Young ordered the Mormons to withdraw. However, they returned in 1870 and enclosed the spring in a fort, named **Winsor Castle** for its first superintendent, which was personally dedicated by Young in a ceremony attended by John Wesley Powell.

In 1907, the federal government established the **Kaibab Paiute Indian Reservation**, which measured eighteen miles by twelve miles and included the spring. No provision was made concerning its water, however, and Mormon cattle ranchers continued to bring their herds here. The situation was further confused in 1923, when spring and fort became a **national monument**, **Winsor Castle**, thanks to the first director of the National Park Service, Stephen Mather, who had discovered its charms after his car broke down nearby. The idea was ostensibly to preserve the fort as a "memorial to Western pioneer life," though the declaration owed as much to its standing halfway between the Grand Canyon and Zion National Park as to any intrinsic interest.

Bitter legal disputes between cattlemen, Paiutes and the park service dragged on for another fifty years, before use of water from Pipe Spring was largely assigned to the Paiutes. The surrounding land, formerly richly grassed, had by then been reduced by overgrazing to virtual desert. Debates over local history still endure, with the Paiute arguing that the fort was built not so much to protect valiant Mormon settlers from Indians, as defiant polygamists from the government. With the monument largely staffed by Paiute rangers, steps have been taken to reflect more of its Native American history, including cultural demonstrations and short walking tours to nearby **petroglyph** sites. The fort itself, the focal point of the monument, remains in good condition, and serves as a not desperately enthralling museum of early ranching life. An Ancestral Puebloan ruin that's said to lie beneath its outbuildings has yet to be excavated.

A quarter-mile north of the monument, the Paiute run a small **campground** (☏928/643-7245), where a site costs $5 per tent or $10 for RVs. During the 1990s Indian gaming boom, they also had a casino, but that is now defunct.

COLORADO CITY

AZ-389 continues northwest from Pipe Spring, and serves as the most direct connection from the North Rim to the I-15 interstate, which runs between Las Vegas and Salt Lake City. A mile or so before it reaches Utah, a spur road to the

POLYGAMY ON THE ARIZONA STRIP

Although it was not officially founded until 1913, as Short Creek, Colorado City had long been an important center of Mormon settlement. After the Mormon church disavowed polygamy in 1890, the Arizona Strip was a major refuge for recalcitrant polygamists. During the 1930s, Short Creek became the home of the Fundamentalist Church of Jesus Christ of Latter-Day Saints, who preached that by maintaining polygamy they were keeping true Mormonism alive. The community's location, spanning the state line, made it easier to avoid outside investigation; residents could simply cross between Arizona and Utah to escape police enquiries. Nonetheless, repeated state and federal enquiries culminated in the Short Creek Raid of 1953, when Arizona governor Howard Pyle ordered a massive police swoop that saw 23 polygamist men hauled off for trial in Kingman.

Pyle's anti-polygamy campaign backfired, amid much negative publicity about separated families, and children left without their fathers. Each of the accused menfolk of Short Creek received a year's probation, while Pyle lost his bid for re-election. To erase the name from public memory, Short Creek voted in 1958 to divide itself in two, becoming Colorado City in Arizona, and Hildale in Utah.

The issue of polygamy in Colorado City resurfaced during Arizona's fall 2002 gubernatorial election. Independent Richard Mahoney alleged that the ultimately successful Democrat candidate, Attorney General Janet Napolitano, was ignoring crimes in polygamist communities – specifically, that for young girls to be obliged to submit to plural marriage amounts to statutory rape – and that her Mormon Republican opponent, Matt Salmon, would be unable to tackle the problem. Both rejected the charges, with the official response being that while it was difficult to develop winnable cases, investigations were still being pursued.

right runs up to the staunchly traditional Mormon community of **COLORADO CITY**. Set beneath the towering bluffs of the Vermilion Cliffs, and devoid of either accommodation or dining options, this is a surreal-looking place, laid out with a small urban grid of extremely broad streets that see very few cars but plenty of gingham pinafores. Everyone will assume you're a magazine journalist hoping to write a sensational article about polygamy, and there's no encouragement to linger.

TOROWEAP

The Arizona Strip holds one tremendous prize for visitors prepared to venture off the paved highways: **Toroweap Point**, the only place where you can drive to the very lip of the canyon's Inner Gorge and peer down sheer 3000-foot cliffs to the Colorado River. As the crow flies, it's slightly under sixty miles west of Bright Angel Point, the main focus for North Rim tourism. By road, it's almost 150 miles, as you have to circumvent the full length of Kanab Canyon by heading all the way north to Fredonia.

Is it worth it? An unequivocal yes – Toroweap is not just another overlook. However, don't underestimate the amount of time and effort it takes to get there. Even a fleeting visit requires at least six hours of laborious driving on gravel roads.

There are two main routes: the eastern **Sunshine Route**, which starts on AZ-389 seven miles west of **Fredonia** and runs for 61 miles southwest, and the more scenic but longer western **Main Street Route**, which takes a total of ninety miles from the heart of **St George**, Utah, but is closed by snow for much of the winter. The account below follows the obvious east–west itinerary for a road trip, by getting there from Fredonia and heading back via St George. A third possibility, the sixty-mile **Clayhole Route** from Colorado City, is not recommended here because it's less convenient for onward travel, and becomes impassable during wet weather.

When open, which in the case of the Sunshine Route is usually all year, these roads are generally passable in ordinary vehicles. If 4WD is necessary at all, it will be for the last few miles only, so if you don't have 4WD you can still reckon on being able to hike along the remainder of the road as far as the overlooks. Be sure to enquire locally about current driving conditions before you set off; to carry all the food, water and gas you might need; and to have a spare tire and emergency repair kit for your vehicle.

The Sunshine Route

The **Sunshine Route** to Toroweap begins with a southward turn off AZ-389 seven miles west of Fredonia, onto **BLM road 109**. This is a broad, well-surfaced gravel road, albeit subject to "washboarding" (corrugated by bone-jarring little undulations), that passes through a succession of wide open valleys first recorded by the Domínguez and Escalante party of 1776 (see pp.120–121). Much of the country here is range land, grazed within an inch of its life. You don't see so much as a tree during the first hour, and precious few thereafter.

Forty miles along, you join **BLM road 5** – the Clayhole Route mentioned above – coming down from Colorado City. The final thirteen miles south to the national park lie just within the eastern boundary of **Grand Canyon-Parashant National Monument**. Halfway down, BLM road 5 veers west towards Mount Trumbull, as described on p.143, so the last few miles are on **BLM road 115**.

TOROWEAP

Tuweep

A sign just over six miles short of Toroweap Point welcomes visitors to the **Tuweep Area** of Grand Canyon National Park. The last six miles to the overlook are by far the roughest stretch of the drive. Expect to take a little under two hours to reach the ranger station from the highway, and then another half-hour to nurse your protesting vehicle to the canyon rim. While the ranger station is not open to any fixed hours, and cannot be contacted by phone, a ranger is in residence year-round, though not always available on site, and there's an emergency phone. A mile before the end, you come to the main section of the park service's exposed **primitive campground**, which holds a total of eleven first-come, first-served sites. One is a group site, which can be reserved on ☎ 928/638-7870. Fires are allowed, but you have to bring your own firewood, and there are composting toilets but no water. **No fee** is charged for day use or overnighting at the campground, but you do need to buy a permit in advance, as detailed on p.207, for **backcountry camping**.

Incidentally, although the Paiute terms "Tuweep" and "Toroweap" are used more or less interchangeably in these parts, strictly speaking, "Toroweap," which means "dry valley," is applied to a valley, the geological fault that created that valley, one of the strata in the canyon as a whole, and an overlook, while "Tuweep," meaning "the earth," referred first to a Mormon settlement in the valley and now to this district of the park.

Toroweap Overlook

What doesn't quite sink in until you reach the end of the road at Toroweap is that this is an utterly unique segment of the Grand Canyon. Everywhere else, there are effectively two canyons in one, consisting of a towering rim, separated by mighty cliffs and, as a rule, a broad plateau, from the deep, narrow chasm that holds the Colorado River. Here, thanks to volcanic action along the **Toroweap Fault**, that high outer rim is absent on the north side of the river, and the road is able to follow the **Toroweap Valley** right to the brink of the Inner Gorge. From the end, it's therefore possible to gaze straight down upon the river.

You come to a halt at a wide, rocky hilltop that holds one or two picnic tables and a couple of campsites detached from the rest. Anyone used to Grand Canyon viewpoints further east may not feel as if this can really be the canyon; there are no buttes and pyramids, or labyrinthine spurs and mesas. Tiptoe to the southern edge of the parking lot, however, and the ground suddenly drops three thousand feet from your feet.

You're now at the **Toroweap Overlook**, which at 4600 feet is the lowest viewpoint within the national park. Though you can see the river approaching from the east and flowing away to the west, it's so directly below that you may have to lie full length and peep over the edge to see it right here. The cliffs on the other side of the river, which belongs to the Hualapai reservation, soar thousands of feet higher.

There's more information about attractions at and the history of the Hualapai reservation starting on p.189.

Lava Falls Overlook

A five-minute hike over the boulder-strewn clifftop west of the Toroweap Overlook – there's no fixed trail – leads to the stupendous west-facing **Lava Falls Overlook**. The view of the river here, turning from green to blue as it recedes towards the horizon, and interspersed with mighty white rapids, is so spellbinding that you may not at first notice the most awesome feature of the landscape. Straight ahead, a few hundred feet below eye level, a colossal black

GRAND CANYON–PARASHANT NATIONAL MONUMENT

President Bill Clinton flew into Toroweap Valley by helicopter on January 11, 2000, to create the vast Grand Canyon–Parashant National Monument, covering over a million acres of northwestern Arizona. Such presidential proclamations skirt the normal legal requirements for public discussion and approval by state legislators; Theodore Roosevelt used the same strategy when he proclaimed the original Grand Canyon National Monument back in 1908. Both the governor of Arizona and the majority of its congressional delegation opposed the Clinton move.

The monument is bounded to the west by the Nevada border, and to the east and northeast by the drainage of the Virgin River (only a tiny portion of which crosses into Arizona). To the south, it either runs up against Grand Canyon National Park at or near the rim of the canyon, or meets, and shares jurisdiction with, the Lake Mead National Recreation Area. It's also scattered with parcels of Arizona state land; a few private landholdings; and several designated wilderness areas. The 808,000 of its acres that lie outside the Lake Mead NRA are administered by the Bureau of Land Management, and the rest by the National Park Service.

The point of creating Grand Canyon–Parashant was not to increase tourist visitation, but to preserve this little-known region's geological, archeological and natural resources. The new monument straddles the boundary between two major geological "provinces": the "Basin and Range" country to the

TOROWEAP

lava cascade spills over the North Rim and pours down to within a few feet of the Colorado.

This lava bears witness to some of the most dramatic episodes in the canyon's history. On at least eight separate

west, and the Colorado Plateau to the east. Its central feature, the Shivwits Plateau, is the westernmost segment of the Colorado Plateau, which drops down the dramatic escarpment of the Grand Wash Cliffs on its western edge to meet the eastern Mohave Desert. While boasting a rich fossil record, it remains home to many rare animal and plant species; some sections have been set aside as sanctuaries for desert tortoises, and the program of re-releasing Californian condors has been active here too (see p.55). Although few visitors are aware that the monument even exists, in terms of protecting the overall ecosystem of the Grand Canyon, ecologists insist it has effectively doubled the size of Grand Canyon National Park.

While the human presence has ranged from early hunters, via Ancestral Puebloans, to Mormon ranchers, the region remains all but uninhabited and only minimally exploited. The new monument is obliged to respect existing grazing and hunting rights, but no new mining or geothermal activity will be permitted.

Very few roads penetrate the monument, and none of them is paved. With a high-clearance 4WD vehicle, it's possible to visit remote western Grand Canyon viewpoints such as Whitmore Point, Twin Point and Kelly Point, but even without hiking, all involve demanding multi-day expeditions for which you'll need strong survival skills. Contact the visitor centers in Kanab or Fredonia before you set off; there's also some information online at Ⓦ www.az.blm.gov/natmon2.htm.

TOROWEAP

occasions, **volcanic eruptions** atop the Esplanade Plateau in this region have filled the Grand Canyon to a depth of as much as 2330 feet, and thus **blocked the Colorado**. The largest flow, around 1.2 million years ago, created the long-vanished **Prospect Dam**, which backed the river up to form a lake that stretched all the way east to Lees Ferry. Geologists estimate that it would have taken 23 years to fill to the brim; then the Colorado burst over the top, and, eventually, wore the dam entirely away. Vestiges of such events can be seen at various heights on the canyon walls – the most recent was around 140,000 years ago – and make it possible to work out the speed at which the canyon grows deeper.

The same lava that dammed the Grand Canyon also filled a number of side canyons up to the brim, including **Prospect Canyon** on the south side and **Toroweap Valley** here. That explains why it's flat enough for the road to run all the way to the rim, and also why you probably won't have noticed that Toroweap Valley even exists. What was once the valley mouth is now topped by a 567-foot cinder cone known as **Vulcan's Throne**, which prevents any water that flows down the valley from reaching the river; instead, after heavy rains a small lake collects on its northern side.

Down below, a solitary black basaltic column called **Vulcan's Anvil** sticks up forty feet from the middle of the river. For rafters, it's a telltale marker that the fearsome **Lava Falls Rapid**, created by debris washed down from Prospect Canyon, lurks just around the next bend. From here, however, you can both see it and hear it roar. Until a flash flood radically redesigned Crystal Rapid in 1966 (see p.282), this was generally recognized as the most difficult whitewater challenge in the canyon.

TOROWEAP

The Main Street Route

Though described here as an alternative route from Toroweap back to civilization, the **Main Street Route** is also the most direct way to approach Toroweap if you're coming from the west, as its terminus, **St George**, Utah, stands on the I-15 interstate between Las Vegas and Salt Lake City. A spectacular ninety-mile, three-hour desert drive on gravel roads, it's very straightforward in summer, but liable to be closed altogether in winter.

Starting from the Tuweep ranger station, you drive 7.5 miles north, and then turn left when you meet **BLM road 5**. This climbs west into the **Uinkaret Mountains**, the volcanic field responsible all those eruptions. Uinkaret is a Paiute word meaning "place of pines"; you'll see why ten miles along, when you reach the high pine-forested saddle between **Mount Logan** to the south and the 8026-foot **Mount Trumbull** to the north. In the late nineteenth century, timber from here was shipped north to construct the Mormon Temple at St George. In another five miles, you crest a final ridge to face a hair-raising descent into the huge **Hurricane Valley**.

Now located within but not part of Grand Canyon-Parashant National Monument, Hurricane Valley used to be home to a Mormon ranching and mining community. Founded by Abraham Bundy in 1916 as **Mount Trumbull**, it was universally known as "Bundyville," as most of its peak of almost three hundred inhabitants seemed to be called Bundy. The settlement lasted for around fifty years, before being defeated partly by drought and partly by the fact that improved roads and vehicles meant ranchers could live in St George and commute to their land.

The flat desolate crossroads in the heart of the valley holds the last remaining vestige of Bundyville, the four-square

Mount Trumbull Schoolhouse, which is generally open during daylight hours. Built in 1922, this was burned to the ground in July 2000, but it has since been rebuilt from scratch, and holds old schoolbooks and an awful lot of photos of Bundys.

Though a sign back at Tuweep warns drivers heading for St George to "watch for the left turn at the old schoolhouse," you need in fact to make a **right** turn, which is still BLM road 5. Head due north, on what eventually becomes **BLM road 1069**, and after passing through the dramatic **Wolf Hole Valley** and down into some eerie gray badlands beside the **Mokaac Wash**, you'll reach the sanctuary of a paved tarmac road in suburban St George after another 49 miles.

TOROWEAP

Flagstaff and Route 66

T hanks to the forbidding terrain not only of the Grand Canyon but also of the Colorado Plateau as a whole, Arizona's northernmost hundred miles remain impassable to east–west traffic. That makes the **I-40** interstate, which runs pretty much straight across the state roughly sixty miles south of the canyon, a crucial lifeline. Before the interstate was pushed through, the legendary **Route 66** followed much the same path; before either road, there was the Santa Fe Railroad; and before the railroad arrived, little more than a century ago, there were no significant Anglo settlements in the region at all.

Of the various communities along this corridor that serve as "gateways" for Grand Canyon travelers, the college town of **Flagstaff** is definitely the pick of the bunch. Set in the world's largest stand of sweet-smelling **ponderosa pine forest** – lumber from which provided the basis for the region's pioneer nineteenth-century economy – it ranks among the Southwest's most appealing small towns, while the deserts just to the east hold the intriguing ancient sites of **Wupatki** and **Walnut Canyon**.

Williams, to the west, is closer to the canyon and the starting point for the steam trains up to the South Rim, but is unlikely to hold your attention for any length of time, while **Ash Fork** and **Seligman** are both tiny desert outposts, and **Kingman**, though larger, lacks much sense of identity. That said, all of these places became reliant on tourism during the heyday of **Route 66**, and driving through any one of them can always bring on a frisson of that era's romance.

Flagstaff

Northern Arizona's liveliest and most attractive town, **FLAGSTAFF**, occupies a superbly dramatic location beneath the San Francisco Peaks, halfway between New Mexico and California. Straddling the I-40 and I-17 interstates, it's a major waystation for tourists en route to the Grand Canyon, just eighty miles northwest, but it's also a worthwhile destination in its own right.

Downtown, where barely a building rises more than three stories, oozes Wild West charm. Its main thoroughfare, Santa Fe Avenue, used to be **Route 66**, while before that it was the pioneer trail west. A stroll around its central few blocks is gloriously evocative of the past, though these days the diners and saloons are interspersed with outfitter stores and coffee bars, and the local cowboys and Indians share the sidewalks with liberal-minded students from Northern Arizona University. Just to add to the atmosphere, the tracks of the Santa Fe Railroad still cut downtown in two, so life in Flagstaff remains punctuated both day and night by the mournful wail of passing trains.

**A map of downtown Flagstaff can be found
at the back of this book (map 8).**

Flagstaff's first settlers arrived in 1876, lured from Boston by widely publicized accounts of mineral wealth and fertile land. Although they soon moved on, disappointed, toward Prescott, they stayed long enough to celebrate the centenary of American independence by flying the Stars and Stripes from a towering pine tree. This flagpole became a familiar landmark on the route west, and as the town grew it inevitably became known as Flagstaff. Right from the start, it was a cosmopolitan place, with a strong black and Hispanic population working in the (originally Mormon-owned) lumber mills and in the cattle industry, and Navajo and Hopi heading in from the nearby reservations to trade.

Modern Flagstaff, with a population of a little over fifty thousand, makes an ideal base for travelers, whether heading to the canyon or not. As well as the abundant hotels, restaurants, bars and shops within easy walking distance of downtown, outlets of the national food and lodging chains line the interstates slightly further afield, and budget travelers too are well catered for by hostels and student diners. There are also a couple of good museums nearby, together with some wonderful scenery and ancient sites in the close vicinity. Just one word of warning: the altitude here is almost seven thousand feet, which means the nights may well be colder than you're expecting. It can even snow in July.

ARRIVAL AND INFORMATION

Though the Santa Fe Railroad is still busy with freight, Amtrak's daily **Southwest Chief** between Chicago and Los Angeles is now the only passenger **train** that stops at Flagstaff's venerable wooden stationhouse, in the heart of

FLAGSTAFF

town. In summer, the eastbound service leaves at 5.15am for Albuquerque and the westbound at 9.26pm for Los Angeles; winter times are one hour later.

Open Road Tours and Transportation (☎ 928/226-8060 or 1-800/766-7117, ⊛ www.openroadtours.com), based at the Amtrak station, runs twice-daily **bus services** via Williams to the Grand Canyon. The first leaves Flagstaff at 8.30am, the second at 3pm; the one-way fare is $20 for adults, and $15 for under-12s. They also offer trips to Sedona ($48), Monument Valley ($89), and around Flagstaff itself ($32). In addition, Open Road runs four daily **buses** between Flagstaff and **Phoenix** ($30), a route on which Northern Arizona Shuttle (☎ 928/773-4337 or 1-866/870-8687, ⊛ www.nazshuttle.com) operate three daily services for the same price. Greyhound, based a few blocks south of downtown at 399 S Malpais Lane (☎ 928/774-4573 or 1-800/231-2222), run four daily buses to Phoenix, and also head west to Las Vegas, LA, San Diego and San Francisco, and east toward Albuquerque.

Flagstaff's helpful **visitor center** occupies the western half of the station at 1 E Route 66 (Mon–Sat 7am–6pm, Sun 7am–5pm; ☎ 928/774-9541 or 1-800/842-7293, ⊛ www.flagstaffarizona.org). Even when it's not staffed, the building itself remains open for Amtrak passengers, so it's still possible to pick up brochures, some of which include **discount coupons** for local motels. There's also a courtesy phone in the Amtrak lobby for making hotel and hostel reservations (daily 8am–5pm).

If you need **Internet access**, head for the self-explanatory *Biff's Bagels & Internet Café*, near the hostels at 1 S Beaver St (Mon–Sat 7am–3pm, Sun 8am–2pm; ☎ 928/226-0424, ⊛ www.biffsbagels.com).

Two local hostels – the *DuBeau* and the *Grand Canyon*, (see below) – arrange inexpensive **excursions for backpackers**.

The least expensive **car rental** is Budget Rent-a-Car, 175 W Aspen Ave (☎928/813-0156); Avis, Hertz, Enterprise and National also have outlets.

Absolute Bikes, 18 N San Francisco St (Mon–Sat 9am–6pm; ☎928/779-5969, ⓦwww.absolutebikes.net), rent out **mountain bikes** for $25 per day, or $90 per week, while Arizona Mountain Bike Tours (☎928/779-4161 or 1-800/277-7985) run local and regional **cycling tours**. Perhaps the best of several local **outfitters** who specialize in selling equipment for outdoors and backpacking expeditions is Aspen Sports, 15 N San Francisco St (☎928/779-1935 or 1-800/771-1935).

ACCOMMODATION

As Flagstaff is considerably more than just another interstate pit stop, its dozens of **motels** and **B&Bs** get away with charging higher rates than its I-40 neighbors. They're still not bad value, however, and **budget** travelers can choose between two hostels as well as a historic hotel that offers hostel-style dorm beds as well as private rooms. Most of the major chain motels are congregated well to the east, along Butler Avenue and Lucky Lane, but staying nearer downtown is much more fun.

If you arrive without a reservation, use the free **courtesy phones** in the local visitor center (see above) to compare options. Above all, plan ahead on summer weekends, when everywhere is likely to be booked solid. When all else fails, Flagstaff Central Reservations (☎928/527-8333 or 1-800/527-8388, ⓦwww.flagstaff-rooms.com) should be able to come up with something.

The best local **campground** is three miles south on US-89A, at *Fort Tuthill County Park* (May–Sept only; ☎928/774-3464), though Flagstaff also holds the year-round

Flagstaff/Grand Canyon KOA at 5803 N AZ-89A (℡ 928/526-9926 or 1-800/562-3524, Ⓦ www.koa.com/az/flagstaff).

Birch Tree Inn
824 W Birch Ave ℡ 928/774-1042 or 1-888/774-1042, Ⓦ www.birchtreeinn.com. Former frat house converted to upmarket B&B, with five tastefully themed guest rooms (two of which share one bathroom), fancy breakfasts, and a wraparound verandah. Shared rooms ❹, others ❻

DuBeau International Hostel
19 W Phoenix Ave ℡ 928/774-6731 or 1-800/398-7112, Ⓦ www.dubeau.com. Welcoming independent hostel just south of the tracks, whose appealingly converted en-suite motel rooms serve as four-person dorms at $16 per bed in summer, $14 in winter, or private doubles at $35. It also runs $18 one-way shuttle rides to the Grand Canyon (full-day tours $43). ❶

Econolodge West
2355 S Beulah Blvd ℡ 928/774-2225 or 1-800/490-6562, Ⓦ www.travelsouthwest.com. Relatively attractive chain motel in white clapboard style, with large rooms and suites, south of downtown near the interstate. ❸

Grand Canyon International Hostel
19 S San Francisco St ℡ 928/779-9421 or 1-888/442-2696, Ⓦ www.grandcanyonhostel.com. Independent hostel, under the same friendly management as the similar nearby DuBeau, and offering the same tours, plus dorm beds at $16 in summer, $12 in winter, and private rooms at $25. Tours to the Grand Canyon ($38) and Sedona ($20), and car rental discounts. ❶

Holiday Inn
2320 E Lucky Lane ℡ 928/714-1000, Ⓦ www.holiday-inn.com/flagstaffaz. Large motel, just off the interstate in a rather characterless area, with a

FLAGSTAFF

150

handful of nearby diners.
Winter ❹, summer ❺

The Inn at Four Ten

410 N Leroux St ☎928/774-
0088 or 1-800/774-2008,
Ⓦwww.inn410.com.
Bright ranch home that's now
a luxurious antique-furnished
B&B; all nine rooms are en-
suite, most have their own
fireplaces, and three have
whirlpool tubs. On summer
evenings, the porch and patio
make welcoming, convivial
retreats. ❺

Little America

2515 E Butler Ave ☎928/779-
7900 or 1-800/865-1401, Ⓦwww
.flagstaff.littleamerica.com.
Large motel-cum-resort near
the interstate, where there's a
good pool, and the 1950s-
style ambience conceals a
higher standard of
accommodation than you
might expect. ❹

Monte Vista

100 N San Francisco St ☎928
/779-6971 or 1-800/545-3068,
Ⓦwww.hotelmontevista.com.
Atmospheric little 1920s

hotel in the heart of
downtown, where the
assorted restored rooms, with
and without attached
bathrooms, are named for
celebrity guests from Bob
Hope to Michael Stipe. Rates
rise by up to $20 at
weekends. ❸–❺

Motel 6

2440 E Lucky Lane ☎928/774-
8756 or 1-800/466-8356.
The cheapest of several *Motel
6*s on the outskirts of town. ❷

Super 8 Motel

3725 N Kasper Ave ☎928/526-
0818 or 1-888/324-9131.
Standard, good-value motel
east of town. Winter ❸,
summer ❹

Super 8 West

602 W Route 66; ☎928/774-
4581.
Smart, good-value chain
motel, arranged around an
enclosed swimming pool,
alongside a Barnes & Noble
bookstore less than a mile
southwest of downtown,
where AZ-89 branches south
to Sedona. ❸

FLAGSTAFF

Hotel Weatherford

23 N Leroux St ⓣ 928/779-1919, ⓦ www.weatherfordhotel.com. Attractive old downtown hotel, with elegant wooden fittings, which bit by bit is restoring its fading rooms to offer tasteful but pretty basic accommodation, without telephones or TVs. The upstairs lounge oozes Wild West charm, but can make for a noisy night. Winter ❷, summer ❸

THE TOWN

Flagstaff's little-changed **downtown** stretches for a few red-brick blocks north of the railroad. Filled with cafés, bars, and stores selling Route 66 souvenirs and Native American crafts, as well as outfitters specializing in tents, clothing and all sorts of contraptions for outdoor adventures, it's a fun place to wander around, even if it holds no significant tourist attractions. Although the visitor center maps out walking tours, few specific buildings are especially historic; by the time you've browsed a few bookstores, downed a few coffees, and peeped into the old *Weatherford* and *Monte Vista* hotels, you may well be ready to move on. Your most lasting impression is likely to be of the magnificent volcanic **San Francisco Peaks**, rising smoothly from the plains on the northern horizon, and topped by a jagged ridge.

Museum of Northern Arizona

The exceptional **Museum of Northern Arizona**, three miles northwest of downtown on US-180, rivals Phoenix's Heard Museum as the best museum in the state (daily 9am–5pm; $5, under-18s $2; ⓣ 928/774-5213, ⓦ www .musnaz.org). Although it covers the geology, geography, flora and fauna of the Colorado Plateau – and can help you come to grips with the various theories that attempt to explain the origins of the Grand Canyon – its main empha-

FLAGSTAFF

sis is on documenting **Native American** life. It provides an excellent run-through of the Ancestral Puebloan past and contemporary Navajo, Havasupai, Zuni and Hopi cultures, with the overview in the initial gallery followed by further rooms devoted to pots, rugs, *kachina* dolls, and silver and turquoise jewelry. There are also temporary shows of local (not always Native American) arts and crafts, a well-stocked bookstore, and a **nature trail** that runs through the small pinon-fringed canyon outside.

Ever since it was established, in 1928, the Museum of Northern Arizona has actively encouraged the development of traditional and even new skills among Native American craftworkers. The exquisite inlaid silver jewelry now made by the Hopi, for example, is the result of a museum-backed program to find work for Hopi servicemen returning from World War II. During its annual Native American Marketplaces, every item is for sale. The **Hopi** show takes place on the weekend closest to July 4, the **Navajo** one at the start of August, the **Zuni** one at the start of September, and the latest addition, the **Pai** event, around Labor Day in late September.

The Pioneer Museum

Alongside US-180, a little closer to town than the Museum of Northern Arizona, an impressive steam train guards the **Pioneer Museum** (Mon–Sat 9am–5pm; donation; ☏928/774-6272). Run by the Arizona Historical Society, and housed in what was once the county hospital, this holds a random but reasonably entertaining assortment of objects and images from old Flagstaff.

Sharing the same grounds, the **Coconino Center for the Arts** is a gallery and concert hall specializing in works by local artists, while just behind it the co-operatively run **Art Barn** (daily 9am–5pm) sells a wide selection of crafts.

FLAGSTAFF

Lowell Observatory

Flagstaff's **Lowell Observatory**, located in the pine forest atop Mars Hill, a mile west of downtown, is famous as the place where the existence of the planet Pluto was first confirmed. Many of the necessary calculations were performed by Dr Percival Lowell, who founded the observatory in 1894 and deluded himself that he'd discovered canals on Mars. Lowell died in 1916 – he's buried in a small domed mausoleum of blue glass on the hilltop – and the ninth planet was eventually spotted in 1930 by Clyde Tombaugh.

From the **visitor center** (daily: April–Oct 9am–5pm; Nov–March noon–5pm; $4, under-18s $2; ☎928/774-3358, ⓦwww.lowell.edu), where only very technically minded visitors are likely to get much joy from playing with computers or watching explanatory videos, the **Pluto Walk** footpath climbs up to the tiny original observatory. Signs tick off the relative positions of the planets, but if it kept going on the same scale, it would have to extend over 600 miles, beyond Boise, Idaho, to show the position of the nearest star, Alpha Centauri.

Astronomy remains a passion in Flagstaff, and the town has won awards for minimizing night-time light pollution. Tourists are welcome to the observatory's regular evening **stargazing sessions** (June–Aug Mon–Sat 8pm; April, May, Sept & Oct Wed, Fri & Sat 7.30pm; Nov–March Fri & Sat 7.30pm; no additional charge).

EATING

Central Flagstaff is surprisingly short of high-end **restaurants**, but more than compensates for that with its lively assortment of both old-style Western **diners** and eclectic **budget** options. Thanks to all those students, the area around San Francisco Street, both north and south of the tracks, is filled with vegetarian cafés and espresso bars.

Alpine Pizza

7 N Leroux St ⓣ 928/779-4109.
Raucous student hangout downtown, with decent pizzas and lots of different beers. Mon–Sat 11.30am–2pm & 5–11pm, Sun 5–11pm.

Beaver Street Brewery & Whistle Stop Café

11 S Beaver St ⓣ 928/779-0079.
Inventive sandwiches and salads, wood-fired pizzas, and outdoor barbecue in the beer garden in summer. Daily 11.30am–midnight.

Black Barts

2760 E Butler Ave ⓣ 928/779-3142.
Enjoyable Western-themed steakhouse, across from Little America on the east edge of town, with a waitstaff who sing and dance on stage in between serving up barbecued steaks, ribs and chickens, for $16–23. Daily 5–10pm.

Cafe Espress

16 N San Francisco St ⓣ 928/774-0541.
Great vegetarian breakfasts, then salads, sandwiches and veggie specials for the rest of the day, plus espresso coffees. Mon, Tues & Sun 7am–3pm, Wed–Sat 7am–9pm.

Charly's Pub and Grill

Hotel Weatherford, 23 N Leroux St ⓣ 928/779-1919.
Café-restaurant in a classy Western setting, serving good, inexpensive meals accompanied by live music (cocktail piano at lunch, bands at night). Mon, Tues & Sun 7am–3pm, Wed–Sat 7am–9pm.

The Cottage Place

126 W Cottage Ave ⓣ 928/774-8431.
Dinner-only European restaurant in a rambling old house a short walk south of the tracks. Most full meals on the very varied Continental menu cost around $20. Tues–Sun 5–9.30pm.

FLAGSTAFF

Dara Thai

14 S San Francisco St
ⓣ 928/774-0047.
Large Thai place just south of
the tracks, where the service
is great and a plate of
delicious pad thai noodles
costs just $6 for lunch, $8 for
dinner. Mon–Sat
11am–10pm, Sun
noon–9pm.

Downtown Diner

7 E Aspen Ave ⓣ 928/774-3492.
Classic Route 66 diner a
block north of the main drag,
featuring leatherette booths
and hefty burgers and
sandwiches. Mon–Sat
7am–9pm, Sun noon–8pm.

Late For The Train

107 N San Francisco St
ⓣ 928/779-5975.
Little coffee bar opposite the
Monte Vista hotel, which
serves very good home-
roasted coffee and pastries to
a slightly older, literary

crowd. Mon–Thurs
6am–6pm, Fri 6am–10pm,
Sat 7am–10pm, Sun
7am–5pm.

Macy's European Coffee House & Bakery

14 S Beaver St ⓣ 928/774-2243.
Not merely superb coffee,
but heavenly pastries to go
with it, in a chaotic but
friendly student-oriented
atmosphere. You can also get
substantial vegetarian dishes
such as black bean pizza, and
even couscous for breakfast.
Mon–Wed & Sun 6am–8pm,
Thurs–Sat 6am–midnight.

Pasto

19 E Aspen Ave ⓣ 928/779-1937.
Downtown dinner-only
Italian joint, with pasta
specials plus chicken, shrimp
or vegetarian entrees for
$13–16. Mon–Thurs & Sun
5–9pm, Fri & Sat 5–9.30pm.

Nightlife

Its streets milling with international travelers in summer,
and students for the rest of the year, Flagstaff has to be the
liveliest **nightspot** between Las Vegas and Santa Fe.

Wander a block or two to either side of San Francisco Street downtown, and you can't go far wrong. Hotel bars which feature live music most nights include both the *Exchange Pub* and the upstairs *Zane Grey Ballroom* at the *Weatherford*, and the *Monte Vista Lounge*.

Flagstaff Brewing Company

16 E I-40 ⊤ 928/773-1442.
Popular downtown pub, with outdoor seating, big windows, and live music Wed–Sat.

The Mad Italian

101 S San Francisco St
⊤ 928/779-1820.
Highly sociable downtown bar with several pool tables.

Monsoons

22 E Route 66 ⊤ 928/774-7929.
Central downtown music venue, with live local bands most nights, plus barbecue.

The Museum Club

3404 E Route 66 ⊤ 928/526-9434.
A real oddity; this log-cabin taxidermy museum somehow transmogrified into a classic Route 66 roadhouse, saloon and country music venue that's a second home to hordes of dancing cowboys. Open daily noon–1am. Call ⊤ 928/774-4444 for a free shuttle service to and from your motel.

Around Flagstaff

The area around Flagstaff is extraordinarily rich in natural and archeological wonders, with three national monuments – **Sunset Crater**, **Wupatki**, and **Walnut Canyon** – within 25 miles, and the **San Francisco Peaks** overshadowing them all. All are generally seen as day-trips from Flagstaff; only Sunset Crater of the monuments has even a campground.

THE SAN FRANCISCO PEAKS

The **San Francisco Volcanic Field**, north of Flagstaff, consists of around four hundred distinct volcanic cones, which have appeared over the past two million years. During that time, the region has also been covered by glacial ice on three separate occasions, shaving around three thousand feet off the top of the volcanoes.

The serrated **SAN FRANCISCO PEAKS**, visible from downtown Flagstaff, are the remnants of a single mountain; their highest point today, at 12,643 feet, is the summit of **Mount Humphreys**. They were named by Spanish missionaries in honor of St Francis of Assisi, though the Hopi already knew them as *Nuvatukya'ovi*, the home of the *kachina* spirits, and to the Navajo this was *Dook'o'oosliid*, one of the four sacred mountains. Seen from afar, topped by a semipermanent layer of clouds, it's obvious why the Hopi and Navajo regarded them as the source of life-giving rain. It's because they were sacred to both that they now belong to neither; federal law dictates that Native American reservations can only include lands of which a tribe can prove it has "exclusive use." The Hopi in particular still make annual pilgrimages on foot from their mesas, 65 miles east, to shrines hidden in the mountains.

Arizona Snowbowl

Considering that the San Francisco Mountain, which has not erupted for 220,000 years, is dormant rather than extinct, the time may come when the gods decide that Flagstaff's own **ski resort**, the **Arizona Snowbowl**, is a desecration no longer to be tolerated. For the moment, it survives, nestling between Mount Humphreys and Mount Agassiz at the end of a seven-mile spur road north of US-180, and featuring ski runs such as "Boo-Boo" and

"Bambi." There's not enough water up here to make artificial snow – another early name for the peaks was the **Sierra Sin Agua**, or "waterless range" – so the season typically runs from mid-December to early April. The *Ski Lift Lodge* provides both food and cabin accommodation (☎928/774-0729, or 1-800/472-3599 from AZ and CA only; Mon–Thurs & Sun $55, Fri & Sat $85), while lift tickets cost $40 for a full day (9am–4pm), or $32 for the afternoon. For more information, contact ☎928/779-1951 or ⓦwww.arizonasnowbowl.com.

In summer, the longest of the Snowbowl's five chair lifts, which climbs to within a few hundred feet of the 12,350-foot summit of Mount Agassiz, remains open as the **Scenic Skyride** (mid-May to mid-Sept daily 10am–4pm, mid-Sept to mid-Oct Fri–Sun 10am–4pm; $9, under-13s $5). To protect the fragile vegetation, you can't hike any further from there, but there are plenty of other **trails** in the mountains, all intended for day use only. One switchbacks right to the top of Mount Humphreys, giving seventy-mile views to the Grand Canyon and beyond.

Sunset Crater Volcano National Monument

The focus of **SUNSET CRATER VOLCANO NATIONAL MONUMENT**, three miles down a side road that heads east off US-89 twelve miles north of Flagstaff, is the youngest of the San Francisco volcanoes. Its most recent eruption, in 1065 AD, had a profound impact on the local population and economy. Thick deposits of ash for miles around opened up previously infertile land to cultivation, accelerating – if not triggering – a land rush that threw different Native American cultures into contact and competition for the first time.

John Wesley Powell named Sunset Crater for its multicolored cone, which swells from a black base through reds and

THE SAN FRANCISCO PEAKS

oranges to a yellow-tinged crest. Unfortunately, however, its shifting cinders are too unstable to allow hikers to climb up to the rim. Instead, the one-mile **Lava Flow Trail** at its base offers a close-up look at the jagged black lava that streamed out across the desert, and the steeper one-mile **Lenox Crater Trail** ascends a lesser cone nearby.

All is explained in the **visitor center** near the start of the road (daily 8am–5pm; ☎928/526-0502, ⓦwww.nps.gov /sucr) opposite the forest service's *Bonito* **campground** (late May to mid-Oct; $10; ☎928/527-0866). The monument admission fee of $3 per person also covers entry to Wupatki.

WUPATKI NATIONAL MONUMENT

A dozen miles north of Sunset Crater, a cluster of several distinct and exceptionally well-preserved ancient ruins, dramatically poised between the volcanoes and the desert, jointly constitute **WUPATKI NATIONAL MONU-MENT**. They appear to testify to a period in which different tribal groups lived side by side in harmony. At some time after the Sunset Crater eruption – though not necessarily because of it, as archeologists formerly believed – the Sinagua people already present here, who surely witnessed the explosion, were joined by many others, including the Ancestral Puebloans and the Hohokam. When the rich new soil had been exhausted, around 150 years later, they all moved on once more.

The first of the five separate pueblo complexes you see as you approach from Sunset Crater, located at the end of its own 2.5-mile spur road, has been named **Wukoki**, a modern Hopi word meaning "big house." Reminiscent of the castle-like structures at Hovenweep in southern Utah, it stands within sight of a procession of rounded cinder cones, but was probably positioned for its commanding prospect of the Painted Desert to the north and east. Windows in its central tower, which is molded to the contours of a red-rock outcrop, and built with bricks of the same material, look out in all directions; the floor is deep in crumbling sand. With the Little Colorado River a full five miles distant, its inhabitants must have been desperately short of water.

The monument's **visitor center** (daily: summer 8am–7pm, winter 8am–5pm; admission $3, including Sunset Crater; ☎928/679-2365, ⓦwww.nps.gov/wupa), back on the highway a short way on, holds informative displays on the history and culture of the Sinagua and their neighbors, updated to incorporate the beliefs and traditions of their modern descendants, the Hopi.

A paved loop trail leads down from the visitor center to the main three-story, hundred-room pueblo block of **Wupatki** ("long cut house") itself, molded once again to a sandstone hillock and thereby concealing a number of natural caves. The site's most intriguing features, however, lie a little further along. First comes what seems to be an amphitheater, a walled circular plaza whose purpose remains unknown. Beyond it is an oval **ball court**, the northernmost such court ever found. Similar arenas throughout central America were used for a game – part ritual, part sport – in which players tried to propel a rubber ball through a stone hoop high on a wall, using their knees and elbows alone, much like modern basketball (except that the losers were sacrificed at the end). Alongside the ball court, cracks in the ground have created a natural **blowhole**, through which air is either sucked or blown depending on pressure and temperature. The audible "breathing" of the earth made this a sacred shrine for Wupatki's ancient inhabitants.

The loop road past Sunset Crater and Wupatki rejoins US-89 twenty miles south of Cameron (see p.107).

Outcrops along its final few miles hold more pueblos, such as one known for obvious reasons as **The Citadel**, perched on and fully occupying a hilltop. While its interior, which appears to hold a large circular *kiva*, remains unexcavated, much of its outer wall is still standing, incorporating striped bands of black lava boulders, and dotted with tiny "windows" that may have served defensive or astronomical purposes.

WALNUT CANYON NATIONAL MONUMENT

Another Sinagua site, even more spectacular than Wupatki, can be seen at **WALNUT CANYON NATIONAL MONUMENT**, just south of I-40 ten miles east of Flagstaff. Between 1125 and 1250 AD, this shallow canyon was home to a thriving Sinagua community, who lived in small family groups rather than in communal pueblos. Literally hundreds of their **cliff dwellings** still nestle beneath overhangs in the sides of the canyon. They simply walled off alcoves where softer strata of rock had eroded away, and put up partitions to make separate rooms.

A large scenic window in the **visitor center** (daily: June–Aug 8am–6pm; March–May & Sept–Nov 8am–5pm; Dec–Feb 9am–5pm; $3; ☏ 928/526-3367, ⓦ www.nps.gov /waca) gives an excellent overall view. **Walnut Creek** itself, long since diverted to provide Flagstaff's drinking water, now runs very dry, but you can still see how fertile this valley must have been when the Sinagua first arrived. Trees cling to the porous rock to shade the ancient dwellings, and the vegetation thickens down to a valley floor dense with black walnut and oak.

The mile-long **Island Loop Trail** drops steeply down from the visitor center and crosses a narrow causeway to an isthmus of rock high above a gooseneck of the creek. Along the path, you can go inside several Sinagua homes; note the T-shaped doorways, which could only be entered headfirst, and the ceilings blackened by the smoke of generations of fires. Petroglyphs have been found in the other ruins visible on all sides, but none remain on the trail.

The main purpose of the separate **Rim Trail**, which follows the edge of the canyon, is to provide a less strenuous walk. It leads to a picnic area and to some surface ruins (in the dissimilar pueblo style, consisting of large clusters of rooms), though you could keep going to turn this into a lengthy hike. There is no accommodation, and only minimal snack food, available at the canyon.

Between June and August each year, rangers lead two- to three-hour **guided hikes** to lesser-known and otherwise inaccessible sites within the monument (Tues, Sat & Sun at 10am; call to confirm).

Williams

Although Flagstaff is generally regarded as the obvious base for visitors to the South Rim, **WILLIAMS**, 32 miles west, is in fact the closest interstate town to the national park. While it can't boast half the charm or pizzazz of its neighbor, it's a nice enough little place, filled with Route 66-era motels and diners but retaining a certain individuality despite the constant stream of tourists. Its setting helps, cupped in a high grassy valley amid pine-covered hills; the largest peak is the 9264-foot **Bill Williams Mountain** to the south, which was named for pioneer trapper and "mountain man" Bill Williams (1787–1849), and gave its name in turn to the town, founded thirty years after his death.

Like Flagstaff, Williams originally based both its architecture and its economy on the ponderosas of the surrounding

forests. Ever since 1901, however, when the Santa Fe
Railroad first connected it with the canyon rim, sixty miles
due north, Williams has lived off tourism. Though the railroad went out of business in 1968, it reopened in 1989 as
the **Grand Canyon Railway**, promoted as a fun ride
rather than a serious means of transportation. Most people
who spend the night in Williams are here to take the
morning train up to the canyon.

ARRIVAL AND INFORMATION

Amtrak's *Southwest Chief* **train** calls in at **Williams
Junction**, three miles east of town, twice daily, heading east
at 4.35am and west at 10.04pm. The *Fray Marcos Hotel* (see
below) runs free connecting shuttle buses into town.

Full schedules and prices for the **Grand Canyon
Railway** (℡928/773-1976 or 1-800/843-8724, Ⓦwww
.thetrain.com), which sets off daily at 10am from the
Williams Depot in the center of town, appear on p.31.

Williams' **visitor center**, near the railroad depot at 200
W Railroad Ave (summer daily 8am–6.30pm, winter daily
8am–5pm; ℡928/635-4061 or 1-800/863-0546), hands
out all the usual brochures, including one detailing a town
walking tour, and doubles as an entertaining **museum** of
neighborhood history. You can find practical local listings
online at Ⓦwww.thegrandcanyon.com.

Marvelous Marv's Tours run daily **guided van tours** of
the South Rim from Williams, with the $70 adult rate
including admission to the park and the IMAX theater in
Tusayan (℡928/635-4061, Ⓦwww.marvelousmarv.com).

ACCOMMODATION

Although the large new *Fray Marcos Hotel* has immediately
established itself as Williams' leading **accommodation**

option, there are plenty of alternatives around. The main downtown streets are lined with vintage motels as well as the odd B&B, while the national chains congregate nearer the interstate exits at either end of town, and the *Red Lake Hostel* to the north caters for budget travelers.

If you're **camping**, you can choose between two *KOA* campgrounds – *Circle Pines*, three miles east (☎ 928/635-2626), and *Grand Canyon*, five miles north (☎ 928/635-2307 or 1-800/562-5771) – or ask at the Chalender Ranger Station, 501 W Route 66 (☎ 928/635-2676), for details of secluded summer-only mountain sites in the Kaibab National Forest.

Best Value Inn
1001 W Route 66 ☎ 928/635-2202.
Small British-owned motel, not far west of the center where the separate carriageways of Route 66 re-join, that's a cut above most of the budget options, with its own pool and spa. Winter ❶, summer ❸

Best Western Inn of Williams
2600 W Route 66 ☎ 928/635-4400 or 1-800/635-4445.
Spacious and very well-equipped motel-resort, with pool and hot tub, perched near I-40 exit 161 at the west end of town. Winter ❹, summer ❻

Downtowner Motel
201 E Route 66 ☎ 928/635-4041 or 1-800/798-0071, ⓦ www.thegrandcanyon.com/downtowner.
Dependable if unexciting old-style motel, stretching between the two one-way streets downtown. Winter ❶, summer ❸

Fray Marcos Hotel
1 Fray Marcos Blvd ☎ 928/635-4010 or 1-800/843-8724, ⓦ www.thetrain.com.
The Grand Canyon Railway's flagship hotel originally opened in 1908; now entirely rebuilt, it's very comfortable without having much character, though the large open lobby is a pleasant

WILLIAMS

enough place to sit, and there's also an indoor pool, spa and saloon. All rooms have two queen beds. Mid-Oct to mid-March ❹, mid-March to mid-Oct ❻

Red Garter Bed and Bakery

137 W Railroad Ave ⓣ928/635-1484 or 1-800/328-1484, ⓦwww.redgarter.com.
Plush four-room B&B in a former downtown bordello, serving fresh-baked breakfasts from its own downstairs bakery. Closed mid-Dec to mid-Feb. ❺

Red Lake Hostel

AZ-64 ⓣ928/635-4753 or 1-800/581-4753,

ⓔredlake@azaccess.com.
Red-painted converted motel adjoining a Mustang gas station at a lonely curve on AZ-64 nine miles north of town, where you can pay $11 for a dorm bed, or $33 to get a private room to yourself. They also offer tent and RV camping. ❶

Super 8

911 W Route 66 ⓣ928/635-4045 or 1-800/800-8000.
Standard, reasonable-quality chain motel – the more central of Williams' two *Super* 8s – not far west of downtown. The interior hallways are rather faded, but the rooms are fine, and there's an indoor pool. Winter ❷, summer ❹

THE TOWN

Williams holds a definite romantic appeal as the very last town on the old **Route 66** to have been bypassed by the I-40 interstate. Until October 13, 1984, when Bobby Troup of *(Get Your Kicks On) Route 66* fame fronted a closing ceremony, the only stoplight on the interstate between Chicago and Los Angeles stood outside the Williams visitor center.

Much of the former Route 66 frontage remains barely changed, with several quirky antiques stores selling both vintage memorabilia and Native American crafts and jewelry. However, while it's fun to explore the central blocks along the two main one-way streets – Route 66, running west to east, is paralleled by the east–west **Railroad Avenue** – an hour's evening or morning stroll is probably enough; Williams is not really a place to spend the day.

For rail enthusiasts, the Williams Depot holds the slowly expanding **Grand Canyon Railway Museum** (daily 7.30am–5.30pm; free). As well as masses of old photos, including some great hand-tinted ones, it's bursting with vintage tools and implements, with cases of ancient arm-rests and window catches. In due course, they hope to unveil a 650-foot model of the whole route up to the canyon.

Twin highlights of Williams' annual calendar are **Rendezvous Days**, on Memorial Day weekend in late May, when locals dress up as pioneer "buckskinners," and the Labor Day **rodeo**.

EATING

The **restaurant** selection in Williams is frankly disappoint-ing. A few places conjure up the feel of its Route 66 hey-day, but there's nowhere that serves interesting food.

Grand Canyon Coffee & Café

125 W Route 66 ⊤ 928/635-1255.

Tiny little downtown café that serves espressos, juices, and pastries through the day, and then switches to simple Asian dishes such as Korean barbecue in the evenings. Daily 8am–8pm.

Max & Thelma's

Williams Depot ⊤ 928/635-8970.

Named for the owners of the Grand Canyon Railway, *Max & Thelma's* is an adequate but boring family restaurant aimed at speedily satisfying hungry tour groups. All-you-can-eat buffets are available for every meal – the dinner one

WILLIAMS

costs $11 – and you can also order predictable a la carte options. Daily 6.30am–9pm.

Pancho McGillicuddy's
141 W Railroad Ave ☎ 928/635-4150.
Popular but very average Mexican cantina, housed in an attractive tin-ceilinged building downtown, with its own authentic-looking saloon. The usual south-of-the border standards, like flautas, tostadas, tamales or carnitas, cost under $10, and there are three possible mixed platters for $12; they also serve steaks and grills. Daily 7am–10pm.

Pine Country Restaurant
107 N Grand Canyon Blvd ☎ 928/635-9718.
Very traditional, very friendly central diner, where the food's not bad, and home-made pies are a specialty. Daily 5.30am–9pm.

Ash Fork

The ranching community of **ASH FORK**, stretched along a brief curving fragment of Route 66 north of the interstate another twenty miles west of Williams, is smaller, less picturesque and far less involved in catering to travelers. By this point I-40 has pulled clear of the forests, and downtown Ash Fork is characterized by buildings constructed with the yellowish local sandstone rather than timber.

The major **motel** chains haven't bothered to set up shop in Ash Fork, but there are still a few homespun alternatives, including the large, pink *Ash Fork Inn*, at the west end of town near I-40 exit 144 (☎ 928/637-2514; ❷), and the *Hi Line*, 124 E Lewis Ave (☎ 928/637-2766; ❷). There's also a *KOA* **campground** at 783 Old Route 66 (☎ 928/637-2521), and a couple of basic diners in the thick of what few things Ash Fork has to its name.

Seligman

Starting a few miles west of Ash Fork, the old Route 66 parallels its modern replacement at a discreet distance for the twenty or so miles to **SELIGMAN**. This flyblown desert halt now feels more than a little stranded, a mile or two north of the interstate, but if you're in the mood to be seduced by its kitsch diners and drive-ins, it makes a mildly diverting stop in a long day's drive. Every business in town strives to outdo the others with eye-catching displays – mannequins of Elvis and Marilyn waving from oddball parked vehicles and the like – and the passing traffic is worth watching too, with all kinds of vintage roadsters making their pilgrimages along the "Mother Road."

You might even choose to follow Route 66's original course as it curves northwards, through a dozen fading villages and part of the **Hualapai reservation** (see p.189), and back south to Kingman. That's a total drive of 88 miles, as opposed to the dreary 65-mile run west on I-40.

Route 66 also provides access to **Havasu Canyon**, in the depths of the Grand Canyon, as detailed in Chapter Six.

Seligman offers the only **accommodation** along the I-40 stretch between Ash Fork and Kingman, though motels like the *Historic Route 66*, 500 W Route 66 (℡ 928/422-3204; ❷), and the *Romney*, 122 W Route 66 (℡ 928/422-7666; ❷), are all much of an indifferent muchness. The wackiest of the local **diners** has to be *Delgadillo's Snow Cap* at 301 E Route 66 (℡ 928/422-3352), where every malt or burger comes with a side order of outrageous puns and put-ons. If you're just looking for a square meal, the *Copper Cart*, in the former railroad station (℡ 928/422-3241), serves a standard all-American menu.

SELIGMAN

Kingman

With a population of over thirty thousand, **KINGMAN**, 65 miles on from Seligman and thirty miles short of California, ranks second to Flagstaff among Arizona's I-40 towns. As all traffic between Phoenix or the Grand Canyon and **Las Vegas** – a mere hundred miles northwest on US-93 – is obliged to pass this way, Kingman also welcomes enough tourists to keep thirty or more motels busy year-round. The best that can be said for it, however, is that it's not particularly ugly – with the exception of the long sprawl beside the railroad tracks north of the interstate – and it's not lifeless. Apart from that, it's a humdrum pit stop with a slight tinge of Route-66 quaintness.

Kingman's main street, curving alongside the railroad tracks, is named in honor of native son **Andy Devine**, the actor who drove the eponymous *Stagecoach* in John Ford's 1939 movie. As the town's promotional brochure puts it, "there must be somebody who hasn't heard of Andy Devine, but that person sure doesn't live in Kingman." His career, the culture and basketwork of the Hualapai, and sundry other unlikely components of Mohave County's heritage, are explored in the **Mohave Museum of History & Arts**, 400 W Beale St (Mon–Fri 10am–5pm, Sat & Sun 1–5pm; $3, under-13s free; ☎928/753-3195). The year 1939, incidentally, was a big one for Kingman: Carole Lombard and Clark Gable were married here on March 29.

ARRIVAL AND INFORMATION

Kingman's large **Powerhouse visitor center** stands at the western edge of downtown, at 120 W Andy Devine Ave (daily 9am–6pm; ☎928/753-6106); as well as the usual brochures, it displays and sells lots of Route 66 memorabilia, and also has its own diner, *Memory Lane*, complete with soda fountain and deli. The old station in the center of town still welcomes Amtrak **trains** between Flagstaff and LA, but only at unearthly hours of the night, while regular Greyhound **buses**, between Phoenix and Las Vegas as well as east–west, use a terminal up near the interstate at 3264 E Andy Devine Ave (☎928/757-8400).

ACCOMMODATION

Granted that you're unlikely to spend more than one night in Kingman – or linger very long in the morning, either – its range of ordinary but inexpensive **motels** should easily meet your needs. There's also beautiful **camping** in the hills five miles southeast of town, in the county-run **Hualapai Mountain Park** (☎928/757-3859), which also holds the *Hualapai Mountain Lodge Resort* (☎928/757-3545; ❹).

Best Western A Wayfarer's Inn
2815 E Andy Devine Ave
☎928/753-6271 or 1-800/548-5695.
Upscale hundred-room chain property, a couple of miles northeast of town near I-40 exit 53, charging very reasonable rates for its smart if anonymous rooms, and offering a pool and indoor spa. ❹

Brunswick
315 E Andy Devine Ave ☎928 /718-1800 or 1-888/559-1800,

ⓦwww.hotel-brunswick.com.
This century-old "historical boutique hotel" offers downtown Kingman's most flavorful lodging, with antique-styled rooms that range from the basic, single-bedded cowboy or cowgirl option, sharing a bathroom, up to lavish suites. Triple-glazed windows keep noise from the nearby railroad to a minimum. All rates include breakfast. ❷–❺

Hill Top Motel
1901 E Andy Devine Ave

KINGMAN

ⓣ 928/753-2198.
Perfectly pleasant, good-value motel, located as the name suggests at the crest of the rise east of downtown and offering a wide range of rooms, which has acquired unwanted notoriety because Timothy McVeigh spent a week here shortly before he bombed the Alfred P. Murrah building in Oklahoma City, in April 1995. ❷

Quality Inn Kingman
1400 E Andy Devine Ave ⓣ 928 /753-4747 or 1-800/228-5151.
Standard motel half a mile up from downtown, with small but adequate rooms, that's given a little character by its strong Route-66 theming,

including vintage gas pumps outside and a retro-styled breakfast room. ❸

Ramblin' Rose
1001 E Andy Devine Ave ⓣ 928/753-5541.
Appealing independent motel, not far east of the center, that's been nicely spruced up to provide some of Kingman's best-value budget rooms ❷

Super 8
3401 E Andy Devine Ave ⓣ 928/757-4808 or 1-800/800-8000.
Reliable, inexpensive chain motel, well out of town just north of the eastern I-40 exit 53. Winter ❷, summer ❹

EATING

Most of the **restaurants** in Kingman play on the Route 66 angle in some form or other. It's all too spread out for you to wander around comparing menus, but hop in your car and you'll find something.

DamBar & Steak House
1960 E Andy Devine Ave ⓣ 928/753-3523.
Classic Western steakhouse at the top of the hill, all sawdust

and bare timber, and serving grilled and barbecued ribs and chicken as well as massive steaks. All entrees come in at under $20 for dinner, more

like $10 for lunch. Mon–
Thurs & Sun 11am–10pm,
Fri & Sat 11am–11pm.

Hubb's Café
Brunswick, 315 E Andy Devine
Ave ⓣ 928/718-1800.
The *Brunswick's* attractively
restored dining room prepares
an eclectic menu of dishes
from around the world, from
rich Continental sauces to
spicy Asian curries, as well as
all the usual American
standards. Few entrees cost
over $15, while lunch specials
can be a real bargain. Daily
except Tues 11am–9pm.

Mr D'z Route 66 Diner
105 E Andy Devine Ave
ⓣ 928/718-0066.

Across from the visitor
center, this loving recreation
of a classic Route-66
roadhouse is bursting with
neon, lurid molded
trimmings, and memorabilia,
and serves up pretty authentic
burgers and shakes, malts and
floats, and fries with
everything. Daily except
Mon 10am–5pm.

Old Town Coffeehouse
616 E Beale St ⓣ 928/753-
2244.
Slightly chintzy café on the
eastern fringes of downtown,
where you can enjoy
espressos, soups and
sandwiches on a small
outdoor patio. Mon–Fri
7am–4pm, Sat 8am–5pm.

KINGMAN

The Havasupai reservation

Havasu Canyon, at the heart of the Havasupai reservation and one of the most spellbindingly beautiful places in the entire Southwest, nestles deep in the Grand Canyon a mere 35 miles west of the national park's headquarters at the South Rim. The only approach is from the southwest, so it's a road trip of almost two hundred miles, the last ninety miles, once you leave the interstate, across the endless Coconino Plateau.

A map of the Havasupai reservation can be
found at the back of this book (map 6).

Those visitors who brave the eight-mile desert hike – the only way down into the canyon – are rewarded by a stunning oasis of **turquoise waterfalls** and lush vegetation, a Shangri-La that has been home for centuries beyond record to the same small group of Native Americans. The five hundred or so **Havasupai** are here thanks to a geological fluke. Although the canyon receives only nine inches of rain each year, all the water that falls for three thousand square miles around funnels down into this one narrow gorge, to create the year-round torrent of Havasu Stream.

Havasu Canyon forms the heart of the **Havasupai Indian Reservation,** said by a 1930s anthropologist to be "the only spot in the United States where native culture has remained in anything like its pristine condition." Since then, tourism has become the mainstay of the tribal economy, but visitor numbers are kept deliberately low, at around 35,000 per year. Suggestions of building a road – or even a tramway – down into the canyon have always been rejected, to minimize the impact on the traditional way of life. Instead, the Havasupai earn their keep by ferrying non-hikers up and down the trail on horses and pack mules, and operating a thriving **campground** beside the stream as well as a comfortable lodge in the village of **Supai**. While visitors should not expect sweeping views of the Grand Canyon itself – or to have much interaction with the tribal members – for spectacular desert scenery, and sheer romance, the Havasupai reservation is beyond compare.

The one crucial factor to bear in mind if you're planning a trip is that you **must** have an advance reservation for either the lodge or campground. That's easier said than done; between May and October, the lodge is almost invariably booked months in advance, and the campground is usually full on weekends. On top of that, the telephone line down to Supai can fail for weeks at a time.

Unless you travel by **helicopter**, as detailed on p.182, it's impossible to visit Havasu Canyon as a **day-trip**; quite apart from the drive to the trailhead, the twenty-mile hike to the falls and back takes well over ten hours.

A HISTORY OF THE HAVASUPAI

Archeologists have identified the earliest inhabitants of Havasu Canyon as the **Cohonina**. Like the Ancestral Puebloans, their neighbors to the east, they are thought to have occupied the region between around 700 and 1100

AD. At some point during that period, a Yuman-speaking group who call themselves the "**Pai**" – a word that simply means "people" – made their first appearance in the Southwest. So little is known about the Cohonina that no one knows whether the Pai were their cousins, their descendants, or an entirely new group.

What is certain, however, is that by 1300 AD, a couple hundred years after the Cohonina abandoned the canyon, a band of Pai had taken their place. The Pai as a whole had by this time quarreled, splitting to form the **Hualapai** ("People of the Tall Pines") of northwest Arizona, and the **Yavapai** ("Almost-People," who no longer quite deserved to be regarded as people) who settled along the Colorado further south. It was a group of Hualapai families who moved into the canyon, to become the **Havasupai** – the "people of the blue-green water." Although not related to any of the many different Pueblo peoples, the Hualapai established close links with the Hopi and the Zuni, from whom they eventually acquired the art of raising sheep, horses, and crops such as peaches.

See "A human history of the Grand Canyon" (p.265), for more information about Native Americans in the region.

Despite taking their name from the turquoise river that watered the fields here, the Havasupai lived on the canyon floor during the summer only, building houses of hide-covered branches. In winter, the canyon made a cold, miserable home, lacking big game and wood for fuel and receiving as little as five hours of sunlight per day. Instead the Havasupai moved up onto the plateau to hunt deer, elk, and antelope, using artificial water holes to lure them closer. Their territory covered perhaps 2.3 million acres, extending far beyond the region now occupied by Grand Canyon

Village to the San Francisco Peaks near modern Flagstaff, and as far north as what's now Tuba City, Arizona.

In June 1776, shortly before the Declaration of Independence was signed in Philadelphia, the Havasupai welcomed their first white visitor. **Father Francisco Tomás Garcés**, a missionary from San Xavier del Bac near Tucson who made several pioneering expeditions into the unknown West, was greeted with five days of feasting. Describing the Grand Canyon as a "calaboose of cliffs and canyons," he dubbed it the Puerto de Bucareli in honor of the viceroy who had despatched him; more enduringly, he was the first to name the **Río Colorado**. Garcés himself traveled eastwards along the South Rim to meet the Hopi, while the rest of his expedition blazed a trail to California, where they founded San Francisco.

The Havasupai then remained undisturbed for another eighty years, before Anglo prospectors and surveyors began to enter the region. Conflict arose in 1866, when, to encourage the spread of the railroads, Congress granted the Atlantic and Pacific Railroad company ownership of swathes of land adjoining its tracks across northern Arizona. Native resistance soon escalated into **war**, and the defeated Hualapai spent several years confined to a reservation near Ehrenberg, 150 miles downstream along the Colorado. Because the Havasupai did not participate in the fighting, they were allowed to remain in their traditional territory, which was then known to the US authorities as **Cataract Canyon**. Only now did they begin to regard themselves as a separate "tribe" rather than just another band of Hualapai.

In negotiations over the extent of a permanent Havasupai reservation, the government was as usual only prepared to acknowledge Native American "ownership" of land that held permanent settlements and cultivated fields. Areas used for hunting, gathering or even grazing, especially if use was

A HISTORY OF THE HAVASUPAI

shared by more than one band, were never included in reservations. Fearful of being deported themselves, the Havasupai settled in 1882 for a tiny plot at the bottom of Havasu Canyon – at a mere 518 acres, it amounted to less than one square mile. Restricted to a fraction of their former range, they were obliged to farm what little land they were granted as intensively as possible.

A century of hardship was to follow, during which the Havasupai repeatedly petitioned to have their reservation enlarged. Suffering great spiritual uncertainty, both the Havasupai and Hualapai took part in the **Ghost Dance** movement in the 1890s, when Native Americans throughout the West joined in trance-like rituals designed to ensure that white men would vanish from the land and the old ways would return. The Havasupai also briefly adopted the rain-making *kachina* dances of the Hopi, until a catastrophic **flood** on January 1, 1910 destroyed their village, which then stood half a mile from its current site.

The creation of **Grand Canyon National Park** in 1919 placed yet more restrictions on Havasupai use of traditional lands. One early supervisor avowed that the Grand Canyon "should be preserved for the everlasting pleasure and instruction of our intelligent citizens as well as those from foreign countries; I therefore deem it just and necessary to keep the wild and inappreciable Indians from off the Reserve." Park proposals during the 1920s to build a direct road along the South Rim and down into Havasu Canyon were probably only thwarted by the Crash of 1929, and resurfaced repeatedly for decades to come.

Although Coconino National Forest, to the south of the reservation, takes its name from the Hopi word for the Havasupai (which also, anachronistically, explains how the Cohonina got their name), tribal members could only graze animals there by annual permit. The Havasupai survived largely through disobeying whatever unenforceable regulations outsiders sought to impose, and continuing to spend their winters up on the plateau. Many Havasupai in due course found jobs in Grand Canyon Village, while tourism to Havasu Canyon itself became an important element in the tribal economy.

Nonetheless, the park service and the Havasupai remained at loggerheads. During the 1950s, the park surreptitiously bought up defunct mining claims in the canyon, and then opened its own campground – the same one that remains in use today under Havasupai control – on a former Havasupai burial ground. Meanwhile, the Havasupai tirelessly petitioned for the return of their lands. It might sound strange now, but their greatest ally was Republican senator **Barry Goldwater**, while ranged against them were environmentalist groups such as the **Sierra Club** and **Friends of the Earth**, who had yet to be convinced that Native Americans could look after wilderness lands as well as the park service.

Despite having agreed in 1968 to accept $1.24 million as final compensation for their lost lands, the Havasupai finally won their battle in 1975. The reservation was expanded by 185,000 acres, and the Havasupai were also awarded rights over 95,300 acres of "traditional use" land that lay within the park. This was the largest tract of land ever returned to Native Americans, but it came with the proviso that it must remain "forever wild." No mining, logging or manufacturing was to be permitted on the "traditional use" lands, and no dams or railroads could be built.

The settlement came only just in time. Almost immediately, the Grand Canyon region experienced a boom in **uranium** mining, with over 3500 claims filed in the Arizona Strip during the ensuing decade. In 1988, Energy Fuels Nuclear was granted rights to develop a uranium mine to be known as **Canyon Mine**, at a site outside the reservation, close to **Red Butte** in the Kaibab National Forest, which is sacred to the Havasupai as *Mat Taav*

A HISTORY OF THE HAVASUPAI

Tijundva. Despite fears that it could contaminate Havasu Stream, Havasu Canyon, and ultimately the Colorado itself, federal courts blocked Havasupai attempts to stop the mine. The mine was built, but never went into operation, thanks to a drop in prices caused by the worldwide glut of uranium. It now belongs to the International Uranium Corporation, which recently denied suggestions that the mine might be reactivated under the Bush/Cheney energy plan of 2001, but still insists that the low price of uranium is the only factor holding it back.

The other major threat facing the Havasupai is that any future tourist development at the South Rim – along the lines of the abortive "Canyon Forest Village" scheme (see p.35) – would be liable to deplete the water table for hundreds of miles around. That could mean that Havasu Stream would finally run dry.

GETTING TO THE RESERVATION

Since the enlargement of their reservation in 1975, the Havasupai have closed all except one of the various possible access routes into their land. Now the only way to get here by road is from **I-40**, turning off at **Seligman** if you're coming from Flagstaff or Grand Canyon Village, or at **Kingman** from Las Vegas or California. Stock up with food, water and gas when you leave the interstate, then follow **AZ-66** – the only surviving segment of Route 66 not to have been superseded by newer roads, and still closely parallel to the main east–west railroad – to the poorly marked intersection with **Arrowhead Hwy-18**, six miles east of **Peach Springs**. From Seligman, that's a straight run of around 29 miles; from Kingman it's more like sixty miles, but there is at least the option of an overnight stop in the *Hualapai Lodge* in Peach Springs (see p.192).

AZ-18 runs for its entire 56-mile length with hardly a

building in sight, across bare sagebrush desert interrupted by patches of thick ponderosa forest. Despite maps to the contrary, it's paved throughout, and there's no possibility of losing your way. Eventually it starts to wind down through burgeoning canyonlands, coming to an end at the large plateau known as **Hualapai Hilltop**. At an elevation of 5200 feet, this commands a long view of the white-walled **Hualapai Canyon**, cutting into the tablelands as it stretches north toward its meeting with Havasu Canyon. Although the hilltop holds no more than a small cluster of dilapidated shacks, with no accommodation, food or gas available, there are usually far more vehicles parked here than you might anticipate for such a remote spot.

From the end of the parking lot, the Hualapai Trail to Supai zigzags steeply down the hillside to the right, and can then be seen threading its way across the valley floor below. As stressed above, do not attempt to go down unless you have already reserved accommodation.

Horse rides and helicopters

Hikers are free to set off from Hualapai Hilltop whenever they choose. If you prefer to **ride** down on either horse or mule, make a reservation at the same time as you book your accommodation. To ride as far as the **village** costs $70 per person one way, and $120 round trip, and should be arranged with the management of the lodge (☎928/448-2111); continuing on to the campground costs $75 one way, $150 round trip, and is arranged by the Havasupai Tourist Enterprise (☎928/448-2121 or 2141). Riders' baggage weighing over ten pounds has to be carried by additional horses, and many hikers also arrange to have their bags carried. One animal can carry up to four packs, for the same charge as a rider. There's a $20 surcharge for leaving the hilltop after noon, or Supai after 10am.

GETTING TO THE RESERVATION

In recent summers, a **helicopter shuttle** service has been intermittently operated between Hualapai Hilltop and Supai village by Skydance Helicopters (☎ 1-800/882-1651). Call to see whether they have reintroduced the service, which in the past has carried passengers on a first-come, first-served basis, without any advance reservations, for a one-way fare of around $70.

Finally, it's also possible to take a helicopter to Havasupai from **Tusayan**, just outside Grand Canyon Village. Papillon Grand Canyon Helicopters (☎ 928/638-2419 or 1-800 /528-2418, Ⓦ www.papillon.com; see also p.11) fly one-day excursions – including a horse ride to Havasu Falls but not meals, which cost $442 for adults, $422 for under-12s – and can also arrange one-night trips when lodge accommodation is available.

THE TRAIL TO SUPAI

Apart from its initial switchbacks down the Coconino Sandstone hillside, the **Hualapai Trail** is not especially difficult. It is, however, a long eight-mile walk, with no shade for the first three miles and no reliable water source until very near the end. Allow around three hours to reach the village (and four or more to come back up again), and be sure to carry all the food and water you will need for a day in the desert.

The route is very obvious, and kept busy throughout the day with small supply trains of mules and horses. Once on the valley floor, it follows the bed of a dry wash between red-rock cliffs that slowly but inexorably climb to form the two walls of the deep, narrow Hualapai Canyon. The sand underfoot is so thick that it splashes at every step, but the potential for flash floods is clear from the much-scoured rocks to either side. Mighty boulders occasionally all but block the path, while solitary cottonwoods reach up toward the thin strip of sky overhead. Atop the Esplanade Plateau straight ahead, the pale, stark butte of **Mount Sinyala** repeatedly looms into view.

After almost seven miles, the trail reaches its intersection with Havasu Canyon; until the disastrous flood of 1910 (see p.178), this was the site of Supai village. All of Havasu Canyon was formerly known as **Cataract Canyon**, but now that old name only applies to its dry segment, to the right of the junction. Whatever you do, don't turn right – it took three weeks to rescue a dehydrated camper who did so in 1975. That said, however, what little tourist traffic the Havasupai received a century ago would arrive this way, along the **Topocoba Trail**, which reaches Cataract Canyon by means of Lee Canyon, at the end of a thirty-mile dirt-road drive from Grand Canyon Village. Although the Havasupai continue to make occasional use of that trail, recreational hikers no longer do so.

Bear left at the trail junction instead, at a dense cluster of small trees. The sound of rushing water soon signals the emergence of **Havasu Stream** from hidden crevices in the rock. Before long it's flowing through the parched landscape in all its blue-green splendor, at an average capacity of an amazing 38 million gallons per day.

Not far beyond, you cross a low rise to be confronted by the meadow that holds the modern village, and the two red-rock pillars that watch over Supai from the high canyon wall on the far side. Known as the **Wigleeva**, these twin sentinels, of which one is considered to be male and the other female, are regarded as the guardian spirits of the Havasupai.

SUPAI

Though located in a superb natural setting – a wide, flat clearing surrounded on all sides by forbidding walls of red sandstone – the village of **SUPAI** is not in itself attractive. The Havasupai were only obliged to build a year-round settlement down in the canyon by the loss of their lands on the plateau above (see p.178), and this site was their second choice after the first proved prone to flooding. It too has suffered repeated damage from floods, including four major inundations over the past decade. It therefore consists of just a scattering of basic timber-frame houses and prefabricated cabins. Even the name itself is a flimsy fabrication: "Supai" is a meaningless abbreviation of "Havasupai," invented by the US Post Office.

Once the Hualapai Trail, running alongside a line of irrigation ditches, has become what's jokingly called "Main Street" and shepherded you into the village, the first building you come to holds the tribal **registration office**. Only campers need to pay the $20 reservation **entrance fee** here; for lodge guests, it's added to their bill. A back room holds a small **museum** (daily 7am–7pm; $1), with a random but reasonably interesting assortment of century-old photographs and newspaper cuttings. Although the Havasupai are famous for crafts such as basket-making, ancient artifacts have become too expensive for the museum to afford.

Fifty yards further on, beyond the only post office in the US that still receives its mail by pack mule, lies Supai's dusty, fly blown **plaza**. Benches outside the village's one **grocery store** on the right form its main social center, where the older Havasupai gather each evening. The younger set, together with a vast population of dogs, are more likely to be found on the terrace of the **café**, opposite. Once past that, the trail skirts the edge of the village school, then branches off left down toward the campground. Visitors are forbidden to wander away from the main trail into the farmlands around the village.

Havasupai Lodge

Havasupai Lodge (☎928/448-2111; ❹) is located slightly apart from things on the edge of the village, close to the canyon wall behind the school. It's a simple two-story structure, built in the style of a functional motel rather than an atmospheric park lodge, where the plain but comfortable air-conditioned rooms are without phones or TVs. All sleep up to four people. As mentioned earlier, advance bookings are essential, and very hard to get between May and October.

Note that the $20 reservation entrance fee is added to all bills at the lodge, which like all prices on the Havasupai reservation are also subject to an additional five percent **tribal sales tax**.

Eating

Although the lodge has a pleasant little garden, the only place to get a **meal** in Supai is at the **Tribal Cafe** (daily: hours vary from 6am–7pm in summer down to 8am–5pm in winter; ☎928/448-2981). The food is far from exciting, with fried breakfasts, and a lunch or dinner of beef stew, fry bread or burritos; pretty much everything seems to cost around $6, or more if you want grated cheese on top.

The **grocery store** across the plaza has a limited selection of processed items, all carried in by mule and priced accordingly.

BELOW SUPAI: THE FALLS

All the **waterfalls** for which the Havasupai reservation is famous lie further down the canyon beyond Supai. Much of the riverbed immediately below the village remains cluttered with fallen trees and undergrowth deposited by the many floods, but after a mile and a half a thundering from the left betrays the presence of **Navajo Falls**. Intervening trees make them hard to spot from the main trail, as they plummet down the far wall of the canyon, but hardy hikers can reach them by picking their way down below the path. Once there, clamber across a minor fork of the stream and you'll come to the foot of the falls, which tumble through a series of pools.

The falls were, incidentally, named for **Chief Navajo**, who led the Havasupai at the time the reservation was first established, and died in 1900. His own confusing moniker is owed to the fact that he was kidnapped by the Navajo as a child, and only returned to his people in adult life.

Havasu Falls

The trail beyond Navajo Falls – which was washed away completely in 1993, and has been reconstructed to follow a course higher up the canyon wall – soon reaches the stupendous double cascade of **Havasu Falls**. First seen from an overlook more or less level with the top, this is an absolutely breathtaking sight. The stream foams white as it hurtles over a 150-foot cliff, to crash into shallow terraces filled with limpid turquoise water. The rock formations all around are formed from water-deposited limestone known as **travertine** – the same stuff that clogs the inside of domestic kettles. It's the light travertine coating on the riverbed that gives the water its astonishing blue-green glow. Be sure not to walk onto it in bare feet, however; travertine is horrendously sharp stuff.

In the days when it they were known to the park service as **Bridal Veil Falls**, Havasu Falls used to be a long, broad expanse of water, which explains the solidified sheets and curtains of travertine that run right across their wide brim. Then a flash flood punched out a notch right in the center, through which the falls now gush to either side of a small outcrop that's knitted together by a frail cottonwood sapling. Side trails off the main path lead down to an idyllic shaded "beach" beside the largest, deepest pool, where the ceaseless roar makes conversation difficult, but swimming is all but irresistible. Cross to the far side of the river, traversing the natural travertine dams that divide the various terraces – partially reconstructed after the 1993 flood, using artificial breakwaters that are now buried beneath new deposits – to reach a group of picnic tables standing in a cottonwood grove at the mouth of a side canyon.

It's possible to take a short **horseback tour** from Supai village down to Havasu Falls, at a cost of $60; for reservations, contact Havasupai Tourist Enterprises (see p.181).

The campground

A short distance beyond Havasu Falls, two miles down from Supai village, you finally reach the Havasu **campground**, set in an especially narrow and high-walled segment of the canyon. Once the tribal cremation and burial ground, this site was excluded from the original reservation on account of its rich deposits of lead, silver, and zinc. After mining activities ceased, and before the Havasupai managed to claim it back in 1975, it fell into the hands of the national park, which turned it into a campground in 1957. As one Havasupai bitterly complained during hearings before the US Senate in 1973, "dead people's things have long since walked off with hikers."

Today, the campground stretches for around three-quarters of a mile, and is capable of holding up to two hundred campers, with tents pitched in clearings in the woods to either side of the stream. Facilities are primitive in the extreme, but it's a wonderful spot, with safe drinking water provided by fresh springs in the canyon wall, and luxuriant cottonwood trees for shade. There are no showers or phones, and fires are not permitted. Although villagers are

BELOW SUPAI: THE FALLS

barred from the area in summer by tribal edict, groups of horses stand tethered at the entrance, waiting to carry campers back up the hill.

Mooney Falls and the Colorado River

Havasu campground is brought to an abrupt end by the precipitous, and once again luridly turquoise, 196-foot **Mooney Falls**. This natural barrier was long regarded, even by the Havasupai, as impassable. Its modern name comes from an unfortunate prospector who fell to his death here in 1880, after a rope snagged as he was being lowered to the bottom. Colorful stories that he dangled for three days before the rope broke are untrue, but it did take several months before his companions managed to bore through the travertine to retrieve his body, which lay by then beneath a fresh coating of limestone.

The trail to the bottom is little better today. Having scrambled down the travertine ledges to reach the two successive tunnels made by Mooney's cohorts that drop through the cliff face, you come to a sheer section that was blasted away in the flood of 1993, and now consists of a vertical series of footholds aided by an iron chain fixed into the rock. The prospect of the climb is terrifying enough for most hikers to turn back at this point.

If you do manage to continue, a further set of swimming holes leads down from the bottom of the falls, while a good dayhike from the campground continues on for three miles to **Beaver Falls**. Negotiating a route beyond this quick-fire set of rapids involves climbing up to and along a high ledge, but keep going for four more miles and you'll eventually reach the Colorado itself. Quite possibly, you'll be greeted by river-runners who preferred to get here the easy way, shooting 157 miles of whitewater from Lees Ferry (see p.112).

The Hualapai
reservation

The **Hualapai Indian Reservation** spreads across almost a million acres of northwest Arizona. Its northern border is formed by a 108-mile stretch of the Colorado River at the extreme western end of the Grand Canyon, from which the reservation extends south on average between twenty and thirty miles. That's just far enough south for it to include curving thirteen-mile segments of both the original old **Route 66**, and the parallel transcontinental **railroad**. The reservation's only town, **Peach Springs** on the highway, is home to just under a thousand of the total Hualapai population of around 1500.

The main business of the tribe these days is **tourism**, specifically promoting a cluster of overlooks above their river frontage as **Grand Canyon West**, or the "**West Rim**" of the Grand Canyon. This canny piece of marketing is aimed squarely at the 35 million tourists who flock to **Las Vegas** each year. The Hualapai reservation is the closest spot to Las Vegas where it's possible to see the Grand Canyon, and most of its visitors are first-time day-trippers who don't realize that they're not seeing the canyon at its best. As it starts to peter out, the canyon here lacks the colossal depth and width of its central section, and it holds none of the towering mesas, buttes and temples so conspicuous from the South or North rim viewpoints.

The Hualapai reservation sadly holds nothing to match the sumptuous waterfalls of the neighboring Havasupai reservation, as described in Chapter Six.

That said, for anyone not used to the canyonlands of the Southwest, the so-called West Rim still makes a tremendous spectacle, and the Hualapai's independent status, outside the national park and free from federal regulations, means they're able to offer two unique enticements: **helicopter flights** that drop below the rim and land by the river, and **one-day whitewater rafting** trips. In addition, unless you fly in, the long dirt-road drive to get here provides a sense of penetrating an unexplored wilderness that you certainly *don't* get from driving to the South Rim. The main drawback is the **cost**: even the most basic admission to the West Rim, which involves a short bus tour, costs $37.

A history of the Hualapai

Though the Hualapai – whose name is pronounced *Wa-la-pie* – are today not as well known as the Havasupai, the latter were originally a minor offshoot of the Hualapai tribe. As detailed on p.176, both were descended from a group known as the **Pai** – "the people" – who make their first appearance in the archeological record shortly after 700 AD. Also called the **Cerbat**, the Pai trace their tribal origin to Spirit Mountain, further down the Colorado near modern Bullhead City, Arizona. The Hualapai lived in the forests of the South Rim from around 1100 AD – hence their name, "People of the Tall Pines." While their original base in the Grand Canyon was **Meriwhitica Canyon**, a side canyon toward the western end of their current reservation, the Hualapai seem eventually to have supplanted the Ancestral Puebloans throughout most of the canyon, in many cases inheriting their crafts skills and survival techniques as well as their homes.

The Hualapai were traditionally a very mobile people, who planted crops and collected wild plants down in the canyon during the summer, and then spent the winter hunting on the plateaus and up into the mountains to the south. Significant contact with outsiders only came in the 1860s, when a wagon route deep into Hualapai territory was established by prospectors in pursuit of the copper, lead, silver and gold deposits in the Cerbat Mountains to the west. Conflict soon escalated into the **Hualapai War**, a guerrilla struggle that lasted from 1865 to 1869. With a quarter of Hualapai men killed in the fighting, and the tribe further decimated by disease, the survivors were rounded up and force-marched into internment at La Paz, near what is today the town of Parker, Arizona. They soon escaped and returned to their ancestral lands, a situation that was formalized in 1883 – two years after the railroad reached Peach Springs – by the creation of their own reservation.

Between the 1950s and 1970s, Hualapai leaders vociferously supported plans to construct the **Bridge Canyon Dam** on their reservation, to block the Grand Canyon at its narrowest point. The Hualapai stood to gain not only in terms of construction jobs but also in long-term royalties and increased visitation, and accused environmental campaigners appalled by the very notion of damming the Grand Canyon of "condemning our families to lifelong poverty by forcing us to keep our homeland a wilderness." When those proposals were eventually defeated, the Hualapai turned their attention to promoting tourism exclusively, and a new generation of leaders now speaks of preserving the canyon intact.

THE HUALAPAI RESERVATION

PEACH SPRINGS

The one sizeable Hualapai community, **PEACH SPRINGS**, is located at the northern extremity of Route 66's sweeping curve away from I-40, 53 miles northeast of **Kingman** (see p.170) and 35 miles northwest of **Seligman** (see p.169). It stands just six miles west of the turn-off for Arrowhead AZ-18, the one road into the **Havasupai reservation**, as described on p.180. Other than in Seligman itself, you may be disappointed by the lack of kitsch Americana along Route 66, but driving the much-mythologized "**Mother Road**" is still an evocative experience, crossing vast wide-open desert expanses with only the railroad for company.

Peach Springs is no more than a straggle of buildings along the highway, of which the most prominent by far is the shiny, modern **Hualapai Lodge**, which opened in 1997. Its sixty good-sized bedrooms are broadly equivalent to what you'd expect to find in one of the slightly more upmarket hotel chains, as is the **dining room**, open daily for all meals (☎ 1-888/255-9550 or 928/769-2230, Ⓔ tourism@ctaz.com; summer ❹, winter ❸).

A desk in the lobby of the lodge serves as the headquarters of the **Hualapai Office of Tourism** (Mon–Fri 9am–5pm; same phone, Ⓦ www.hualapaitours.com). As well as organizing the rafting trips described below, this office sells **permits** for visits to Grand Canyon West (though most drivers heading there don't come via Peach Springs – see p.195), and for backcountry sightseeing ($5 per day) and camping ($10, including sightseeing fee) on Diamond Creek Road (see p.194). The tribe's separate **Wildlife Office**, a short distance west across the highway (Mon–Fri 8am–4.30pm; ☎ 928/769-2227), issues similar sightseeing permits for explorations elsewhere on the reservation, and also fishing (an extra $8 per day) and hunting (up to $20,000 for a trophy bighorn sheep) permits.

The one-day rafting trip

Under the name of **Hualapai River Runners** (☎1-888 /255-9550 or 928/769-2219, ⓦwww.river-runners.com), the Hualapai tribe run the only **one-day rafting trip** it's possible to take within the Grand Canyon – a 35-mile ride from **Diamond Creek** to **Quartermaster Canyon** that includes significant stretches of whitewater. The price is a hefty $262.50, and no rowing or paddling is involved; instead they use motorized pontoon rafts, capable of carrying up to ten passengers aged 8 or over. At a potential cost of over $1000 for a family of four, it makes a very expensive day out, and simply getting here in the first place takes quite a commitment too, but the trips have become popular nonetheless with those who lack the time to take a longer river trip.

When the trips first started, in 1973, it was with a permit from the National Park Service, which is officially responsible for the whole width of the Colorado River. The Hualapai later decided to claim that their reservation extends not merely to the banks of the Colorado, but to a notional line in the middle of the river itself, so they didn't require permission. These days, the park service tacitly tolerates the situation, its sensitivity to charges that the tours are not properly regulated outweighed by its being even more sensitive to accusations of provoking conflict with the canyon's rightful "owners."

Daily between mid-March and mid-October, the trips depart at 8am by van from the *Hualapai Lodge*. After a ninety-minute drive down to meet the river at Diamond Creek, you board the rafts to be confronted immediately by

PEACH SPRINGS

whitewater. During the first ten miles, you negotiate the final ten rapids of the Grand Canyon, with a maximum difficulty rating (see p.252) of 7. A picnic lunch by the river, and an optional short hike, are followed by a tranquil 25-mile float onwards to Quartermaster Canyon, where you're flown up to the canyon rim by **helicopter**. It's a two-hour drive back to Peach Springs, with a typical return time of around 7pm. Many passengers spend a night at the lodge before or after the trip.

For more on river rafting, see Chapter Nine.

Diamond Creek

The unpaved twenty-mile road that heads due north of Peach Springs to the river at **Diamond Creek** is used almost exclusively by rafters, either leaving the Colorado after multi-day expeditions or taking one of the Hualapai's own one-day trips. With the appropriate permit from the lodge, however – see above – it's possible simply to drive down to take a look.

Thanks to the deep gorge cut by **Peach Springs Canyon**, Diamond Creek is the only place within the Grand Canyon where a road runs all the way to the river, dropping three thousand feet en route. Not much of a road, though: the views as the canyon walls soar to either side are great, but the surface is terrible, and liable to be rendered impassable for ordinary cars by the slightest rain. The final two miles are frequently washed out altogether by summer flash floods.

Despite the difficulties of the terrain, there was a hotel down here between 1884 and 1889, before access to what's now called the South Rim became easier. These days, there's just a rather rudimentary tribal **campground**, set just back from the river amid the sand dunes ($10 per night).

GRAND CANYON WEST

Grand Canyon West, also known as the "**West Rim**," is a remote group of inner-canyon viewpoints located roughly fifty miles northwest of Peach Springs and 120 miles east of Las Vegas. If you're touring the Grand Canyon region, the West Rim is perhaps the least essential stop to include on your itinerary; its sole *raison d'être* is to earn the Hualapai a little money by enabling tourists from Las Vegas to get a glimpse of the canyon in an easy day-trip. And it's only easy if you come by air; by car, it's a very long detour down unpaved and potentially treacherous roads.

While **Guano Point**, the centerpiece of Grand Canyon West, is unquestionably a great vantage point for seeing the canyon's inner gorge, the canyon as a whole here is simply not as majestic as in its better-known segments. Come expecting wonders, and you may well end up feeling short-changed. The one thing you won't find anywhere else, however, is the chance to ride a **helicopter** all the way down to the canyon floor.

Driving to Grand Canyon West

In terms of road quality, the best driving route to Grand Canyon West approaches not via Peach Springs, but from the west. The paved **Pierce Ferry Road** heads east from **US-93**, the main highway between Arizona and Las Vegas, thirty miles north of Kingman and forty miles south of the Hoover Dam. Twenty-eight miles along, by which time the road has veered due north, you turn right (east) onto the unpaved **Diamond Bar Road**. After a rocky fourteen-mile climb through foothills scattered with Joshua trees and up the Grand Wash Cliffs, you enter the Hualapai reservation. The road surface then becomes paved once more, and reaches the airstrip and headquarters for Grand Canyon West five miles along.

Three alternative routes involve significantly more driving on dirt roads: the fifty-mile **Buck and Doe Road**, which heads north from Route 66 four miles west of Peach Springs and meets Diamond Bar Road three miles short of the end; **Antares Road**, which also turns north from Route 66, eighteen miles northeast of Kingman, and meets Pierce Ferry Road 33 miles up, still 26 miles short of Grand Canyon West; and the forty-mile **Stockton Hill Road**, which runs due north from central Kingman and joins Pierce Ferry Road at much the same juncture. Inquire about current driving conditions locally before you take any of them.

Flying to Grand Canyon West

Several companies offer day-trip **air** tours **from Las Vegas** to the rudimentary airstrip alongside the West Rim headquarters. Both Air Vegas Airlines (☎702/736-3599 or 1-800/255-7474, ⓦwww.airvegas.com) and Maverick Helicopter Tours (☎702/261-0007 or 1-888/261-4414, ⓦwww.maverickhelicopter.com) provide **helicopter** tours starting at around $250. **Fixed-wing** operators, using small airplanes, include Scenic Airlines (☎702/638-3200, ⓦwww.scenic.com), who charge $199 with the bus tour described below, or $259 with a helicopter flight into the canyon, and The Missing Link Tours (☎1-800/209-8586, ⓦwww.tmltours.com), who only offer the $199 ground-tour option.

To no fixed seasonal or daily schedules, both Papillon Grand Canyon Helicopters (☎928/699-3993 or 1-800/528-2418, ⓦwww.papillon.com) and Sundance Helicopters

(☎ 702/736-0606 or 1-800/653-1881, ⊛ www.helicop-tour.com) operate **helicopter flights** down to the Colorado River from the Grand Canyon West terminal. The typical price for a quick hop to the canyon floor and back would be around $79, while tours that include a brief foray out on the river on a motorized pontoon raft start at around $149.

Exploring Grand Canyon West

Your initial impression of Grand Canyon West will be of the featureless gray desert plateau that leads to the edge of the abyss. All visitors to the area report to a small single-story building to the right of the highway, a few hundred yards short of the rim, which serves as the **terminal** for both the airstrip across the road and the helicopter launch-pad right outside, and also the **tribal headquarters** for tours and permits.

To reach the two main viewpoints, further down the road, you have to join a pricey Hualapai-run **bus tour** from the terminal (daily 10.30am–3.30pm; $37, under-13s $24.50; ☎ 1-888/255-9550 or 928/769-2230, ⊛ www.hualapaitours.com).

The first, **Eagle Point**, a short way along, is located not right out on the rim, but facing across a narrow, unnamed side canyon. In the right light – especially in the morning – the long knife-edge spur of sandstone that forms the canyon's opposite wall bears an uncanny resemblance to a massive eagle with its wings outstretched.

The principal destination for the buses is at the dead end of the road, two miles from the terminal: the appetizingly named **Guano Point**. This windswept rounded headland, poised atop sheer 3000-foot cliffs, surveys long stretches of the Colorado in both directions. Though the Grand Canyon looks as if it could go on forever, in fact it comes

GRAND CANYON WEST

to an end not far beyond the next bend in the river to the west, where it bisects the Grand Wash Cliffs.

Follow the short trail that loops just below the tip of Guano Point, and you'll find large pylons and chunks of abandoned machinery littering the landscape. Dating from the 1940s and 1950s, these are relics of the days when guano – bat dung, an excellent fertilizer – was commercially mined from the so-called **Bat Cave**, still visible on the far side of the river. A cable car carried the congealed dung across the canyon. The mine was eventually shut down after a rabies scare, while the cables themselves were severed by a low-flying airplane in 1951.

Unlike the National Park Service, the Hualapai allow
USAF fighter planes to operate training missions within
the canyon, so West Rim visitors often see military aircraft
flying below the rim.

An ugly, rather futuristic shelter on the point serves the **barbecue lunches** – chicken and ribs – included in the bus-tour prices.

A third viewpoint at Grand Canyon West, **Quartermaster Point**, is not included on the bus tours, but can be reached via a two-mile spur road that heads north from the approach road a mile before the terminal. Anyone who has already paid for a bus tour can drive there for free. If you haven't – not that there's any point driving this far and not taking the tour – you can buy a separate $10 permit that entitles you to go. Perched just west of deep Quartermaster Canyon, the overlook commands views straight up Burnt Canyon, across the Colorado, toward the long promontory of Kelly Point on the North Rim. All that indubitably makes an impressive sight, and one worth seeing granted that you're in the vicinity, but once again it doesn't really merit a special trip from the interstate.

CANYON
ACTIVITIES

CANYON ACTIVITIES

Hiking the inner canyon

What seemed to be easy from above was not so, but instead very hard and difficult.

Don García López de Cárdenas, 1540

I
f there's one sure remedy for the often-heard complaint that it's hard to appreciate or even comprehend the Grand Canyon as you gaze down from the rim, that's to **hike** down into it. Walking any of the park's magnificent and very varied array of **trails** is rewarded with much more than just another view of the same thing. Instead you pass through a sequence of utterly different landscapes, each with its own distinct climate, wildlife and topography. However, while the canyon is a magnificent, enticing wilderness, it can also be a hostile and very unforgiving environment, grueling even for expert hikers.

Detailed hiking maps for the inner canyon appear at the back of this book (maps 9 and 10).

Park rangers have one simple message for all would-be hikers: **don't try to hike to the river and back in one day**. It might not look far on the map, but it's harder than running a marathon. Several hikers each year die in the attempt, and several hundred more receive emergency medical treatment.

Whatever experience you may have had anywhere else, the Grand Canyon is different. Most hikers are far more familiar with walking up hills and mountains, when it's the initial climb that's most demanding, and if your energy levels start to flag you can simply turn around and walk back to base. Canyon hiking is deceptively seductive. The descent seems easy, and your progress quick. There's always another great view a little further on, and the lure of the river beckons you forward. Eventually, however, you have to pay; start the climb back out when you're already tired, and the midday heat of the inner canyon has set in, and you're in for a murderously long haul. With the South Rim standing 7000 feet above sea level, and the North Rim 8000 feet, the **altitude** alone is fatiguing.

The best hiking seasons are **spring** and **fall**, when the temperatures are cooler, the trails less crowded, and there's more water around. Inevitably, however, most visitors are here in the **summer**. At that time of year especially, avoid hiking in the middle of the day. Set off very early in the morning – well before 7am if you're heading down, and before 5am if you're climbing out.

Rewarding but much less demanding hikes at rim level, which do not involve a descent into the canyon, include the trails to Shoshone Point on the South Rim (see p.71) and Cape Final on the North Rim (see p.96).

CHOOSING A TRAIL

All your hiking should be on designated **trails**. What's more, the park service divides the canyon terrain into four zones of difficulty. First-time hikers are advised to restrict themselves to the **Corridor Zone**, where the Bright Angel, South Kaibab and North Kaibab trails are well maintained, regularly patrolled and offer facilities like emergency phones and piped water. Almost all the other trails reviewed in this chapter lie within the **Threshold Zone**, where the trails tend to be less even underfoot and shorter on water, toilets and formal campgrounds, though a few pass wholly or partly through the **Primitive Zone**, where facilities are non-existent and you may need route-finding skills to keep on the right track. Only absolute experts should venture into the **Wild Zone**, which holds virtually no formal trails or even water sources.

Thanks to the canyon's geology, the main trails from the **South Rim** are broadly similar, taking between seven and ten miles to drop to the Colorado. An initial burst of steep switchbacks culminates in a dramatic overlook around 1.5 miles down at the top of the Coconino Sandstone layer; there's another waystation around three miles down when you reach the Tonto Platform; and if you hike another couple of miles to the edge of the platform, you're rewarded with a view of the Inner Gorge before taking the final plunge to the river. Almost all are **drainage** trails, which use water-cut cracks in the canyon walls to make their descent, and therefore offer only intermittent views; the exception is the South Kaibab Trail, which follows the crest of a high ridge with views most of the way down. The **North Rim** being set back further from the river, its trails are proportionately longer at around fourteen miles, and thus require at least one overnight stop en route.

It's best not to be too ambitious on your first canyon hike. Even if you're sure you want to go as far as the river at some point during your stay, you won't regret having a practice **dayhike** before the main event. On that first day, choose a round trip of not more than six miles, and only venture further if you're absolutely sure of your stamina and your supplies. On the South Rim, most first-timers opt for the **Bright Angel** or **South Kaibab** trails, but both the **Grandview** and the **Hermit** offer equally good short trips. On the North Rim, the **North Kaibab** is the only sensible option.

Die-hard wilderness enthusiasts frequently grumble that the sheer mass of hikers in summer, especially on the trails to and from Phantom Ranch, impairs their enjoyment. If that strikes a chord with you, then you may prefer to hike a lesser-known trail at that time instead. For most casual visitors, however, the heavy traffic on the Corridor Trails is not a problem; it's not *that* bad, and it has the compensation of offering a greater sense of companionship and solidarity.

HIKING SAFETY

The secret to successful hiking is to **plan ahead**. As a rule of thumb, you should allow twice as much time to climb back up as it takes to hike down. That means turning back after a third of your allotted time; if you plan a six-hour hike, reckon on two hours hiking down and four hours to hike up. Rangers say the average speed is two miles per hour on the way down, and just one on the way up.

Assuming that you're adequately equipped with water and other supplies, as outlined below, the best way to guarantee your safety is to never leave the trail. If you imagine you've spotted a short cut, you're wrong; leaving the trail will make you much harder to find in an emergency. That's especially true for solo hikers, who form a large proportion

HIKING SAFETY

of canyon casualties. Ideally you shouldn't hike alone; if you must, stick to the busier trails and, preferably, dayhikes.

On a more general level, try to walk slowly, so you're never out of breath. If you're having trouble maintaining an ordinary conversation, you're walking too fast. And take at least one five-minute break every hour, ideally lying down with legs raised above the level of your heart.

Water and food

The sheer quantity of **water** that you have to carry – and drink – when hiking in the Grand Canyon almost defies belief. In typical summer temperatures of over 100°F, your body loses a phenomenal four pints of fluid during every hour spent on the trail. To keep up with that sort of demand, you should reckon on drinking **one gallon** for each day's hiking in summer, down perhaps to half that in cooler conditions.

You should always know whether water will be available on your chosen trail – park rangers keep abreast of the latest conditions – and carry at least two pints with you at all times, even if you expect to be able to pick up more en route. Only the Bright Angel and North Kaibab trails offer piped drinking water en route, and even that can be unexpectedly cut off if the pipeline breaks. On those other trails where water is to be had, you'll have to **treat** it first, either by boiling it for at least five minutes, or cleansing it with iodine-based purifying tablets or a Giardia-rated filter, available from any camping or sports store.

Pre-hydrate before a big hike, by drinking large amounts the night before. Once you set off, drink regularly, even if you don't feel thirsty. Early symptoms of **heat exhaustion** include loss of both appetite and thirst, so it's possible to become seriously dehydrated without feeling thirsty. Among subsequent signs to watch out for are nausea, dizziness, headache, cramps, and strangely cool skin. The best indicator of whether you're drinking enough is your **urine**; its frequency and quantity should be the same as normal, and it should remain clear rather than discolored.

Just to confuse things, there's also the risk of **hyponatremia**, or **water intoxication**, which in its first stages closely resembles heat exhaustion, and happens if you drink too much without eating. As hikers can burn up to a thousand calories per hour, expect to eat at least twice as much **food** as normal, both during your hike and also, ideally, before it. Salty snacks such as cookies, crackers and trail mix are recommended, as well as jerky or salami and dried ready-made meals. **Electrolyte replacement** drinks, which you can buy either ready-prepared or as powder to add to water, are a great help, but it's best to avoid salt tablets, as taking salt on its own can do more harm than good.

In addition, whenever you come to a water source within the canyon, **soak yourself** – your head, your hair, your clothing, everything. That will keep you much cooler as you hike onwards.

Finally, it's easy to forget that at the end of a long hike there may be no facilities at the trailhead. Don't forget to leave some food and water in your vehicle as well.

Snakes and creepy-crawlies

No one is known to have died in the Grand Canyon from being bitten or stung by a snake, scorpion, or indeed any other form of reptile, insect or spider.

Although the canyon is home to several species of **snake**, including three kinds of rattlesnake, bites are extremely rare and almost invariably the result of misguided attempts at handling. If you do get bitten, current medical thinking rejects the concept of cutting yourself open and attempting to suck out the venom; in most cases, in fact, no venom is injected. You'd do better to stay calm, apply a cold compress to the wound, constrict the area with a tourniquet, drink lots of water, rest in a shady area, and send for help.

Scorpion stings, especially from bark scorpions, are more common. Their poison is nasty, but causes nausea rather than serious illness or death. When camping, be sure to shake out your shoes, clothing and bedding before use.

To avoid painful bites from **red ants**, tidy up any crumbs or spillages after you eat, and don't sit or sleep on the same spot afterwards.

Security precautions

Despite issuing permits to all backcountry hikers, the park service doesn't formally keep track of what happens to each group. There's no official checking in or out, so no one will necessarily notice if you fail to return. It's therefore essential to leave details of your planned itinerary with your family, your friends or your workplace, and to arrange to call when you've emerged safely from the canyon. If you fail to do so, they can then raise the alarm, by calling the park service at ☎ 928/638-2477. Stick to the itinerary – you'll be held liable for the cost of any search and rescue operation, which can run to thousands of dollars, especially if helicopter evacuation becomes necessary.

Note that cell phones are very unlikely to work; most areas even along the rim, let alone down in the canyon, are too remote to get a signal. Satellite phones are somewhat more reliable, but often fail in the gorge.

BACKCOUNTRY CAMPING

To restrict numbers, **backcountry camping** within Grand Canyon National Park – as opposed to camping in the developed *Mather Campground* and *Desert View* sites on the South Rim, and the *North Rim Campground* near Bright Angel Point – is by **permit** only. Demand is very high, and slightly more than half of all applications are turned down. Anyone overnighting in the canyon without a permit, other than guests in the cabins or dorms at Phantom Ranch, is subject to a heavy fine.

Permits cost a flat fee of $10, plus an additional $5 per person per night for sites below the rim, or $5 per group per night for undeveloped campsites on the rim. Applications are accepted **in person**, by **mail** (PO Box 129, Grand Canyon, AZ 86023), or by **fax** (Ⓕ928/638-2125), but not by email or phone. Full details, including the relevant form, can be found online at Ⓦwww.nps.gov/grca/backcountry, or in the park's free *Backcountry Trip Planner* newspaper, available from all visitor centers.

All applications have to specify an exact **itinerary**, with precise details of where you'll spend each night. Depending on where you're hiking, this will be either named campgrounds, or the wide-ranging "Use Areas" you'll find coded on official park maps, also available online. Between March and mid-November, there's a limit on the most popular trails of two nights per party per campsite, whether or not those nights are consecutive. Up to three alternative dates and routes can be suggested. You'll also be asked for the number in your group – which can't exceed eleven – and even the license plates of your vehicles. The fee is payable in advance, by credit card or check, and is non-refundable. Frequent Hiker Membership, costing $25 per year, spares you paying the $10 fee each time, but confers no other benefits.

Mailed or **faxed** applications are accepted for dates until the end of the fourth complete month after they're submitted. Thus in January you can apply for nothing later than the end of May, while if you're planning a trip in the peak month of July you'd better mail your application on March 1. Both mail and fax applications are responded to by mail.

To apply **in person**, turn up at either the **Backcountry Information Center**, in the Maswik Transportation

Center near *Maswik Lodge* in Grand Canyon Village (daily 8am–noon & 1–5pm; ☎928/638-7875; Mon–Fri 1–5pm only); the **North Rim Backcountry Office**, a quarter-mile north of the *North Rim Campground* (daily 8am–noon & 1–5pm; ☎928/638-7868); or the Forest Service's **Kaibab Plateau Visitor Center** in Jacob Lake (see p.122; daily 8am–5pm; ☎928/643-7298, ⓦwww.fs.fed.us/r3/kai).

While both the park offices accept advance applications, you're more likely to be hoping for a **last-minute cancellation**. Even in peak season, your chances of being able to hike within a day or two are pretty good, especially if you're flexible as to which trail you go on. Your name is added to a waiting list, and each morning at 8am that day's cancellations are reassigned – though you have to be there on the spot to get one.

Where to camp

The most popular campgrounds within the canyon are the three located along the rim-to-rim Corridor Trails – *Indian Garden* on the Bright Angel Trail, *Bright Angel Campground* near the river, and *Cottonwood Campground* on the North Kaibab Trail. Camping in other areas varies between similar permanent campgrounds, designated campsites – where the spots at which you can camp are specified by the park service, though they hold no facilities – and wilderness camping. Wherever you camp, minimize your impact on the canyon. Camp where someone else has camped before, and make no additional physical changes.

No **fires** are permitted within the canyon, except in emergencies, though camping stoves are allowed. Human waste should be buried from four to six inches deep, at least two hundred feet from the nearest water supply, while all trash, including toilet paper, should be packed out.

Flash floods, which can appear from nowhere, are most

BACKCOUNTRY CAMPING

likely in July and August. Fatalities are rare, but they have occurred during the last decade on both the Bright Angel and North Kaibab trails. Survivors tend to report having had just a few minutes' warning, in the form of a loud rumbling roar heading downstream along the nearest watercourse. The one major precaution you can take is always to camp well above the bed of even the driest-seeming wash. If you hear any ominous noise, head immediately for high ground, and don't attempt to cross flooded areas until the water has receded.

WHAT TO TAKE

Exactly what **equipment** you need will depend on which trail you're taking, for how long, and in what season. Bear in mind that it's usually around 30°F warmer beside the river than it is up at the rim; be prepared for both extremes.

For a **dayhike**, essentials include dependable **hiking boots** that you've already broken in, worn for blister protection with two pairs of **socks**, thick on the outside and thinner within; a **long-sleeved shirt** and **pants** for sun protection, together with a broad-brimmed **hat**, **sunblock** and **sunglasses**; containers for carrying up to a gallon of **water**, plus, if necessary, a water purification system; substantial **food**; a **pocket knife**; and a **flashlight**, plus a **signal mirror** and/or **whistle** for emergencies. On trails without pit toilets, you'll also need **toilet paper**, and **Ziploc bags** in which to store that and other waste.

All hikers should carry a **first-aid kit**, at its most basic including bandages and moleskin for blisters plus painkillers and anti-inflammatories such as Advil, and extending to knee and ankle wraps. A hiking **staff** or pair of ski poles can be invaluable on knee-jarring downhill stretches.

While you're very unlikely to lose your way on the main trails, a good **map** will greatly improve your sense of where you are. Earthwalk Press's *Bright Angel Trail* (1:24,000), which covers the three Corridor Trails, and Trails Illustrated's wider-ranging *Grand Canyon National Park* (1:73,530), are both recommended.

The major decision for **backpackers** is whether to bring a **tent**. While it's certainly necessary in winter, protection against cold is not a factor in summer. However, rain is always a possibility, in July and August especially, and you

GRAND CANYON FIELD INSTITUTE

The perfect way for inexperienced hikers to get a first taste of the Grand Canyon, or for more experienced ones to improve their skills, is to join one of the many expeditions led each year by the **Grand Canyon Field Institute**. Co-sponsored by the Grand Canyon Association and the National Park Service, this friendly, enthusiastic organization offers an extensive program of well-priced, expert-led **guided tours and hikes** in and around the canyon. All participants receive detailed advice on how to prepare and what to bring.

Different tours, some of which are restricted to women only, specialize in geology, history, natural history, photography, wilderness techniques, and other topics. Most involve camping and backpacking, others include lodge accommodation or even llama trekking; all are graded according to the difficulty of any hiking involved, and your acceptance is subject to completion of a detailed health questionnaire. Typical prices include $305 for a three-night hike down to Indian Garden; $495 for a four-night rim-to-rim backpack, including shuttle service; and $475 for a seven-night off-trail adventure in the wilderness of the western canyon.

For full details, access Ⓦ www.grandcanyon.org/fieldinstitute, or write to PO Box 399, Grand Canyon, AZ 86023 (Ⓣ 928/638-2485, Ⓕ 638-2484).

WHAT TO TAKE

may also prefer to be sealed away from the desert wildlife, so a **rain fly** or waterproof **bivy sack** may suit you. A **sleeping bag** is always recommended – though in summer it could simply be a light cotton sleeping sack – as are a foam pad or air mattress to put it on, and a ground cloth beneath that. As for a cooking **stove**, hot food may be more bother than it's worth in summer, but it's a life saver in winter. **Sandals** make a welcome change for camp use.

Equipment rental

Outfitters the world over should sell any specialized equipment you need, and there are several good stores nearby in **Flagstaff** (see p.149). The **General Store** next to the *North Rim Campground* (see p.86) stocks a fairly limited range, while the **Canyon Village Marketplace** on the South Rim (formerly known as Babbitts; see p.49) has a very good selection. The Village Marketplace also **rents** equipment, including day packs and backpacks, stoves, sleeping bags and tents; typical rates for a tent would be $15 for the first day and $9 for each subsequent day. Rental reservations are only accepted between one and five days in advance (☎928/638-2262).

The Corridor Trails

So called because they form the only continuous route between the South and North rims, the three **Corridor Trails** – the **Bright Angel**, **South Kaibab** and **North Kaibab** trails – are deservedly the most popular hiking trails within the park. All provide a wonderful inner-canyon baptism for **backpackers**, with well-equipped campgrounds en route, and the lure of **Phantom Ranch** down by the river, while also offering good short **dayhikes** for novice canyoneers who don't have the time or energy to complete the entire routes.

Because most hikers want to start from and finish at the South Rim, the most common itinerary is to hike **down the South Kaibab**, spend a night or two by the river, and then back **up the Bright Angel**. That's certainly better than doing it the other way round: the climb up the South Kaibab is a real killer. The reason more people don't do the **rim-to-rim** hike, from the South Rim to the North or vice versa, is partly because it's longer, as the North Kaibab Trail takes at least two days in itself, and also because you end up over two hundred driving miles from where you began. As detailed on p.82, however, there is a rim-to-rim **shuttle bus** service, costing $65 one way.

Be warned that the Corridor Trails are also the only ones on which **mules** are allowed; for details of mule trips see p.61 (South Rim) and p.82 (North Rim). Hikers are expected always to give way to mule trains, by standing quietly at the side of the trail.

THE BRIGHT ANGEL TRAIL

Map 10, B9.

Trailhead Grand Canyon Village.
Length (one way) Indian Garden 4.6 miles; Plateau Point 6.1 miles; Colorado River 7.8 miles; Phantom Ranch 9.6 miles.
Elevation Trailhead 6860ft; Indian Garden 3060ft; Colorado River 2450ft.

By far the busiest inner-canyon hiking route, the **Bright Angel Trail** starts in Grand Canyon Village, beside the wooden shack that once served as the Kolb photographic

studio (see p.60). Although the side canyon immediately
below the village makes access to the Tonto Platform relatively straightforward, it's still a long hard climb, with **water**
available en route between May and September only. Most
day-hikers content themselves with walking to either of
the two resthouses in the first three miles, but with an early
start you should be able to manage the round trip of nine
miles to **Indian Garden**, or even, in summer, the twelve
miles to **Plateau Point**. As stressed above, don't even consider hiking to the Colorado and back in a single day. Only
try to reach the river if you've reserved accommodation
down there for the night.

The "Bright Angel" name, first ascribed by John Wesley
Powell to the tributary stream that flows down from the
North Rim, is so ubiquitous in the Grand Canyon that it's
very easy to get confused. The Bright Angel Trail doesn't
start from Bright Angel Point, which is on the North Rim,
and it doesn't quite reach, let alone follow, Bright Angel
Creek. Technically, it ends where it meets the Colorado,
7.8 miles from the rim, and the 1.8-mile hike from there to
Phantom Ranch, beside the creek, is on the separate **River
Trail** (see Map 10, C7). The Bright Angel Trail does,
however, launch itself into the canyon from a couple of
hundred yards west of *Bright Angel Lodge*, and most crucially
of all, it owes its existence to the geological fault line that
made rim-to-river access possible at this point, the **Bright
Angel Fault**.

As one of the "easiest" natural routes into the canyon,
the trail down to Indian Garden was known to the
Ancestral Puebloans a thousand years ago, and was still in
use by the **Havasupai** when prospectors Pete Berry and
Niles and Ralph Cameron improved it in 1890. Ralph took
it over in 1903, exploiting spurious mining claims to charge
riders a toll of $1 each, and it only passed on to the park in
1928.

There's no gentle introduction to the trail, which hurtles straight into a long, exposed set of switchbacks down the dry rocky hillside. Both the two short **tunnels** within the first mile mark transitions between geological layers, the first from Kaibab Limestone to the Toroweap Formation, and the second on to Coconino Sandstone.

Soon after dropping down that steep, dark cliff, you reach **Mile-and-a-Half Resthouse**, a basic waystation that offers water (May–Sept), restrooms and emergency phones. By now, wildlife is much more abundant, including pesky squirrels and ravens. A similar onward haul, through first the Hermit Shale and then the Supai Formation – look out for the rock surfaces along the way that hold a few **pictographs**, all but obscured by graffiti – brings you to the equally self-explanatory **Three-Mile Resthouse**, which has water (again in summer only) and phones but not restrooms.

As is readily apparent from its sweeping canyon views, Three-Mile Resthouse marks the final boundary between forest and desert. Below it lies the precipitous **Redwall Limestone**, the major obstacle to inner-canyon access throughout the park, breached here thanks to the Bright Angel Fault. Even so, it takes the forty tight switchbacks of **Jacob's Ladder** – the most murderous stretch of the return journey – to carry you down to the gently sloping bed of Garden Creek below.

Indian Garden

Though you'll almost certainly have spotted it from the rim above, the verdant green strip of **Garden Creek** still makes a welcome surprise at the foot of those baking-hot switchbacks. Soon after a host of prickly pears appears, along with other yellow- and red-blossomed cactuses, you hear the astonishing sound of trickling water. The streambed is lined with dazzling green cottonwood trees.

Native peoples really did grow crops at **Indian Garden**, 4.6 miles from the rim. As well as the creek, there's also a perennial **spring**, where seepage from the more porous rock layers above collects atop the impervious Bright Angel Shale. Originally planted in prehistoric times, the "garden" was continuously used by the Havasupai from around 1300 AD until the modern era; early tourists admired the ancient stone granaries. Theodore Roosevelt is said to have curtly instructed their leader in 1905 to "get your people out"; they were finally evicted in 1928, by which time they were no longer farmers but dependent on the tourist trade.

These days this unexpected little oasis holds a year-round water supply, a ranger station, restrooms, separate **camping** and day-use areas, and a staging post for mules. Forever filled with hikers, backpackers, and mule-riders, it's not exactly pristine wilderness, but it's such a well-shaded and attractive staging post for weary trail-users that no one's complaining.

Plateau Point

While the Bright Angel Trail continues on down to the river from Indian Garden, as described below, if you head west on the **Tonto Trail** (see p.241), by turning left across Garden Creek at Indian Garden, you come three-quarters of a mile along to an obvious spur trail to the right. This takes 0.8 miles to thread its way out to **Plateau Point**, a superb overlook above the Inner Gorge from which it is not possible to descend any further.

Constructed to give day-tripping mule-riders a view of the river, the **Plateau Point Trail** also makes an ideal route for hikers. However, although it involves almost no additional elevation change, the round trip still adds three very exposed miles to any dayhike. For that reason, it's not recommended between June and August. At other times, allow at least eight hours to get to Plateau Point and back from the rim.

Barren even by inner-canyon standards, the Tonto Platform landscape is spectacular, with agave and yucca plants shooting up from the sandy soil, and the mighty red buttes and mesas of the canyon now framed against the blue sky. Shortly after you get your first awesome glimpse of the black tumbling walls of the gorge, the trail comes to a dead end. Precariously perched on the rocky outcrops, you can see a long stretch of the dark-green Colorado, though both the bridges and Phantom Ranch lie out of sight around the next promontory to the east. With binoculars, you can just make out the buildings back at the top of the South Rim, six miles away.

Taking the Tonto Trail **east** from the Bright Angel Trail, across the flat, arid Tonto Platform enables you to link up with the **South Kaibab Trail** after 4.1 miles, at the Tipoff (see p.221).

Devil's Corkscrew and the Colorado River

Flowing down from Indian Garden, Garden Creek has cut a narrow cleft into the Tapeats Sandstone below. With the Bright Angel Trail alongside, it swiftly enters a secluded little gorge known as the **Tapeats Narrows**. This is among the most delightful segments of any inner-canyon trail – if you could somehow arrive here without having hiked down, you'd never imagine you were deep in the Grand Canyon. The temptation to linger beside the babbling stream is irresistible, but don't drink from it – you've just seen where it's been, beside the mule pen.

At the lower end of the narrows, Garden Creek veers into a tangle of rocks as it tumbles to meet **Pipe Creek**. Humans, however, have to take the slow way down, along

THE BRIGHT ANGEL TRAIL

one last searing set of switchbacks, the **Devil's Corkscrew**, which were hacked into the rock to create a shortcut to the river during the 1930s. (Before that, river-bound Bright Angel hikers took the Tonto Trail to join the South Kaibab Trail.) Beyond the **Columbine Spring** waterfall at the bottom, the gradient becomes much less severe, and you crisscross Pipe Creek repeatedly as it meanders down its own pleasant side canyon to reach the Colorado at **Pipe Creek Beach**, 3.2 miles from Indian Garden. The small **River Resthouse**, with a phone but no water or restrooms, is located just before the river.

It's a breathtaking moment when you first find yourself in the **Inner Gorge**, with thousand-foot walls of gnarled gray **Vishnu Schist** granite soaring on both sides of the river. Only here at its very bottom, with the rims obscured from sight and only the occasional butte or temple rearing its head above the inner walls, can the Grand Canyon ever feel at all gloomy or oppressive, but a more common response for hikers is exhilaration at finally being down in the ancient bowels of the planet. It takes a good ten-minute walk along the **River Trail**, undulating over the rocky debris slopes, before you round a corner to see a bridge in the distance, and another mile or so, through sandy dunes, before you reach it.

The slender, see-through **Bright Angel Suspension Bridge**, also known as the **Silver Bridge**, was built in the 1960s to carry the **pipeline** from Roaring Springs, high on the North Kaibab Trail (see p.224), by which the South Rim receives all its water. Mules quite sensibly balk at the way both pipeline and river are clearly visible between the slats, and how the whole bridge bounces with every tread. They therefore continue eastward along the River Trail to join the South Kaibab Trail less than a mile along. Hikers, however, invariably cross here, eager to reach the **Phantom Ranch** area on the far side.

THE SOUTH KAIBAB TRAIL

Map 10, D9.

Trailhead Yaki Point.

Length (one way) Cedar Ridge 1.5 miles; Skeleton Point 3 miles;
Tipoff 4.6 miles; Colorado River 6.4 miles; Phantom Ranch 7.1 miles.

Elevation Trailhead 7200ft; Cedar Ridge 6060ft; Skeleton Point
5160ft; Tipoff 4000ft; Colorado River 2460ft.

The **South Kaibab Trail** – the most direct route from the
South Rim to Phantom Ranch – is the only major park trail
never to have been used by the canyon's ancient inhabitants.
Rangers hacked it out of the bare rock in 1924, when it
looked as though they'd never wrest control of the Bright
Angel Trail away from Ralph Cameron (see p.214). Whereas
all Ancestral Puebloan trails follow natural drainage channels down into the canyon, the South Kaibab stays atop the
narrow, exposed **Cedar Ridge**. That means the views are
fabulous, but with a pitiless lack of shade and not a drop of
water en route, it's a grueling trek. The park service recom-
mends that no one should try to hike up it in summer, and
all year it's used principally by backpackers who descend
this way and return via the Bright Angel Trail; mule-riders,
climbing back out after spending the night at Phantom
Ranch; and dayhikers, venturing just a short way down to
enjoy those views. For all but the very shortest dayhikes,
reckon on carrying a gallon of water per person.

You can only drive to the trailhead, four miles east of
Grand Canyon Village at **Yaki Point**, between December
and February. All year, however, you can get there on the
free park shuttle buses – either the **Kaibab Trail Route**,
or, ideally, the early-morning **Hikers Shuttle**, both of
which are detailed on p.37 – or by **cab** (see p.39).

Starting from beside Yaki Point's mule corral – not the
main overlook – the trail drops down the western flank of

the promontory, negotiating the off-white Kaibab Limestone layer via a long but not all that steep switchback. This first stretch is easy going underfoot, with the path graded and lined with neat boulders. Three-quarters of a mile along, it reaches the tip of the promontory, where for the first time massive views open to the east as well as the west. The park service has recently taken to calling this **Ooh Aah Point**; it's a dramatic enough spot, but the new name was partly in order to give day-hikers the sense of having reached an important destination.

Turn back now, and you've had a satisfying taste of what it's like to see the canyon from the inside. Otherwise, the scale of the task that lies ahead is very apparent. Reaching the level plateau of **Cedar Mesa**, down below, involves a sharp, three-quarter-mile zigzag descent of the red Coconino Sandstone layer. Allowing an hour to get there from the trailhead, and two hours to climb back up again, that makes a good half-day hike. Once again, the views from this scraggy, russet mesa-top – which holds pit toilets but no other facilities, and very little shade – are tremendous. As well as seeing thirty miles up the canyon in either direction, and straight up Bright Angel Canyon towards the North Rim on the far side, you can look down to the Tonto Trail snaking across the Tonto Platform, and the Devil's Corkscrew on the Bright Angel Trail to the west.

A dire park-service warning sign ("STOP – Heat Kills") makes one last attempt to deter day-hikers before the trail drops off the east side of Cedar Mesa. The next segment is in fact relatively mild, consisting of a roughly forty-minute traverse along the flank of the mesa, which skirts the 6071-foot pinnacle of **O'Neill Butte**, and then levels out on another small plateau dotted with towering agave.

Just after you plummet off the tip of this little plateau, **Skeleton Point**, comes your first glimpse of the Colorado River. A succession of major switchbacks, interspersed with a brief saddle or two where you can catch your breath, now cuts down through a notch in the Redwall. After perhaps three hours' hiking from the trailhead, a total distance of 4.4 miles, you come out on the **Tonto Platform**, to meet the **Tonto Trail** a short way ahead.

While hardy backpackers can connect with the Grandview Trail (see p.234) by hiking 18.5 miles **east** along the Tonto Trail, the obvious way to go is **west**. Were you to keep going for four miles, you'd reach **Indian Garden** (see p.215), where you could join the Bright Angel Trail and follow it back up to the village. However, you're much more likely to be heading for the river. It's now less than two miles away, but the most hair-raising section of the South Kaibab Trail is still ahead.

The launch-pad for Inner Gorge hikers is a spot known as the **Tipoff**, a cleft in the rock that's located just beyond a set of pit toilets and is equipped with an emergency phone. Turn right off the Tonto Trail here, head a couple of gray switchbacks down, and you're suddenly confronted by an absolutely petrifying long traverse, where the trail seems barely scraped into the red dust of the Hakatai Shale layer as it curves above an abysmal drop. Here and there, a few mighty blocks of blackened Tapeats Sandstone (see "The geology of the Grand Canyon," p.280) teeter above your head. Walking this stretch is not quite as bad as it looks, but then little here could be. Attaining the haven of the broad promontory at the far end is rewarded with a prospect of the full majesty of the **Inner Gorge**, with Phantom Ranch spread out invitingly.

Further steep switchbacks fly by during the final descent, which culminates first with a rendezvous with the **River Trail** (which connects with the Bright Angel Trail, as described on p.218), and then with the forty-yard tunnel that brings you to the broad, green Colorado itself. The slender 400-foot **Kaibab Suspension Bridge** here, hanging from eight 1.5-inch-thick cables and also known as the **Black Bridge**, was set in place in 1928 to replace a makeshift cable car. Each cable weighs over a ton, and was carried down the Kaibab Trail on the shoulders of 42 Havasupai. The bridge of choice for the canyon's picky mules, it stands 78 feet above the water, and makes a great vantage point for spotting exhilarated river-runners as they round the last curve before Phantom Ranch.

THE NORTH KAIBAB TRAIL

Map 10, E2.

Trailhead North Kaibab Trailhead.

Length (one way) Coconino Overlook 0.7 miles; Supai Tunnel 2 miles; Roaring Springs 4.7 miles; Cottonwood Campground 6.9 miles; Ribbon Falls 8.4 miles; Phantom Ranch 14 miles; Colorado River 14.4 miles.

Elevation Trailhead 8250ft; Supai Tunnel 6840ft; Roaring Springs 5040ft; Cottonwood Campground 4040ft; Colorado River 2460ft.

Some version of the **North Kaibab Trail**, following **Bright Angel Creek** down from the North Rim to the Colorado, has been in use for over a thousand years. At one time, the park-service trail started several miles east of Bright Angel Point, and traced the creek's entire course to the river; its current route, which begins by descending through **Roaring Springs Canyon**, was established in the late 1920s, to be more accessible from the epicenter of North Rim tourism, and also to shorten its overall length to 14.5 miles from rim to river. Old and new routes combine at the actual **Roaring Springs**, just under five miles down, which is the very furthest you should aim for on a dayhike. In fact, with the first few miles being the steepest of all, it's more realistic to settle for the four-mile round trip as far as the Supai Tunnel.

The trail starts from a wooded parking lot at a curve in AZ-67 just under two miles north of *Grand Canyon Lodge* (see p.83). In summer, when the lot tends to fill early, many hikers simply leave their vehicles by the roadside, but even that alternative is soon exhausted, in which case you'll have to park at the lodge or campground and walk from there. A limited, early-morning **hiker shuttle** service leaves *Grand Canyon Lodge* at 5.20am and 7.20am daily, and costs $5 for the first person in each group, plus $2 per additional passenger. Notices at the trailhead, filled with somber advice about heat and water, recommend that all hikers should set off by 6am.

At first, the trail remains within the pine forest, with thick sandy dust underfoot as it zigzags steadily downwards through the Kaibab Limestone layer. Views at this stage are mostly of Roaring Springs Canyon itself, which was created by its own separate geological fault.

Many people go no further than the **Coconino Overlook**, a flat slab of rock just off the trail 0.7 miles down. Marking the bottom of the Toroweap Formation and the top of the Coconino layer, this high eminence surveys the junction of the two canyons, Roaring Springs and Bright Angel. Just over a mile beyond that, a total of around an hour's walking from the top, you reach an open clearing equipped with a summer-only water tap and pit toilets, which is where the mule-riders on half-day trips turn back (see p.82).

Immediately around the corner lies the brief **Supai Tunnel**, bored through the rock in the 1930s, which though less than twenty yards long seems to carry you into another world. Below it, long and very exposed switchbacks take roughly half an hour to plummet down the red Supai Sandstone layer, until they come to the **Redwall Bridge**. After much of the trail at this point was destroyed by flooding in 1966, the bridge was built to provide a safer crossing over Roaring Springs Creek.

THE NORTH KAIBAB TRAIL

It takes another hour, via a reasonably gentle and consistently spectacular traverse of the Redwall Limestone, to reach the **Roaring Springs**, a quarter-mile off to the left of the trail. Water from this open cascade irrigates a pleasant little oasis, and is also pumped up to the *Grand Canyon Lodge*, as well as piped down the trail and up to the South Rim. The park-service employees who keep the pumphouse working live nearby. With picnic tables alongside, Roaring Springs makes a good point to head home on a dayhike, or halt on a longer expedition, but don't expect deep enough pools to swim.

Roaring Springs Creek is subsumed soon afterwards into the much more substantial stream of Bright Angel Creek. The trail remains on its western side through the slender Tapeats Narrows, then crosses over to the east bank just after its confluence with the lesser Manzanita Creek.

Cottonwood Campground, 1.4 miles past that bridge and 2.5 miles beyond the springs, is a major overnight halt for trans-canyon hikers. Laid out in the 1930s by the Civilian Conservation Corps, it's an attractive spot, located at one of the canyon floor's broader moments, right beneath Bright Angel Point. It holds a summer-only water faucet and restrooms, but only the ranger station benefits from the shade of the eponymous Fremont cottonwoods; the actual campsites stand amid rather sandy scrub.

The highlight of the final seven-mile segment to Phantom Ranch is the lacy **Ribbon Falls**, 1.5 miles below the campground and 0.3 miles up a spur trail west into a side canyon. Of the two alternative trails that lead across the creek to the falls, only the first, at a very obvious junction where the main trail is about to climb a short hill, is recommended. That one has a footbridge, whereas the other involves a dangerous fording of the water. Ribbon Falls is a beautiful spot, a double cascade tumbling around a hundred feet over shiny, moss-stained cliffs surrounded by rich vegetation. Small wonder that one clan of the Zuni people, who now live two hundred miles southeast in New Mexico, traces its origins here.

The North Kaibab Trail finally enters the Grand Canyon's Inner Gorge in **The Box**, squeezing for almost four muddy miles between twin thousand-foot walls of the ancient black Vishnu Schist. That eventually opens out again a mile or so short of Phantom Ranch, with the last stretch consisting of a level, sandy stroll alongside the delightful babbling creek. Your first intimation of the ranch ahead comes with the sudden reappearance of dramatic cottonwood trees.

Finally, when the North Rim is closed during the winter (see p.79), it's still possible to walk *up* the North Kaibab Trail from Phantom Ranch. What's unpredictable is quite how far you'll get; depending on the season, you'll probably be stopped by heavy snow and ice somewhere above Roaring Springs. Ill-equipped hikers who climb too high on this trail have been known to die from hypothermia.

The Clear Creek Trail

Map 10, D7.

Inner-canyon trails are few and far between on the north side of the canyon, and even fewer offer the chance to explore parallel to the river rather than simply heading to or from the rim. The **Clear Creek Trail**, which heads east from the North Kaibab Trail just under half a mile north of Phantom Ranch, is therefore the most popular side-hike for backpackers basing themselves in the ranch area.

Not that it's an easy option: it starts with a very stiff thousand-foot climb up from the Inner Gorge to the Tonto Platform, and continues for a total of nine miles one-way as it meanders eastwards beneath the Brahma and Zoroaster temples. The views are superb, both down into the gorge and also across the vastness of the inner canyon.

THE NORTH KAIBAB TRAIL

When the trail was built by the Civilian Conservation Corps in 1933, the idea was to provide access to the canyon's highest free-falling waterfall, **Cheyava Falls**, which cascades off the Walhalla Plateau and achieves peak flow in late spring. However, the falls lie another four miles of fierce scrambling up the bed of Clear Creek from the official end of the trail, so it requires a 26-mile round trip from Phantom Ranch – and thus a multi-day wilderness camping expedition – even to get a glimpse of them.

Phantom Ranch area

The only place where inner-canyon hikers and mule-riders can not only cross the Colorado River but also camp and even sleep in a real bed at the bottom of the canyon, lies at the confluence of the Colorado with **Bright Angel Creek**. **Phantom Ranch**, at the rendezvous of the Bright Angel, South Kaibab, and North Kaibab trails, is a venerable park-service lodge that provides individual and dorm accommodation in log cabins, and also has a restaurant. In addition, up to 92 campers per night can sleep in the stream-side **Bright Angel Campground**.

Although **Bright Angel Creek**, which flows down Bright Angel Canyon from the North Rim, is usually just a few feet wide by the time it meets the Colorado, the sandy deposits around its mouth stretch for a few hundred yards in either direction. The journals of John Wesley Powell, who spotted it on August 15, 1869, record "We discover a stream entering from the north, a clear beautiful creek coming down through a gorgeous red canyon." He named it to contrast with the muddy Dirty Devil River, upstream in Utah.

Hikers who arrive on the North Kaibab Trail will be prepared for the rich riparian habitat of the riverbanks; if you've come down the South Kaibab, this feels like an amazing oasis. Majestic willows and cottonwoods offer welcome shade, and small animals scurry through the dense undergrowth. The **ecology** down here is, however, both threatened and changing. Before Glen Canyon Dam was completed in the mid-1960s, the Colorado would carry an average of 380,000 tons of earth and rock past Phantom Ranch each day. On one single day in 1921, 27 million tons went hurtling by. Now it's more like 40,000 tons per day, all from rivers that meet the Colorado below the dam, such as the Little Colorado. Trees are establishing themselves that would previously have been swept away, and fish adapted to suit muddy waters are becoming extinct.

Be warned that while it's always a relief to reach the river, it's often too **hot** to do very much of anything down here. Temperatures at river level tend to be around 20°F higher than on the South Rim, and more like 30°F higher than the North Rim, which means that between mid-May and late September it's likely to be over 100°F. Cooling off in the shallow waters of Bright Angel Creek is a popular pastime, but don't venture into the Colorado itself. Thanks to the dam, that stays at an icy 45°F year-round; if the currents don't kill you, hypothermia may.

THE RIVERBANK

The most interesting portion of the Colorado riverbank in the vicinity of Phantom Ranch lies just across the **Kaibab Suspension Bridge**, at the foot of the South Kaibab Trail. Immediately west of the bridge, it's still possible to discern the outline of a small **Ancestral Puebloan settlement**, first described by John Wesley Powell in 1869. Consisting of five linked rooms plus a *kiva* (ceremonial chamber), it was home to perhaps three or four families for a forty-year period between 1060 and 1150 AD. Just beyond that is the **Boat Beach**, in frequent use by canyon rafting expeditions, for whom this represents the first place passengers can leave the river in the 87-mile run from Lees Ferry.

If you arrive across the **Bright Angel Suspension Bridge** instead, after descending the Bright Angel Trail, a short trail leads past park-service facilities including ranger accommodation, a small mule corral, and public restrooms. It then crosses Bright Angel Creek to meet the trail from the Kaibab bridge, and both run together up the east side of the creek toward the campground and ranch.

BRIGHT ANGEL CAMPGROUND

A quarter-mile up from the confluence, a small footbridge crosses to the west bank of Bright Angel Creek, where you enter the **Bright Angel Campground** at its northern end. Thirty-two separate sites, each with its own picnic table, are ranged below the cottonwoods beside the creek, and there's a central restroom complex with running water. Camping at this beautiful spot is by **permit** only, as detailed on p.207. Do not hike down without a reservation.

The site started out in 1933 as a base for Civilian Conservation Corps workers, who were improving the park's trail network. They even built a swimming pool down here, but that was filled in in 1972.

PHANTOM RANCH

Another quarter-mile north of the campground, and thus set half a mile back from the Colorado, **Phantom Ranch** itself is the only accommodation option within the canyon. Clustered around a central lodge, its various cabins, corrals and outbuildings stand amid huge cottonwoods and fruit orchards that were planted early in the twentieth century, to shade a group of tents known as Rust's Camp. Renamed Roosevelt's Camp after a visit by Theodore Roosevelt in 1913, this was in turn replaced by Phantom Ranch in 1922, designed as something of a dude ranch by Mary Jane Colter for the Fred Harvey Company. She used uncut river stone and natural timbers to blend in with the surroundings, and continued to add more buildings over the succeeding years until the complex reached its present size.

First call on Phantom's fully equipped individual **cabins** (❹) goes to riders on Fred Harvey **mule trips** – full details, including prices, appear on p.61. When available, however, which is more likely in winter, they're also let to hikers, and rafters who need to spend a night here before or after a river trip. You can also get a bed in one of the four ten-bunk, single-sex **dormitories** (❶) – two for men and two for women – with bedding, showers, towels and soap provided.

Reservations, as for the South and North-Rim lodges, are handled by Xanterra Parks & Resorts, PO Box 699, Grand Canyon, AZ 86023 (☎303/297-2757 or 1-888/297 -2757, ⓦwww.grandcanyonlodges.com). Once again, you must not hike down without a reservation; even if you do have one, it's essential to **reconfirm** between one and three days before your stay, either in person at the transportation desk at *Bright Angel Lodge* or by calling ☎928/638-3283.

As a rule, Phantom Ranch is booked way in advance, but if you're spending a few days at the canyon it's worth inquiring about **cancellations** for dorm beds and, conceivably, cabins. These are handed out first-come, first-served at the *Bright Angel Lodge* early each morning. Check what time they'll be opening the night before – it can be as early as 6am.

Phantom's main lodge building acts as **dining room**, **bar**, and **store**. Meals are served communally at long tables, and at set times; all must be reserved in advance, ideally at

PHANTOM RANCH

the same time as you book your accommodation, and they're also available to campers. All supplies get here the same way you do, so food is expensive. The price for **dinner** depends on your main course, and includes vegetables, salad, dessert and coffee for $20-$30. The 5pm sitting offers either a 12oz steak for just under $30 or a vegetarian alternative, with lentil loaf, for just over $20, while a beef stew is served at 6.30pm, again for just over $20. **Breakfast**, served well before dawn, includes eggs, pancakes and bacon for about $17, and you can also pick up a **sack lunch** to carry with you on the trail for $9.

Outside meal times, the counter in the lodge sells simple snacks, like trail mix and cookies; drinks including beer and wine; first-aid supplies such as bandages and sun cream; and accessories like camera film, batteries, flashlights and sun-hats (daily: April–Oct 8am–4pm & 8–10pm, Nov–March 8.30am–4pm & 8–10pm). They'll also have details of the daily program of **ranger talks** about aspects of the canyon, mostly held in the grounds nearby.

Finally, you can arrange to have a large bag carried in or out of the canyon for you, by some unfortunate mule. So-called **duffel service** costs just over $53 each way, though as you'll still have to carry your own food and water you may not be able to reduce your load all that significantly.

Other South Rim trails

While the two corridor routes, the Bright Angel and the South Kaibab, are always the busiest South Rim trails, there are plenty of equally appealing alternatives even for first-time hikers. All the trails described below – which are listed from east to west – are officially "unmaintained," which means they can be hard to follow and may even be blocked altogether by rockfalls. In practice, however, they see regular traffic, and in their upper reaches especially, where they're frequented by day-hikers, they shouldn't tax your route-finding abilities. The two most obvious dayhikes are as far as **Dripping Spring** via the **Hermit Trail**, and down to Horseshoe Mesa on the **Grandview Trail**.

THE TANNER TRAIL

Map 9, L7.

Trailhead Lipan Point.

Length (one way) Seventy-five Mile Saddle 1.9 miles; Redwall 3.5 miles; Colorado River 7.6 miles.

Elevation Trailhead 7360ft; Seventy-five Mile Saddle 5600ft; Redwall 5600ft; Colorado River 2700ft.

The easternmost of the South Rim's inner-canyon trails, the **Tanner Trail**, follows a former Hopi route that was improved by prospector Seth Tanner (see p.107) during the 1880s to provide access to his copper-mining claims. Fortune seekers in search of John D Lee's supposed hidden gold mines also passed this way, and it's said that rustlers and bandits combined it with the Nankoweap Trail on the far side to make the self-explanatory Horsethief Trail. Today it's in reasonable condition for an unmaintained park trail, but it's a steep haul, and with no water and precious little shade available en route it's used almost exclusively by hardened canyon backpackers.

From the trailhead at **Lipan Point** – as described on p.75 – the path swiftly drops down the eastern flank of the promontory. It takes around an hour of stiff switchbacks to reach level ground at the **Seventy-five Mile Saddle**, named for Seventy-five Mile Creek which starts to the west and joins the Colorado just after river mile 75. Beyond that,

THE TANNER TRAIL

there's little elevation change for the next 1.6 miles, as the trail skirts around the bases of first **Escalante Butte** (6536ft) and then **Cárdenas Butte** (6281ft) – Don García López de Cárdenas being the Spanish would-be conquistador credited with first seeing the Grand Canyon from somewhere nearby (see p.269). Grassy natural depressions near both make ideal campsites for backpackers on the long climb out of the canyon.

Day-hikers should go no further than the top of the **Redwall**, just beyond Cárdenas Butte. Even that seven-mile roundtrip can prove a grueling trek in the heat of summer, though the views from here, down to where the river makes its crucial westward bend at **Tanner Rapid**, are magnificent. The most difficult stretch of trail comes immediately afterwards, with an extremely steep plummet down a crack in the crumbling Redwall Limestone. The river itself is four miles down, and the gradient barely relents. At the bottom, sandy, dune-fringed **Tanner Beach** is a popular campsite for both hikers and rafters, while a twenty-mile round-trip hike to the north along the **Beamer Trail** (see Map 9, M5), which starts from here and runs parallel to the Colorado, can bring you to the mouth of the Little Colorado River.

THE NEW HANCE TRAIL

Map 9, J9.

Trailhead Off Desert View Drive, near Moran Point.

Length (one way) Coronado Butte Saddle 1.2 miles; Redwall 2.9 miles; Colorado River 6.8 miles.

Elevation Trailhead 6982ft; Coronado Butte Saddle 5900ft; Redwall 4850ft; Colorado River 2600ft.

The most demanding of all the South Rim trails, the **New Hance Trail** bears the name of one of the Grand Canyon's great characters, **Captain John Hance**, who looked the very picture of the eccentric white-bearded prospector and spent his old age as a treasured Fred Harvey employee, spinning tall tales of his adventures for any tourists who would listen. In 1883, he created the Old Hance Trail to help him reach his asbestos mine across the river; building a cabin at the trailhead, he became the canyon's first white resident. He went on to guide pioneer sightseers down his trail, though by the turn of the century it had eroded and collapsed so completely that not a trace now remains.

By all accounts the old trail was exceptionally steep and dangerous; Hance's replacement, originally known as the Red Canyon Trail but now named for its creator, remains extremely difficult. Sections of its switchbacks have crumbled away, and you often have to scramble over minor rockfalls. It's not a hike to undertake lightly, and if you're using it as part of a longer itinerary, by combining it for example with an expedition along the Tonto Trail, it's one much better used to go down rather than up.

No parking is permitted at the unmarked New Hance trailhead, which lies a quarter-mile off the highway along a disused road. Leave your vehicle either at Moran Point, and walk the 1.6 miles southwest from there, or at the Buggeln Picnic Area another mile southwest. As with the Tanner Trail, the route consists of two distinct sets of fierce switchbacks, one down to the saddle below **Coronado Butte**, and the other two miles further on where it drops off the **Redwall**. This time, though, the stretch in between the two is hardly less demanding, so even a dayhike to the brink of the Redwall is far from easy. The final couple of miles to the river, beside the verdant Red Canyon Wash – which doesn't flow year-round – are the most attractive part of the hike, but even those involve some difficult scrambling. At the far end, the roiling waters of **Hance Rapid** await.

THE GRANDVIEW TRAIL

Map 9, H8.
Trailhead Grandview Point.
Length (one way) Coconino Saddle 0.8 miles; Horseshoe Mesa 3.2 miles.
Elevation Trailhead 7406ft; Coconino Saddle 6300ft; Horseshoe Mesa 4932ft.

The **Grandview Trail** provides a rare opportunity to explore one of the many wooded mesas dotted around the inner canyon, the double-pointed **Horseshoe Mesa**. Although it's possible, by connecting with other trails, to use the Grandview to find your way down to the Tonto Platform and thus eventually to the Colorado, this is not a rim-to-river route. Involving a shorter trek, and less of an elevation change, than the other major South Rim trails, it's therefore one of the most popular **dayhikes** in the park. Which doesn't mean it's easy; the trail itself is in worse condition than you'll be used to if you've only tackled the Corridor Trails, and the climb back out is tough by any standards. Reckon on six hours for the whole round trip.

Peter Berry first improved the trail in 1892, to aid operations at his Last Chance copper mine out on the **Horseshoe Mesa**. He made enough money to finance construction of the *Grandview Hotel* at the top, which lasted a little longer than the copper but was eventually bankrupted by the arrival of the railroad to the west. While the trail is no longer officially maintained, evidence of Berry's work remains very visible. Several of its switchbacks were constructed by inserting metal rods deep into the canyon wall, then covering them with juniper logs, stones and dirt. At times it can be a little hair-raising, but it has stayed surprisingly sturdy for over a century.

THE GRANDVIEW TRAIL

As described on p.73, the best views come at and just below the trailhead, beside the parking lot at Grandview Point. Below that, narrow cobbled switchbacks cling to the canyon's wall of Kaibab Limestone, with steep drop-offs to the side. It takes something under an hour to reach the refuge of the **Coconino Saddle**, a spur between Grapevine Canyon to the west and Hance Canyon to the east where the trees offer some very welcome shade. In due course the switchbacks grow shallower, and you're faced instead with some long, exposed traverses along the red Supai Sandstone layer, where the path dwindles to just a couple of feet wide and gravel skitters over the edge with every step.

Another saddle, three miles from the rim, leads onto Horseshoe Mesa, with a short drop still to go before you reach the pit toilets (with no water) that mark the start of what used to be the active mining area. The ruddy soil is scattered with mineral-rich flecks and outcrops of copper ore, and the ruins of miners' cabins are everywhere you look. Makeshift trails meander around the whole mesa-top, passing abandoned workings and mysterious caves; investigating any of these is officially forbidden, and would be an extremely perilous undertaking.

If you're planning a backpack further into the canyon, the best route down to the mesa – signed to Cottonwood Creek – heads off to the left (west) close to the restrooms. A seven-mile **loop** around the foot of Horseshoe Mesa, at the Tonto Platform level, will bring you back to meet the Grandview Trail a few hundred yards higher up. Alternatively, you could join the **Tonto Trail**, and head either seven miles east to meet the New Hance Trail beside the Colorado, or twenty miles west to join the South Kaibab Trail.

THE HERMIT TRAIL

Map 9, B7.

Trailhead Hermit's Rest.

Length (one way) Santa Maria Spring 2.3 miles; Hermit Creek 7.7 miles; Colorado River 8.7 miles.

Elevation Trailhead 6640ft; Santa Maria Spring 5000ft; Hermit Creek 3000ft; Colorado River 2400ft.

Equally appealing to both day-hikers and long-distance backpackers, the **Hermit Trail** is another unmaintained trail that dates from the days when the obstreperous Ralph Cameron controlled access to most of the prime rim-edge sites (see p.214). Having started life as the El Tovar Trail, used from 1912 onwards by the Fred Harvey company for its mule excursions, it was soon renamed in honor of the reclusive French-Canadian prospector Louis Boucher, a familiar figure in its early days. Though abandoned in 1931, much of the trail's engineering remains in good shape, and even if the views are seldom as spectacular it makes a good alternative to the often-overcrowded Bright Angel and South Kaibab trails. The best **dayhikes** go to either Santa Maria Spring on the main trail (4.5 miles round trip), or Dripping Spring on the side trails described below (6.5 miles round trip). Water from both is drinkable if treated.

The trail begins from Hermit's Rest, at the far end of Hermit Road (see p.68); in winter, when the shuttle buses aren't running, trail users can drive to a separate parking lot beyond the shuttle stop. Immediately rough and rocky underfoot, it starts by switchbacking down the eastern flank of Hermit Basin, feeling a long way removed from the central Grand Canyon as it slowly descends a high rock wall far above Hermit Creek. It's joined from the south by the **Waldron Trail** 1.5 miles along – mapped out in 1896 as the original route down into Hermit Basin but now seldom used – and then passes the spur trail to **Dripping Spring** a quarter-mile further on. Upheavals in the cobbled pathway, and rockfalls from above, tend to make for slow progress.

Beside **Santa Maria Spring**, another half-mile along, there's shade in a vine-covered resthouse, though the spring itself often amounts to little more than a steady drip. Day-hikers should turn back here; the trail onwards is gentle at first, but after around a mile it reaches further steep switch-backs and then a tricky downward scramble through fallen rocks. It eventually hurtles down the Redwall below Pima Point by means of the cramped **Cathedral Stairs** switch-backs, to meet the Tonto Trail a total of 6.4 miles from the trailhead.

Between 1913 and 1931, mule-riders would spend the night deep in the inner canyon at the permanent **Hermit Camp**, a mile west of the Tonto Trail junction, which was provisioned by cable car from Pima Point. Only the outline of its sturdy stone walls remains in place, however, so mod-ern backpackers congregate instead at the **Hermit Creek Campground**, a few hundred yards on. Though its much-loved natural swimming pool was destroyed by a flash flood in 1996, it's still a spectacular spot, with dramatic views of the cliffs that soar above it to the rim.

The most direct route down to the Colorado on the Hermit Trail has you turning right into Hermit Creek just before Hermit Camp, but you can also get there by follow-ing the creek down from the campground. Either way, you reach the river in a little over a mile, at the rocky beach just short of **Hermit Rapid**, whose wave-like surge can reach over twenty feet high.

THE HERMIT TRAIL

THE DRIPPING SPRING TRAIL

Map 9, B7.
Trailhead Hermit's Rest.
Length (one way) Dripping Spring 3.2 miles.
Elevation Trailhead 6640ft; Dripping Spring 5800ft.

The delightful and none-too-strenuous expedition to **Dripping Spring** ranks among the best mid-length day-hikes in the Grand Canyon. The spring itself, which was home to the "hermit" Louis Boucher between 1891 and 1912, is only a few hundred yards beneath the rim, but the nearest road-accessible trailhead is at **Hermit's Rest**, and it's necessary to approach the spring from below, so it's still a round trip of 6.5 miles.

Turn left at the junction described above, almost two miles down the Hermit Trail, and follow the narrow path as it clings to the contours of two successive wooded amphitheaters. After a mile, you meet the **Boucher Trail**, and turn left again, joining it on its upward course back toward the rim. Not far up, the spring cascades from the ceiling of a large overhanging alcove in the Coconino Sandstone wall, amid eruptions of ferns and tiny blossoms. Boucher used this perennial water supply to irrigate gardens and orchards along the creek.

THE BOUCHER TRAIL

Map 9, B7.
Trailhead Hermit's Rest.
Length (one way) Boucher Trail Junction 2.8 miles; Yuma Point headland 5 miles; Tonto Trail 8.2 miles; Colorado River 10.8 miles.
Elevation Trailhead 6640ft; Yuma Point headland 5400ft; Colorado River 2325ft.

Strictly speaking, the **Boucher Trail**, which runs a mile or so west of, and roughly parallel to, the Hermit Trail, begins at a remote trailhead above Dripping Spring. It began life as Louis Boucher's "Silver Bell Trail," the most direct route down to his stream-side base. These days, however, access is so much easier from Hermit's Rest that it's used almost invariably as part of longer, multi-trail itineraries, which most commonly involve going down to the river via the Boucher Trail and then climbing back out again on the Hermit.

In its earlier stages especially, the Boucher Trail is not a hike for canyon novices. As soon as you turn right onto the trail, three miles down the Dripping Spring itinerary described above, you're obliged to totter along the very brink of an extremely steep drop. In icy winter conditions, this long traverse of the west wall of **Hermit Basin** is truly terrifying. Conditions improve when you round the headland beneath **Yuma Point** at the far end, but you still have to negotiate long, difficult scrambling descents before you meet the **Tonto Trail**. Half a mile on from there, turn right and pick your own way along the boulder-strewn Boucher Creek streambed to reach the river close to the **Boucher Rapid**. Alternatively, a 4.5-mile eastward hike on the Tonto Trail will bring you to the **Hermit Creek Campground** on the Hermit Trail (see p.237).

THE SOUTH BASS TRAIL

Trailhead Bass Camp.
Length (one way) Esplanade Rim 2.7 miles; Tonto Trail 6 miles; Colorado River 7 miles.
Elevation Trailhead 6646ft; Esplanade Rim 5400ft; Colorado River 2200ft.

Over a century ago, the **Bass Trail** was the most important trans-canyon hiking route. Now located way to the west of the current center of tourist activity, and all but reverted to wilderness, it no longer even crosses the canyon at all. Its early promoter, former cowboy **William Bass**, set up the long-defunct **Bass Camp** tent village near **Havasupai Point** in 1885, and soon instigated a regular stagecoach service from Williams. He would lead intrepid visitors down the ancient Indian trail he had improved to reach his copper and asbestos mines, and ferry them over the river either by boat, when the water was low, or via cable car.

Bass went out of business after the railroad reached the South Rim, but his trail remains in reasonable condition for experienced inner-canyon hikers who have the route-finding abilities to negotiate its occasional obliterated segment. Many do still complete the rim-to-rim trip by hitching a ride with the river-runners they chance upon down by the Colorado. However, that route is generally regarded as two separate hikes – the **South Bass Trail**, described here, and the **North Bass Trail**, as outlined on p.244.

The main obstacle to hiking the South Bass Trail is not the absence of water anywhere above the river, but the sheer remoteness of the trailhead. When you ask about current trail conditions at the park visitor center, get a ranger to describe the access route in detail. It's a thirty-mile drive off US-180, of which the first 26 miles are on Forest Service road 328, which heads west from Tusayan just south of *Moqui Lodge*, and the final four, north from Pasture Wash, are so rough that a **high-clearance 4WD** vehicle is essential.

Havasupai Point, two miles east of the trailhead, is reachable via an equally problematic dirt road that branches off to the right shortly before Bass Camp. It marks a natural boundary between the eastern Grand Canyon, characterized by massive indented amphitheaters, isolated buttes, and generally tangled topography, and the western canyon, which consists of a much simpler, broad valley known as the **Esplanade**, with the deep **Granite Gorge** still at its core. That's why the ridge immediately east of the trailhead is known as the **Grand Scenic Divide**.

The trail takes almost three miles to zigzag down through the woods and reach the edge of the Esplanade, alongside the towering butte of **Mount Huethawali**. This spot offers the first and best views of the vast sweep of the canyon, making it clear how abruptly the mesas and buttes disappear as the river heads west. Down below you, the trail plunges deep into **Bass Canyon**, whence it emerges after three miles to meet the Tonto Trail. Follow the bed of the often dry wash for two miles downwards, and it ends at a lovely little riverside **beach**, often used by passing rafters for overnight stays.

THE TONTO TRAIL

The **Tonto Trail** is an exception to the other South Rim trails described here, in that it has no contact with the canyon rim. Neither, for the vast proportion of its length, does it approach the river. Instead it runs parallel to both rim and river, meandering along the Tonto Platform at a typical elevation of around 4000 feet. That means it stays mostly on the parched, cactus-strewn Bright Angel Shale layer, which spreads out below the Redwall and Muav Limestone strata and above the Tapeats Sandstone layer and the Inner Gorge. It doesn't mean, however, that it's an easy hike. With streams and earthquake faults forever cutting down toward the Colorado, the Tonto Trail is repeatedly forced either to cut down into lesser gorges and then climb out again, or to circle endlessly back around the head of each successive amphitheater. Water is scarce and facilities non-existent.

THE TONTO TRAIL

As it stretches for a phenomenal 92 miles, almost no one walks the full length of the Tonto Trail. Canyon hikers tend simply to cross it at some point en route to or from the river, or at best join it for a small connecting stretch between two major trails. There's no trailhead as such, but technically it begins, as the **Tonto East Trail** (Map 9, I7), at the foot of the **New Hance Trail**, heading west to meet the **Grandview Trail** in seven miles and the **South Kaibab Trail** another twenty miles after that. Its central portion, the part officially called the Tonto Trail, runs for four miles from the Tipoff on the South Kaibab to Indian Garden on the Bright Angel Trail; thirteen more miles to join the Hermit Trail; and six miles beyond that to connect with the Boucher Trail. The Tonto West Trail then takes up the baton, running for a full thirty miles to connect with the South Bass Trail, and another twelve miles to Garnet Canyon, where it meets the Royal Arch Route for the lengthy climb out.

Other North Rim trails

While the **North Kaibab Trail** (see p.222) is by far the most popular inner-canyon trail to start from the North Rim, two others lie within reach of hikers eager to experience greater solitude – and a tougher physical challenge. Both the **Nankoweap Trail** and the **North Bass Trail** demand considerable confidence and self-sufficiency, and both are much more suitable for backpackers planning multi-day itineraries than they are for day-hikers. Be sure to ask about current conditions when you pick up your permit.

THE NANKOWEAP TRAIL

Trailhead Saddle Mountain.
Length (one way) Saddle Mountain Saddle 1.4 miles; Tilted Mesa 6.8 miles; Nankoweap Creek 10.6 miles; Colorado River 13.9 miles.
Elevation Trailhead 8848ft; Saddle Mountain Saddle 7500ft; Tilted Mesa 6450ft; Nankoweap Creek 3350ft; Colorado River 2800ft.

Located far to the north of all other Grand Canyon trails, the dramatic **Nankoweap Trail** is unique in not only providing access to the seldom visited upper reaches of the canyon, but also offering tremendous panoramas out across the Marble Platform and upstream toward Lees Ferry. With its hair's-breadth ledges and sickeningly high drop-offs, however, it's not recommended for anyone with even the slightest fear of heights. **Charles Doolittle Walcott**, who with John Wesley Powell improved the trail during their geological expedition of 1882, called it "utterly frightful," and its early stages remain every bit as terrifying. Only true canyon veterans should even consider attempting it.

Though the **trailhead** is less than three miles north of Point Imperial (see p.94), it can only be reached by driving fifteen miles along the graveled Forest Service road 610, which heads east from AZ-67 a mile south of *Kaibab Lodge* (see p.123); the route is normally passable in ordinary vehicles. It takes a mile for the trail itself to begin in earnest; first you have to negotiate a steep little hill, which involves a brisk climb. Then comes the hard part, a heart-stopping sidle along a narrow exposed ledge of Esplanade Sandstone. A brief respite at **Marion Ridge**, a camping spot overlooked by some striking misshapen rock pillars, is followed by more tremulous ledge work, as far as **Tilted Mesa** at the outer limit of the Redwall.

Beyond Tilted Mesa, a very steep set of switchbacks – which at least are in good condition – brings you down onto the terrace where at length you meet the verdant **Nankoweap Creek**. Three more miles down the trackless but mostly gentle streambed, at spreading, sandy Nankoweap Delta, you arrive at the Colorado itself, to be confronted by the towering eastern wall of Marble Canyon on the far side. Minor trails lead downstream beside the river for around a mile, but in due course you have to turn around and climb back the way you came. Note that there are no designated campsites along the trail; instead you're free to select your own site in the wilderness.

THE NORTH BASS TRAIL

Trailhead Swamp Point.
Length (one way) Muav Saddle 1 mile; Redwall 4.5 miles; Colorado River 13.5 miles.
Elevation Trailhead 7520ft; Muav Saddle 6750ft; Redwall 5100ft; Colorado River 2200ft.

The North Rim counterpart to William Bass's South Bass Trail (see p.239), the **North Bass Trail**, starts from the overlook at **Swamp Point**, which as described on p.102 is a twenty-mile dirt-road drive west of AZ-67 that's only suitable for 4WD vehicles. As with the South Bass, this trail is recommended for veteran inner-canyon hikers only – in many places, the trail is liable to have vanished completely, so you'll need route-finding skills, considerable energy for scrambling down talus slopes and through thick brush, and a head for heights.

From Swamp Point, a mile of comparatively well-maintained switchbacks drop down to the **Muav Saddle**, where a long-abandoned park-service cabin dating from 1925 is still used by overnighting backpackers. A minor dead-end trail leads up from the cabin onto **Powell Plateau** (see p.102), but the main route now descends **Muav Canyon** in earnest, along the rocky bed of **White Creek**.

When you've covered the total of almost five miles to the top of the **Redwall**, you've cleared the most difficult section of the trail – several short *uphill* stretches won't have improved your mood – and you've also finally reached some superb inner-canyon views. Swift switchbacks then carry you down the Redwall, where you rejoin White Creek. In theory the trail strays away from the creek onto the nearby plateau, but it's much easier simply to follow the streambed all the way down to **Shinumo Creek**, another five miles on. William Bass planted melons, corn and squash down here, along with peach orchards, at a spot he found by tracing ancient Indian irrigation ditches; in his day, intact cliff-dwellings and granaries were still visible nearby. The Colorado is reached via a final steep descent, which ends at a sheltered riverside grove much frequented by rafters. Both here and all along the trail, there are no officially designated campsites, so follow usual wilderness-camping protocols.

THE NORTH BASS TRAIL

Rafting the Colorado River

I conclude the Colorado is not a very easy stream to navigate.

Diary entry of George Bradley, member of the first Powell expedition,
at the end of the first-ever day's boating on the Colorado

Part white-knuckle ride, part leisurely scenic cruise, **rafting** the **Colorado River** through the Grand Canyon has been repeatedly rated among the greatest outdoors adventures our planet has to offer. Yes, you can admire the canyon from the safety of the rim, but only once you've raced its every rapid, drenched to the skin and deafened by its thundering roar, can you truly claim to know it inside out. And there's much more to a river trip than pure adrenaline: there's also picnicking on sandy riverside beaches; camping beneath the stars; hiking into little-known side canyons to reach hidden waterfalls, mysterious caves, and narrow slot canyons; swimming in streams and water holes; and generally escaping from the modern world into a remote, timeless wilderness.

When **John Wesley Powell**'s crew set out in 1869 to become the first party to travel down the Colorado by boat (see p.270), they had no way of knowing whether such a voyage was possible. All the way, they were haunted by the fear that a mighty waterfall might lie around the next bend, or that some fearsome rapid might fill the canyon wall-to-wall at a point where there was no way to climb out. As it turned out, there were fortunately no waterfalls, and it *is* possible to float the full length of the Colorado. It's still far from easy, of course, and not something you could even dream of attempting without the most expert guidance and advice. Nevertheless, river craft and techniques have become so refined that professional rafting companies can carry thousands of inexperienced passengers through the canyon each year in guaranteed safety. Yet as weather and water levels fluctuate, and flash floods reshape the canyon's contours, the thrill of uncertainty remains, and every trip presents a new challenge.

The prime reason rafting the Grand Canyon is so exciting is the estimated 161 sets of **rapids** along the way. The Colorado here is what's known as a **"pool and drop"** river, meaning that it consists of tranquil lake-like sections, where it meanders along at an average speed of around six miles per hour, that alternate with hectic rapids, when it's constricted into a narrower, debris-strewn channel. These occur where rocks washed down the side canyon by a tributary stream have tumbled into the riverbed. The resultant **whitewater** flows at perhaps twenty or thirty miles per hour, creating an obstacle course of concealed boulders and treacherous whirlpools that canyon boatmen learn to navigate by both instinct and experience.

The **rafting season** begins in mid-April, and runs until mid-September for motorized trips, and as late as early November for oar-powered expeditions. The busiest period is **summer**, between June and August. However, daytime temperatures during that period tend to exceed 100°F, and there's a greater likelihood of thunderstorms from late July into September. In **spring** and **fall**, when temperatures are cooler and the canyon quieter, many operators offer longer trips to allow for extra hiking, and spring also sees the canyon flora at its most colorful. Typical daytime highs would be in the 60–80°F range in April and November, more like 70–100°F in May, September and October. Nightly lows vary from as low as 40°F in April up to a sweaty 90°F in July. Whenever you come, however, you need to be prepared for extremes of both heat and cold, and also potential rain. Although the Colorado itself remains consistently cool year-round, barely straying from 48°F – which is cold enough to cause hypothermia – streams and pools in the side canyons allow for great swimming in summer.

There are two basic kinds of rafting trip, both strictly regulated by the park service – you certainly can't just turn up at the Colorado with your own raft and set off. You can either join a **commercial** trip, with one of the accredited concessionaires listed on p.253, or, if you have a great deal of whitewater experience and an even greater amount of patience, put together your own **non-commercial** party and join the waiting list for a time slot. As it currently takes around twelve years to get to the head of the line, the commercial option is much more realistic.

COMMERCIAL RAFTING TRIPS

Anyone planning to take a commercial rafting trip down the Grand Canyon faces a fundamental choice between joining a **motorized** or an **oar-powered** expedition. Both typically cost between **$200 and $250 per person, per day**, though oar-powered trips tend to cost a little more per day, and take longer overall. On a motorized trip, the professional guides are entirely responsible for the actual work of running the river; on an oar-powered one, you don't necessarily have to do any rowing, but many allow passengers to paddle some or even all of the way. As a rule, the **minimum age** for participants on motorized trips is 8, while on oar-powered trips it's 12.

Although purists insist that the comparative silence, and sense of physical involvement, of an oar-powered trip provides a far more "authentic" river-running experience than a motorized one, the actual day-to-day routine is not all that different whichever type you choose. Even the fastest trips of either kind tend to spend little more than five hours actually on the river each day; it's taken for granted that everyone wants to stop for picnics and hikes.

The boats

For the most part, commercial operators use different kinds of **inflatable rubberized rafts**. Powell's wooden boats were built for speed, very hard to maneuver, and rowed by two men, seated in traditional rowing-boat style with their backs to what lay ahead. Modern rafts are flat-bottomed, extremely maneuverable, and capable of bouncing undamaged off obstacles; the single boatman faces forwards, and often slows down by paddling against the current, jockeying for position until a route through opens up.

Motorized trips, not surprisingly, travel significantly faster; each raft can be up to thirty feet long, equipped with outriggers for extra stability, and carry up to ten passengers. The park service has long seemed sympathetic to the idea of banning motorized craft altogether, arguing that they increase both noise and environmental pollution. Industry lobbyists have so far managed to stymie any complete ban, but motorized expeditions are currently restricted both in terms of the total number permitted each year, and in terms

COMMERCIAL RAFTING TRIPS

of the season they can operate, from mid-April to mid-September.

Non-motorized or **oar-powered** rafts are more like eighteen feet long, and are usually rowed and steered by a single guide with the only oar, while the four or five passengers simply enjoy the ride. Some outfitters also offer **paddle boats**, however, of a similar size and number of passengers, but with the difference that everyone has their own paddle, and the guide's responsibility is strictly for steering. Adventure-sports enthusiasts tend to prefer **paddle-only** trips, in which the paying customers are expected to paddle all the way; it's also possible to take a **hybrid** trip, in which both types of vessel are taken along, and individual passengers can choose each day whether to ride in a paddle boat or be rowed by a guide.

For those determined to echo the conditions experienced by the early river pioneers as closely as possible, two operators, **Grand Canyon Expeditions** and **O.A.R.S.** (under the name Grand Canyon Dories), also offer rowing trips in hard-bodied **dories**. These are the closest modern approximation to Powell's boats, albeit extensively adapted for Grand Canyon use. Because dories require such skilled handling, they can only be rowed by the crew rather than the passengers, and tend to be significantly more expensive.

Choosing a trip

The Grand Canyon is officially 277 miles long, with each river mile being numbered downstream from Mile 0 at **Lees Ferry** (see p.112). Itself just under sixteen miles downstream from Glen Canyon Dam, Lees Ferry is the only spot from which it's possible to **launch** a rafting expedition. (Passengers can join an existing trip at Phantom Ranch, but there's no way to get a boat down to the Colorado at that point.) Boats and/or passengers can, however, **leave** at various different junctures. The canyon ends at Mile 277, where the Colorado emerges onto the open waters of **Lake Mead**; three miles on, at Mile 280, a paved road reaches the edge of the lake at **Pierce Ferry** (also spelled Pearce Ferry). However, for the final 43 miles of the canyon, the true river channel is submerged beneath the waters of Lake Mead. Many river trips therefore end at **Diamond Creek**, on Hualapai land at Mile 226, where boats and passengers can be driven out of the canyon along a gravel road. Recently, some operators have begun to curtail their trips even sooner, at **Whitmore Wash** at Mile 187, scooping customers up from river level by helicopter and taking them to the **Bar 10 Ranch** on the North Rim, where an airstrip makes it possible to fly on to Las Vegas or elsewhere. There's also one other potential stopping place en route: **Phantom Ranch**, at Mile 87, from where passengers can hike out to either the South or the North Rim.

The permutations for possible trips are endless. What are advertised as full-length Grand Canyon expeditions may be 187, 226 or 280 miles long and take anything from six motorized days to 22 oar-powered days. (The record, incidentally, for the full 277 miles is just under 37 hours, by an unauthorized expedition undertaken during dangerous 1983 flooding, when the canyon was closed to all craft.) Most operators also offer an **Upper Canyon** option, starting at Lees Ferry and ending with a hike out from Phantom Ranch, which typically takes three nights, four days, and a **Lower Canyon** trip, starting by hiking down to Phantom Ranch, and taking out somewhere downstream after four or five nights.

You can also take a **one-night**, two-day river trip if you fly down into the canyon at Whitmore Wash with Arizona River Runners (see p.255), or a **one-day** trip from Diamond Creek with Hualapai River Runners (see p.193).

Neither an Upper nor a Lower Canyon trip is "better"

than the other. If you take the Upper Canyon trip, you'll know that all your fellow passengers are starting at the same time as you, as opposed to joining an established group, and you'll also get a gentler, more progressive introduction to the canyon and its rapids. On the other hand, there's less placid water overall, and you'll have to hike out at the end. A Lower Canyon trip will give you a slightly longer ride, but also plunge you straight away into some really major rapids.

Although whitewater experts traditionally grade the difficulty of rapids on the world's rivers on a scale of one to six, on the Colorado they're ranked from one to ten, so a "4" here won't be the same as one elsewhere. Both the Grand Canyon's two unquestioned tens lie downstream from Phantom Ranch – **Crystal Rapid** at Mile 98, created by a flash flood in 1966, and **Lava Falls Rapid** further west at Mile 179, which is visible from Toroweap Point (see p.135). There are, however, a couple of almost-as-intense rapids in the Upper Canyon: **Hance Rapid** at Mile 76, and **Sockdolager Rapid** – named by Powell for a contemporary word meaning "knockout punch" – just after the start of the Granite Gorge at Mile 78.

Other highlights in the Upper Canyon include **Vasey's Paradise**, a flower-filled natural garden at Mile 31; the **Redwall Cavern** at mile 33, a vast sand-floored alcove which Powell overeagerly estimated could hold fifty thousand people; and the confluence with the **Little Colorado** at Mile 61, where, thanks to a rich concentration of salts from springs not far upstream, the tributary flows in from the east as a resplendent turquoise stream. The biggest treats for **hikers** come in the Lower Canyon, with the successive **Olo**, **Matkatamiba** and **Havasu** canyons between miles 145 and 156. Both the first two are narrow "slot canyons," interspersed with hidden pools and waterfalls and boasting rock walls sculpted by flash floods into beautiful swirling patterns; the splendors of Havasu Canyon are described in full in Chapter Six, though rafters seldom hike any further up the canyon than to Beaver Falls, four miles up, but two miles below Mooney Falls.

Commercial rafting operators

A complete list of all operators authorized to conduct commercial river trips within the Grand Canyon appears below; you can also find the current list online, with active links, at ⓦ www.nps.gov/grca/river/river_concessioners.htm. For an overview of what's available at any one time, contact **Rivers and Oceans**, 12620 N Copeland Lane, Flagstaff, AZ 86004 (ⓣ 1-800/473-4576 or 928/526-4575, ⓦ www.rivers -oceans.com), a travel broker that specializes in making bookings with them all.

In choosing which company to go with, be sure you're clear whether their published rates include any **transportation** and/or overnight **accommodation** that may be required before or after your trip. While you might be tempted to cut costs by driving yourself to Lees Ferry, that can leave you with a serious logistic problem. Also, if you're a long way from home, taking a trip that includes round-trip transportation to and from Flagstaff or Las Vegas can spare you from having to pay for a **rental car** you won't be using for several days.

All rates include unlimited **food** and **beverages** for the duration, though you have to supply any alcoholic drinks yourself. You should, however, check exactly what **equipment** is included in the price. Some operators charge rental fees to passengers who don't bring their own sleeping bags and mats, others provide everything.

Individual companies also provide checklists of what you should and shouldn't bring. Recommended **clothing** includes a full set of raingear, long insulating underclothes, a fleece jacket and hat, a swimsuit, and sandals with soft rubber soles. Among items not to carry are mobile or satellite phones, radios and other electrical devices.

Finally, bear in mind that it's customary to **tip** your river guides between five and ten percent of the total cost at the end of your trip.

Aramark-Wilderness River Adventures

PO Box 717, Page, AZ 86040
ⓣ 1-800/992-8022 or 928/645-3296,
ⓦ www.riveradventures.com.
Aramark offer both oar-powered and motorized trips. The oar-powered ones, using six boats each capable of carrying 4–6 passengers, set off every 2–3 weeks between mid-May and mid-September. They cost around $1500 for the 5-day Upper Canyon ride; $2400 for the Lower Canyon, from Phantom Ranch to the Bar 10 Ranch, with a flight out to Las Vegas or Page; and $3000 for the 12–14 days of the full-length Grand Tradition. Motorized expeditions, using two 15-passenger boats, run regularly between mid-April and mid-September, taking 3.5 days for the Upper Canyon ($950);

4.5 days for the Lower Canyon ($1800); and 7–8 days for the whole thing ($2200).

Arizona Raft Adventures

4050-F E. Huntington Rd, Flagstaff, AZ 86004 ⓣ 1-800/786-7238 or 928/526-8200, ⓦ www.azraft.com.
ARA's motorized voyages operate between May and mid-August, costing around $1900 for the 8-day standard trip or one devoted specifically to natural history, or $2200 for the 10-day Hiker's Special in August. Paddling trips, for riders who want to paddle all the time, leave once monthly between May and mid-September, at around $1500 for 6 days, $2150 for 9 days, and $2750 for 14 days. For the same rate, you can also join one of a dozen hybrid trips between May and September, on which passengers choose each

day between riding in an oar-powered raft, or actively crewing a paddle boat.

Arizona River Runners

PO Box 47788, Phoenix, AZ 85068-7788 Ⓣ 1-800/477-7238 or 602/867-4866, Ⓦ www.raftarizona.com.
Motorized trips down the full length of the canyon, available between May and September, cost $1600 for 6 days, $1750 for 7 days, or $1800 for 8 days. Oar-powered expeditions, run four times between June and October, though not in mid-summer, and are $1200 for the 6-day Upper Canyon voyage; $1600 for the 8-day trip from Phantom Ranch to Diamond Creek; and $2500 for the full 13-day voyage from Lees Ferry to Diamond Creek. Every few days between May and September, they also do a 3-day "Grand Canyon Escape" from Las Vegas, in which you fly to the Bar 10 Ranch and spend a night there, then take a helicopter down to the river for a 1.5-day trip and return to Las Vegas from Lake Mead, all for $790.

Canyon Explorations/ Canyon Expeditions

PO Box 310, Flagstaff, AZ 86002 Ⓣ 1-800/654-0723 or 928/774-4559, Ⓦ www .canyonexplorations.com.
An extensive program of river trips of differing lengths is available between April and October. All begin and end in Flagstaff, and several are extended to allow for extra hiking. Hybrid trips, which include not only oar boats and a paddle boat but also inflatable kayaks, range from $1450 for 6 days, via $2150 for 9 days, up to $3100 for 15 days, while all-paddling expeditions cost from $1550 for 6 days up to $3300 for 15 days. Kayakers can join any trip, at the same rates as for the paddle trips.

Canyoneers

PO Box 2997, Flagstaff, AZ 86003 Ⓣ 1-800/525-0924 or 928/526-0924, Ⓦ www.canyoneers.com.
Canyoneers, who also run the *Kaibab Lodge* (see p.123) and the *Kaibab Camper Village* (see p.123) near the North Rim, specialize in sending

COMMERCIAL RAFTING TRIPS

massive powered pontoons down the Grand Canyon. Weekly between mid-April and early September, they run its entire length in 7 days (6 nights) for $1800. In June and July, they also offer a handful of shorter trips, with a $700 2-day, 2-night sprint through the Upper Canyon and a $1400 5-day, 4-night trip through the Lower Canyon. The 13-day, $3350 Hiker Special trip, in early May, allows time to hike into many side canyons. In September only, they also offer oar-powered trips, costing $1350 for the 5-day Upper Canyon segment and $2200 for the 8-day Lower Canyon stretch. All trips start and end in Flagstaff.

Colorado River & Trail Expeditions

PO Box 57575, Salt Lake City, UT 84157-0575 ☎ 1-800/253-7328 or 801/261-1789, ⓦ www.crateinc.com. Weekly motorized expeditions between mid-May and the end of August, at $900 for the 4-day Upper Canyon; $1400 for the 6-day

Lower Canyon run; and $1900 for the whole thing, in either 8 or 9 days. Rates for their first trip of the season, at the end of April, are a little lower, even though it lingers 5 days over the Upper Canyon and 7 in the Lower, to give more scope for hiking. In August, they also offer a single hybrid trip, costing $1200 for the 5 days from Lees Ferry to Phantom Ranch; $2100 for the 7 days from Phantom Ranch to Whitmore Wash; and $2650 for the 11 days from Lees Ferry to Whitmore Wash.

Diamond River Adventures

PO Box 1300, Page, AZ 86040 ☎ 1-800/343-3121 or 928/645-8866, ⓦ www.diamondriver.com. Female owned and managed rafting company, which offers Grand Canyon expeditions of between 4 and 13 days by either oar or motorboat. The season runs from May to early September, with motorized trips setting off more or less weekly, and oar-powered ones somewhat less frequently. Four-day Upper

Canyon motorized trips start at around $800, while to run the full length with a motor takes 7 days and costs $1800. By oar, it's 10 days and $2600.

Grand Canyon Expeditions Company

PO Box 0, Kanab, UT 84741 ☏ 1-800/544-2691 or 435/644-2691, ⓦ www.gcex.com.

A huge number of motorized expeditions, with 65 departures between April and mid-September each year. Some are devoted to special interests like ecology, archeology and photography, and thereby offer longer pauses at, and extra hikes to, sites of particular significance, with guidance from experts in the relevant field. The 8-day run from Lees Ferry to Lake Mead costs $2000. They also offer four rowing trips each summer, in May, June, July and September, using modern dories, which take 14 days and cost $3000.

Hatch River Expeditions

PO Box 1200, Vernal, UT 84078 ☏ 1-800/433-8966 or 435/789-3813, ⓦ www.hatchriverexpeditions.com.

Hatch River Expeditions run regular 7-day, 188-mile motorized trips between Lees Ferry and Whitmore Wash; passengers leave the canyon well before the end, via helicopter, for connecting flights to Las Vegas or Marble Canyon. Taking the whole cruise costs $1625, or you can take a 4-day version, entering or exiting at Phantom Ranch, for $850.

High Desert Adventures

PO Box 40, St George, UT 84771-0040 ☏ 1-800/673-1733 or 435/673-1733, ⓦ www.boathda.com.

Utah-based company which offers a relatively small program of both motorized and oar-powered trips, all including transportation to and from Las Vegas. On the 8 oar-powered trips between May and October each year, you can either take the first 6 days, from Lees Ferry to Phantom Ranch, for $1750; the last 8 days, from Phantom Ranch to Pearce Ferry, for

COMMERCIAL RAFTING TRIPS

$2350; or stay aboard for the whole 14-day trip for $3250. The seven 8-day motorized trips, available between June and September, cost $2150, and you can also arrange a made-to-measure charter trip.

Moki Mac River Expeditions

PO Box 71242, Salt Lake City, UT 84171-0242 ☎1-800/284-7280 or 801/268-6667, ⓦwww.mokimac.com.

Each summer, Moki Mac run eleven 14-day oar-powered trips between Lees Ferry and Lake Mead – priced at $2950 for the whole thing, $1500 for the Upper Canyon, and $2000 for the Lower Canyon – and nine 8-day motorized trips on the same route, only sold as the entire trip and costing $1950. All rates cover round-trip transportation to and from Las Vegas.

O.A.R.S.

PO Box 67, Angles Camp, CA 95222 ☎1-800/346-6277 or 209/736-2924, ⓦwww.oars.com.

Adventure-tour operator, active through the West,

whose Grand Canyon trips use modern dories and are also sold under the name of Grand Canyon Dories. Their very flexible program runs from mid-April into early November. A full canyon voyage from Lees Ferry to Lake Mead can take 15 days ($3900), 17 days ($4100), or 22 days ($4800), while the many shorter stretches on offer include the usual Lees Ferry to Phantom Ranch stretch in 6, 7 or 8 days ($2050–2350); Phantom Ranch to Diamond Creek (9 days, $2700); or Whitmore Wash to Lake Mead (5 days, $1450).

Outdoors Unlimited

6900 Townsend Winona Rd, Flagstaff, AZ 86004 ☎1-800/637-7238 or 928/526-2852, ⓦwww.outdoorsunlimited.com.

Oar-powered trips, all of which take at least one paddle boat along, and some of which are all-paddling. The standard trip from Lees Ferry to Lake Mead costs $2900 for the full 13 days, or you can pay $2300 for the 9-day Lower Canyon segment or

$1350 for the 5-day Upper Canyon run. An all-paddling trip is slightly more expensive, while at the start or end of the season you can pay a little more again to join an extended trip that offers more opportunities for hiking.

Tour West

PO Box 333, Orem, UT 84059 ☏ 1-800/453-9107 or 801/225-0755, Ⓦ www.twriver.com. Between April and mid-September, Tour West send 33 motorized expeditions down the canyon; a 6-night trip costs around $1900, or you can take a 3-night jaunt ending either at Lake Mead ($950) or the Bar 10 Ranch ($1050). In June and July each year, they also offer three 12-night rowing trips, for $2600.

Western River Expeditions

7258 Racquet Club Drive, Salt Lake City, UT 84121 ☏ 1-800/453-7450 or 801/942-6669, Ⓦ www.westernriver.com. Western River runs a very slick program of brisk, motorized Grand Canyon expeditions, offering just two basic choices on almost fifty separate expeditions between mid-April and September each year. You can either take the 6-day run from Lees Ferry to the Bar 10 Ranch, which involves being helicoptered out of the canyon 187 miles along, just after Lava Falls; or be choppered in at that point, for a 3-day float down to Lake Mead. The former costs around $2000, the latter more like $1000; both are ten percent cheaper in April.

One-day trips

No **one-day** rafting trips are available within Grand Canyon National Park. There are, however, two alternatives if you only have a day to spare, one at either end of the canyon.

In an entirely separate operation to their multi-day expeditions detailed on p.254, Aramark-Wilderness Adventures (☏928/645-3279) also offers one-day **float trips** that start

COMMERCIAL RAFTING TRIPS

immediately below **Glen Canyon Dam** and take out at **Lees Ferry**. There's no whitewater along the way, and strictly speaking you never enter the Grand Canyon, but it's still a very pleasant cruise between imposing high-canyon cliffs. Participants rendezvous at Aramark's headquarters at 57 S Lake Powell Blvd in Page, Arizona, not far from the dam, daily at 11am between March and early November. The cost is $59 for adults, $49 for children aged 12 and under. Water and sodas are provided, but you're expected to bring your own picnic lunch.

Further west, the Hualapai River Runners run daily 35-mile motorized trips through the western end of the canyon, including several rapids. You'll find full details in the **Hualapai reservation** chapter on p.193.

NON-COMMERCIAL TRIPS

Between 250 and 300 **private rafting expeditions** are allowed onto the Colorado River each year, with a maximum of sixteen participants each. The park service maintains a **waiting list** of around 7600 applicants eager to organize their own trips. They estimate that someone who signs up now will take more than twelve years to reach the top of the list.

To add your name to the list, contact the Grand Canyon River Permits Office, Grand Canyon National Park, PO Box 129, Grand Canyon, AZ 86023 (☎1-800/959-9164 or 928/638-7843, ⓕ928/638-7844). Applications are only accepted if they're postmarked or faxed in the month of **February**, and there's a $100 fee to join. In addition, you have to submit a **Continuing Interest** form every year, to arrive by the end of January; miss this deadline more than once in any four-year period, and you'll be dropped from the list.

When your name finally does rise to the top, you'll be invited to pick a date within the next two years. A further fee of $100 per person is payable ninety days in advance. No participant on any trip can have been on another non-commercial trip within the last four years, and places are transferable only in very tightly controlled circumstances.

Around seventy **cancellations** come through each year. The freed-up dates are assigned to those on the waiting list only, who have to call on Friday evenings or all day Saturday or Sunday. Names higher up the list are favored, but if you're very flexible you may even get a cancellation the year you apply.

CONTEXTS

A human history of the Grand Canyon

The Grand Canyon might seem like a supremely inhospitable pristine environment, but it has been home to humans for around twelve thousand years. Native Americans once farmed along the canyon floor, across its plateaus, and up on the rims, while Spanish adventurers arrived here eighty years before the *Mayflower* set sail. Only within the last hundred years, however, has it occurred to anyone to come here for fun.

Native peoples

The oldest traces of a human presence at the Grand Canyon are a handful of flaked-stone spear-points that date back to around 10,000 BC. They were produced by the so-called **Clovis** culture, which spread throughout North and South America until around 8000 BC. Living in small groups, constantly on the move, Clovis hunters pursued their prey across large distances. They seem to have been such successful killers that they drove the indigenous fauna – which also included giant sloths, camels and even horses – to extinction.

As the large animals died out, the inhabitants of the Grand Canyon adapted to become **hunter-gatherers**, who migrated seasonally between the canyons and plateaus in search of fresh food. Judging by the small figurines that have been found in caves in Marble Canyon and elsewhere – made from split willow twigs to represent deer and bighorn sheep, and often run through by little "spears" – they developed shamanistic rituals to encourage hunting success.

The so-called Archaic era was brought to an end by the infiltration of influences from Mexico, and especially **agriculture**. The skill of growing **corn**, passed northwards from group to group, accompanied by the prayers and rituals necessary to ensure a good harvest, reached the canyon around 1000 BC. At first, a low level of farming merely supplemented the traditional diet; large-scale cultivation of corn and also **squash** probably began around 100 BC. The people responsible – known as the **Basketmakers** – lived in extended family groups, in shallow **pithouses** – rectangular pits, two to six feet deep, with earthen roofs that rose above ground level. They hunted using the *atlatl* – a spear-throwing device – and cooked by dropping hot rocks into yucca-leaf baskets lined with waterproof pitch. They also domesticated **dogs**, for hunting, and **turkeys**, used for feathers rather than food.

Pottery arrived a few centuries later, and with it the ability to boil **beans**, the third great staple Southwestern food. By around 500 AD, the Basketmakers were also growing **cotton**, and using **bows and arrows**. Sizeable **villages** (what the Spanish later called **pueblos**) started to appear. Each focussed around one pithouse, larger than the rest, that was set aside for public or ritual use. These were the first *kivas* – the ceremonial underground chambers still at the heart of Pueblo religion. By 700 AD, the Grand Canyon was populated by the ancestors of the modern Pueblo Indians, a people now known as "**Ancestral**

Puebloans" in preference to the previously common term
"**Anasazi**," which comes from a Navajo word meaning
"enemy ancestors."

The heyday of agriculture in the Grand Canyon came
roughly one thousand years ago, when increased levels of
precipitation meant that corn, beans and squash could be
planted throughout the canyon. The deltas at the mouths of
major side canyons, such as **Unkar Creek** and **Chuar
Creek**, made prized living spots. Modern visitors can see
typical Puebloan dwellings both down in the canyon, close
to Phantom Ranch (see p.226), and up on the plateaus,
most notably at **Tusayan Museum** on the South Rim (see
p.74) and **Walhalla Glades** on the North Rim (see p.97).
Ancestral Puebloans seemed to have roamed readily
between rim and river; their ladders and even footbridges
still survive in certain well-hidden places, while their trails
form the basis of almost all the park's hiking routes.

By around 1150 AD, rainfall had diminished once more,
the soil was becoming depleted, and an exodus from the
region began. There are also indications of conflict for scant
resources between competing groups. The Ancestral
Puebloans of the canyon can be subdivided into the
Kayenta peoples of its eastern and central reaches, and the
Cohonina further west, who with less fertile farmland
depended to a greater extent on roasting wild agave plants.
Fortified watchtower-like structures along the rim suggest
that these previously amicable neighbors may have fallen
out, or that perhaps the Cohonina left the canyon earlier
than the Kayenta, and were supplanted by the less friendly
Cerbat people. The **Paiute** also made their appearance
around this time, along the western end of the North Rim.

Although only a minimal population remained in the
canyon proper by 1250 AD, Puebloan groups have maintained close spiritual links ever since. The many distinct
Pueblo peoples that survive today came into being when

groups of migrants coalesced in various locations well to the east of the canyon between around 1100 and 1300 AD. Geographically the closest are the **Hopi**, whose mesas lie sixty miles east. They regard the dome-shaped hot spring known as the *sipapu*, not far up the Little Colorado from its confluence with the Colorado, as the hole through which they entered the world, and still make pilgrimages into the Grand Canyon along the **Salt Trail**. Some **Zuni**, who now live in New Mexico, also trace their origins back to the canyon, and particularly to Rainbow Falls below the North Rim.

Further west, the Cerbat never left the vicinity of the canyon. Their descendants became the **Hualapai**, and also the **Havasupai**, whose continued existence deep in Havasu Canyon represents the closest modern approximation to the ancient way of life.

The coming of the Spanish

In 1540 – less than twenty years after Cortés conquered the Aztecs of Mexico, and before any European settlements had been established anywhere in what's now the United States – the first **Spaniards** reached the Southwest. An expedition led by **Francisco Vásquez de Coronado**, hoping to find cities of gold and consisting of over three hundred Spanish soldiers plus hundreds more Native American "allies" and servants, marched up through Arizona and reached the Zuni pueblos on July 7. After a bloody battle – the first ever fought between Europeans and Native Americans – secured the area as a temporary base, exploring parties were sent out in all directions.

One such group was told at the Hopi mesas of a great river not far to the west, inhabited by people with very large bodies (presumably the Havasupai, who tend to be significantly bigger than the Hopi). Four men, under

García López de Cárdenas, were dispatched to investigate. They reached the Grand Canyon after twenty days, a puzzlingly long march that suggests their Hopi guides were deliberately leading them astray. The Spaniards were assured that no trails down to the river existed, and taken to a spot where none was visible; no one knows exactly where, but it's generally reckoned to have been somewhere near Grandview Point.

Cárdenas' men spent three days on the South Rim, searching for a route to the bottom. Three eventually made an abortive attempt, only to discover that "some huge rocks on the sides of the cliffs [that] seemed to be about as tall as a man ... were bigger than the great tower of Seville." They turned back a third of the way down, concluding that "it was impossible to descend."

The Spanish hoped to find a river route to the so-called "South Sea," the Gulf of California, and identified the Colorado as being the Tíson or "Firebrand" River, up which a simultaneous naval expedition was attempting to sail. It managed 225 miles, reaching the modern site of the Hoover Dam. Cárdenas himself, who seems to have been an unsavory character, rejoined Coronado, and was later responsible for burning two hundred Indian hostages alive at the pueblo of Tiguex.

Although Coronado's expedition ultimately failed, the Spaniards returned in force in 1598 to establish the colony of **New Mexico**, the boundaries of which nominally included the Grand Canyon. However, no further Spanish visits to the canyon are recorded before **1776**, when a group of explorers from Santa Fe, led by the Franciscan friars **Domínguez** and **Escalante** (see pp.120–121), set out to map what later became the Old Spanish Trail to California. On their return they wandered extensively across the Arizona Strip, and failed to cross the river at the site of Lees Ferry. That same year, **Father Garcés** from

Tucson penetrated what he called a "calaboose of cliffs and canyons" to visit the Havasupai in the western canyon.

John Wesley Powell

One or two "mountain men" or trappers may have seen the Grand Canyon during the first half of the nineteenth century, but by the time jurisdiction over the region passed from Mexico to the United States in 1848, it had never been surveyed, and did not even have a fixed **name**. To the Havasupai, it was Wikatata ("Rough Rim"); Spanish maps showed it as Río Muy Grande ("Very Big River"); and Yankee prospectors knew it as the Big Cañon.

The first serious attempt to explore it came in 1857, when **Lieutenant Joseph Christmas Ives** was instructed by the War Department to find out if the Colorado River was navigable by **steamboat**. Like his Spanish predecessors, he got little further than the Hoover Dam site, but he then continued on foot all the way to the Little Colorado River. An accompanying geologist made the first accurate scientific observations of the canyon, but the expedition is best remembered for Ives' own very negative assessment: "The region is, of course, altogether valueless … Ours has been the first, and will doubtless be the last, party of whites to visit this profitless locality."

The name **Grand Canyon**, first used on a map in 1868, was popularized by the one-armed Civil War veteran **John Wesley Powell**, whose dramatic 1869 boat trip along the fearsome and uncharted Colorado captured public imagination. Such a trip had long been mooted, but in the words of John Frémont, the legendary "Pathfinder" of the West, "no trappers have been found bold enough to undertake a voyage which has so certain a prospect of a fatal termination."

Powell's ten-man **Colorado River Exploring Expedition** set off from Green River, Wyoming on May

24, 1869. This was just two weeks after the completion of the transcontinental railroad, which carried his four heavy "Whitehall" oak rowing boats here from Chicago. Another expedition, led by Thomas Hook, set off a few days later, but was abandoned almost immediately after Hook was drowned in a rapid. Powell himself soon lost one of his boats, but he reached what became Green River, Utah on July 13; the previously unseen confluence of the Green and the (larger) Grand rivers, which marks the start of the Colorado, on July 16; and the mouth of the San Juan on July 31. From what's now Lees Ferry, he launched himself into the Grand Canyon on August 5.

It was a grueling, even nightmarish trip, for which Powell's boats were wholly unsuitable. His crew counted a total of 476 rapids, 62 of which they had to "portage" – that is, physically pick their boats up, and carry them over the riverside rocks. Eventually, however, the bedraggled, ravenous crew emerged from the canyon on August 29. In a dreadful irony, three members of the party, terrified by the interminable prospect of yet more rapids, had abandoned the river the day before, only to be murdered as they hiked out of Separation Canyon. Their deaths have traditionally been blamed on Native Americans, but compelling recent evidence suggests that they were in fact killed by Mormon settlers.

Powell was both a genuine hero and a consummate self-publicist, who, thanks in part to the acclaim he received for his journals – an unacknowledged amalgam of both this voyage and a second two years later – later became director of both the Bureau of American Ethnology and the US Geological Survey. He returned repeatedly to the canyon with scientific teams, one of which, in 1875, also included the artist **Thomas Moran**. Moran's paintings and engravings, and the detailed geological report prepared by **Clarence Dutton** in 1880–81, which was the first to give

A HUMAN HISTORY OF THE GRAND CANYON

quasi-religious names to the various "temples" and monuments below the rim, did much to place the canyon firmly in the American consciousness.

The growth of tourism

As the Grand Canyon was being recognized as the most extraordinary natural wonder in the US, settlers moved to the vicinity in ever greater numbers. Isolated Mormon communities sprang up across the Arizona Strip, on the plateaus of the North Rim, while pioneers from the east began to stake their claims close to the South Rim. There has been tension ever since between this new permanent population, determined to survive in such an unforgiving environment, and visitors hoping to find unspoiled wilderness. Broadly speaking, **logging** and **grazing** interests long retained control of the plateau forests, while in the canyon itself most attempts at **mining** were defeated by the difficulty of the terrain, and **tourism** soon proved a far more lucrative proposition.

When the **railroad** first crossed northern Arizona in 1882, visitors were taken by stagecoach from **Peach Springs**, the nearest station to the Grand Canyon, to stay at the *Diamond Creek Hotel* by the river. With the growth of the timber towns to the east, that locality soon declined; by the 1890s, **Flagstaff** was the main terminus, connected to the canyon by three weekly stages. The railroad reached the canyon itself, via a branch line from **Williams,** in September 1901. That triggered the growth of **Grand Canyon Village**, built under the auspices of the Fred Harvey Company, a subsidiary of the Santa Fe Railroad, and dependent on water carried by rail from Del Rio, 120 miles away. The company's grand *El Tovar Hotel* – still the showpiece canyon-edge lodging – opened in January 1905, and its early marketing strategies influence the experience of Canyon visitors to this day. Following an internal memo to "get some Indians to the Canyon at once," the Hopi House souvenir store was built, modeled on the Hopi village of Old Oraibi, and staffed with Hopi craftspersons. Similarly, Navajo weavers were exhorted to produce rugs to suit tourist tastes, using previously unfavored "earth" colors such as brown. Pseudo-Pueblo architecture became the dominant theme, in line with the vision of architect Mary Jane Colter (see p.58).

Late nineteenth-century proposals to create a **Grand Canyon National Park** aroused vigorous local opposition. In due course, however, naturalist **John Muir** – who had earlier championed Yosemite Valley in California, and declared the Grand Canyon to be "unearthly … as if you had found it after death, on some other star" – found a powerful ally in **Theodore Roosevelt**. Presidential authority only entitled him to protect sites of historical, rather than geological, interest, so Roosevelt used the pretext of preserving Ancestral Puebloan ruins to proclaim the creation of **Grand Canyon National Monument** in 1908. Having failed to persuade the Supreme Court to overrule the president, Arizonan politicians finally came around to the idea of a national park after Arizona achieved statehood in 1912. Even so, by the time the boundaries of the new **Grand Canyon National Park** were fixed in 1919, they had trimmed away large tracts of grazing land. The park covered only around 1000 square miles, and included just 56 miles of the actual canyon.

Meanwhile, tourism to the South Rim had not stood still. **Ralph Cameron** had been accumulating bogus mining claims along the South Rim since 1890, which enabled him to charge a toll of $1 to riders using the Bright Angel Trail. In 1905, he built his own hotel alongside the railroad terminal, thereby forcing the Fred Harvey Company to relocate the station out of sight of their upstart rival. When the national park came into being, Cameron continued to be a thorn in its side. Elected to the US Senate in 1920, he spent a few years hacking at the park's budget before his mining claims were eventually invalidated. His presence had by then spurred the development of the **Kaibab Trail**, stretching from rim to rim by way of the Kaibab suspension footbridge. Plans to pave that route never materialized, but a small enlargement of the park in 1927 permitted the construction of a road east to Desert View, which, with the completion in 1928 of the **Navajo Bridge** across Marble Canyon, reduced what had been a 600-mile drive between the rims to a more feasible 215 miles.

The first **automobile** showed up at the canyon in 1902, despite running out of gas twenty miles short. By 1926, more visitors were coming by car than by train, and Flagstaff was once again the major point of access. By 1938, the throngs of visitors had made advance reservations for both mule rides and lodging necessary. Annual visitor numbers first exceeded a million in 1956, and ran at over five million through most of the 1990s. Anticipating that visitation would continue to increase at an exponential rate, the park service drew up plans around the turn of the millennium to build a huge new tourism complex close to the South Rim, to be known as "**Canyon Forest Village**," and also a **light rail** network. In fact, however, numbers have now dropped back down below five million – no one's sure why, though the downward trend has continued since the September 11 attacks – and the political will to make major changes seems to have disappeared.

Environmental issues

The biggest issues to face the Grand Canyon during the twentieth century centered on the **environment**. The 1935 damming of Black Canyon, just west of the Grand

Canyon, by the **Hoover Dam**, inspired a spree of dam-building in the western US. Bureau of Reclamation proposals included damming the Green River in northwest Colorado, the San Juan in New Mexico, and the Colorado itself in both Bridge Canyon in Arizona and Utah's Glen Canyon. The axe eventually fell on **Glen Canyon**, which, although it had entranced John Wesley Powell, remained almost completely unknown; in fact, Sierra Club director **David Brower** campaigned for both Glen Canyon and the Grand Canyon to be dammed in preference to the Green River site, which lay within Dinosaur National Monument.

On the day that Glen Canyon Dam first stopped the Colorado River, in January 1963, President Kennedy's Secretary of the Interior, Stewart Udall – the great-grandson of John D Lee, of Lees Ferry fame – announced plans to build two more dams within the Grand Canyon. By now, the Sierra Club had realized its mistake – yet promptly made another. This time it argued for building coal-burning power stations instead of hydroelectric dams. The Navajo Nation, imagining that nuclear power might soon render its mineral resources worthless, decided to cash in by permitting the construction of the Navajo Generating Station outside Page, which was completed in 1976. Pollution from that plant remained barely controlled until 1999, when scrubbers were finally installed under the provisions of the federal Clean Air Act. At least no further dams have been built, with opposition from environmentalists eventually killing plans to construct the **Bridge Canyon Dam** on the Hualapai reservation in the 1970s, despite the eagerness of the Hualapai themselves (see p.191).

By the time Lake Powell was filled to the brim, in June 1980, David Brower was calling his support for Glen Canyon Dam "the greatest sin I have ever committed." Since 1996, the Sierra Club has campaigned for Lake

Powell to be drained so that both Glen Canyon and the Grand Canyon can regenerate. It's easy to forget that although the Grand Canyon has not itself been dammed, the character of the Colorado River within it, and thus the ecology of the inner canyon, has been utterly changed by Glen Canyon Dam (see p.278).

Commercial **logging** and **mining** were finally banned from the Grand Canyon when the park boundaries were redrawn and enlarged in 1975. President Clinton also followed Roosevelt's tradition in 2000 by using his presidential prerogative to protect two vast enclaves within the overall Grand Canyon ecosystem, proclaiming the 294,000-acre **Vermilion Cliffs National Monument** (see p.118) and the million-acre **Grand Canyon–Parashant National Monument** (see p.140). Fears persist, however, that **uranium mining** may return to areas just outside the park along the South Rim, as evidenced by the Havasupai concern over the prospective **Canyon Mine** (see p.179).

The geology of the Grand Canyon

T he merest glance at the Grand Canyon reveals that this vast landscape is composed of layer upon layer of different kinds of rock, each with its own distinct color and texture. Some layers form thin stripes, some sheer cliffs hundreds of feet tall; others vary in width, and in places may disappear altogether. Taken as a whole, however, the consistency of these horizontal bands, identifiable throughout the canyon, acts as a reassuring counterpoint to the bewildering complexity of the terrain, with its tangle of buttes, mesas, and side canyons.

Geologists often talk of "reading" the various strata like a book, which tells the story not only of the canyon but of the earth itself. What makes the Grand Canyon such a good read is that it's very rare for such an even, undisturbed set of rock layers to exist so high above sea level, and unique for them to be exposed to view to such an amazing depth. Common sense tells us that the deepest layers are the oldest, and the saga does indeed start at the bottom, almost **two billion** years ago. What's less obvious, however, is that in geological terms the canyon is not old, but very **new**. The processes that put all those buried strata into place were entirely separate from those that created the canyon itself.

At various times, the spot that now holds the Grand Canyon has lain underwater, or at the edge of a very different continent, or even embedded in the planet's one massive super-continent. As it swirled around the globe, it also spent long periods at the equator. Until less than six million years ago, there was no canyon here. Then the **Colorado Plateau** started to rise, somehow climbing several thousand feet without greatly deforming its thick layers of sedimentary rock, and its many rivers began to cut deeper and deeper.

While scientists still can't decide quite how it happened, the canyon took shape quickly. It had acquired essentially its present form a million years ago, and since then has only burrowed a further fifty feet. Finally, a new phase began in 1963, when the completion of the **Glen Canyon Dam** rendered the Colorado River barely capable of maintaining the canyon, let alone enlarging it.

The story in the stone

Almost every rock layer visible from the rim of the Grand Canyon is **sedimentary**, and was originally deposited on the bed or along the shoreline of some shallow primeval sea. Such rocks can be further subdivided into **sandstone**, which consists mostly of sand, perhaps mixed with a little silt or clay, and cemented with silica or calcite; **limestone**, which is largely biological, made up of dead sea creatures and, especially, their shells; and **mudstone** such as shale and siltstone, carried down to the sea by rivers as mountain ranges rise and fall.

There are two other types of rock in the canyon. **Igneous** – fire-formed – rocks well up from the depths of the earth, both in the ocean along the edges of the lithospheric plates that hold the separate continents, and also via volcanic action on the surface. **Metamorphic** rocks are those that have been altered by heat and pressure over time, which happens especially when continents collide.

The oldest rocks of all, in the **Vishnu Schist** layer, are both igneous and metamorphic. This gnarled, dense bed of dark granite – which is not only exposed at river level, but forms the entire thousand-foot-deep **Inner Gorge** – was originally deposited by lava flows 1.84 billion years ago. (While that makes it old by any standard, the oldest visible rocks on the planet, dating back almost four billion years, lie along the shore of the Great Slave Lake in Canada's Northwest Territories.) The Vishnu Schist subsequently metamorphosed when the seabed on which it rested collided with what became the North American continent around 1.7 billion years ago, and the schist became threaded with veins of pink Zoroaster Granite. Life had already established its first tentative foothold on earth during this **Precambrian era**, but no fossils could hope to survive such an inferno of molten rock.

In parts but not all of the canyon, a further medley of both igneous and sedimentary Precambrian rocks lies immediately above the Vishnu Schist. Where it exists, as for example in the vicinity of Desert View, this **Grand Canyon Supergroup** is immediately recognizable because, unusually for the canyon, the normally horizontal strata are tilted at a twenty-degree angle.

If we think of each layer as being a "page" of the canyon's great geological textbook, then we have to bear in mind that many pages are missing altogether. Just as there are eras when new strata are being added, there are also periods, like our own, when not only is nothing new being deposited, but pre-existing layers are exposed to the elements and erode away. Such gaps in the record are known as **unconformities**. The most obvious, dubbed the **Great Unconformity** by John Wesley Powell, is the line that

THE GEOLOGY OF THE GRAND CANYON

separates the Precambrian rocks of the Inner Gorge from the sedimentary strata of the **Paleozoic** era above. It's especially striking when the Grand Canyon Supergroup is absent, in which case it represents an interlude of a billion years.

During the Paleozoic epoch, which lasted from 550 million until 250 million years ago, much of what's now North America was covered by water. The oldest Paleozoic groups consist of three consecutive strata – the **Tapeats Sandstone**, the **Bright Angel Shale**, and the **Muav Limestone** – which collectively form the **Tonto Group**, as seen in the broad Tonto Platform at the four-thousand-foot elevation. Each in turn was created further offshore, which is thought to reflect increasingly high water levels, possibly due to melting polar ice caps.

Next comes another unconformity, followed by the **Temple Butte Formation** from the Devonian era, and the distinctive **Redwall Limestone** layer, responsible for the 500-foot cliffs that pose such a problem on many inner-canyon trails. Despite its namesake color, the Redwall is not naturally red, but dyed by leaching from the iron-rich rocks of the thick **Supai Group** above. These mingle limestone, sandstone, shale and siltstone, testifying to an era when the coastline repeatedly rose and fell.

The Paleozoic ends with a final four-part sequence: the **Hermit Shale**, left by rivers on a coastal plain; the pale **Coconino Sandstone**, the solidified dunes from a windswept ancient desert; the **Toroweap Formation**, a mixture of limestone and shale that once more lay beneath the waves; and the **Kaibab Formation**, a similar but harder blend that tops the canyon rim all the way from Lees Ferry to the heart of the national park.

And there the story stops, roughly 250 million years ago, at which point all the world's land masses were jammed together to form a giant super-continent now known as **Pangea**. Although only the tiniest traces of anything newer survive at the Grand Canyon, it's thought that another four or five thousand feet of rock was deposited on top, during the Mesozoic era. Those are the rocks that form the **Navajo Sandstone** of Arizona's spectacular Canyon de Chelly, and the multicolored shales of the nearby **Painted Desert**. The canyon is rich in marine fossils, but it holds nothing from the age of the dinosaurs, which ended a mere 65 million years ago.

Those final blank pages do hold one last footnote, however. A series of **lava cascades** inundated the western canyon during the last three million years, culminating around 1.2 million years ago when the largest flow created the **Prospect Dam**. That backed up the Colorado into a lake that stretched even further upstream than the modern Lake Powell, and took around twenty thousand years to erode away. Volcanoes remain active in the vicinity; **Sunset Crater**, near Flagstaff (see p.159), last erupted in 1065 AD.

The power of erosion

The physical mechanisms that have sculpted the Grand Canyon are well understood, not least because they can still be observed in action today. All fall under the broad heading of **erosion**, with **water** as the dominant force. Whatever intuition might suggest, however, the Colorado River alone did not carve the canyon. The river only operates at river level, so while it's responsible for the **depth** of the canyon – and continues to scour its way deeper – it did little to create its **width**. The fantastic pyramids and mesas that tower above the central gorge are the result of the interplay of water, wind, and gravity, and extreme cycles of heat and cold.

Erosion is often pictured as a gradual process, under which grains of sand tumble one by one from the rim. In fact, the canyon has been shaped to a much greater extent by cataclysmic events, and none more so than **flash floods**.

The very fact that the Grand Canyon is located in a desert means that what rain does fall can have a disproportionate impact. There's little soil cover to absorb the monsoon-like thunderstorms that hit the region each year, especially in late July and August. Instead they pour onto bare stone, and quickly gather into storm channels that feed in turn into side canyons and the main canyon. Vast quantities of mud and rock are picked up and swept along in these violent upheavals, widening the old routes down to the river and battering out new ones.

An even more fearsome phenomenon is the **debris flow**, in which a morass of gravel, stone and sand becomes sufficiently sodden after rains that it begins to flow like concrete. Such flows occur somewhere in the canyon roughly twice every year. One created Crystal Rapid in 1966; another, in Monument Creek in 1984, threw boulders weighing as much 37 tons each into the Colorado.

Subtler activity can produce equally spectacular results. Some of the water that falls as rain or snow finds its way into cracks in the earth. As it subsequently freezes and expands, the water chisels vast slabs of stone away from their moorings, unseen and unsuspected until one day a mighty rockfall shatters the peace of the canyon.

Many of the **side canyons** in which so much of this activity takes place follow courses that were originally created by **earthquakes**, and only later widened by water. Major cracks include the **Bright Angel Fault**, which made possible the "Corridor" hiking trails between the South and North rims, and the **Toroweap Fault** downstream, and seismic action, including the occasional earthquake, still continues. The side canyons tend to be so barren and dry that visitors are inclined to think of them as somehow peripheral to the Grand Canyon proper; see them roar into life after a storm, and you'll be in no doubt as to the important part they've played in its creation.

THE GEOLOGY OF THE GRAND CANYON

The effects of erosion vary according to the different rock strata. **Cliffs** are usually composed of sandstone or limestone that's been deposited in broad bands and erodes only slowly, whereas **slopes** form from constantly crumbling shales. Assorted combinations of rock, piled up like a layer-cake and then eroding at differing speeds, have resulted in the bizarre monuments so conspicuous toward the eastern end of the canyon. Broad, flat, hard-capped **mesas** erode to form smaller **buttes**, taller than they are wide, or potentially the pyramids known at the Grand Canyon as **temples**. It was Clarence Dutton, a student of comparative religion who wrote the first Geological Survey report on the canyon in 1881, who started the custom of naming prominent canyon features – **Brahma Temple**, **Shiva Temple**, **Vishnu Temple**, and so on – for religious architecture. His tradition was followed by later cartographers such as François Matthes, who named **Krishna Shrine** and **Walhalla Plateau**.

To return finally to the Colorado River, even if it hasn't been so very instrumental as an erosive force, the crucial role it *has* played is to carry all the debris away. It would take around a thousand cubic miles of rock to fill in the Grand Canyon as we see it today; and that's how much the Colorado has taken away. Originally the debris was all deposited toward the river mouth in the Gulf of California, thus renewing the cycle of sedimentation. After 1935, the Colorado set about filling in **Lake Mead**, behind the Hoover Dam. What now worries scientists is that the Colorado simply isn't itself anymore. Flash floods still sweep the side canyons and hurl debris into the Colorado, but the cold steady stream that's allowed through the Glen Canyon Dam no longer experiences surges of its own, and it no longer has the brute strength necessary to clear away the obstacles thrown into its path. Any year now, some new debris flow may create a monster rapid that the river can't remove.

THE GEOLOGY OF THE GRAND CANYON

The creation of the canyon

Despite their success in explaining how its building blocks were put in place, and even how they were subsequently eroded away again, geologists have yet to agree how the canyon itself came into being. At least they know what set the ball rolling: the **Laramide Orogeny**, which began at the end of the Mesozoic era, 65 million years ago. An "orogeny" is an ongoing period of upheaval and mountain-building; this one, caused by the Pacific plate colliding with the North American plate and slipping beneath it, was primarily responsible for creating the Rocky Mountains, but also had the effect of delineating the **Colorado Plateau**. Later on, within the last five or six million years, that plateau has been rapidly lifted several thousand feet higher. As it has risen, its rivers, the Colorado amongst them, have become incised ever more deeply into the earth.

The crucial mystery, however, is that the Colorado Plateau in the Grand Canyon region is not flat. It's an enormous hill, known as the **Kaibab Plateau** from a Paiute word meaning "mountain with no peak," which slopes southwards from a ridge that runs roughly a dozen miles north of the North Rim, more or less along the national park boundary. Thus the Colorado has eaten away a chunk of the hillside, around a third of the way up the southern slope – which explains why the North Rim is a thousand feet higher than the South. The pivotal point in the course of the modern Colorado comes when it hits the Kaibab Plateau, close to Desert View, and rather than veering away, perhaps to the southeast, turns west instead and cuts directly into it.

Why, or how, the Colorado River slices straight through that hill has long taxed the scientific imagination. The oldest serious theory proposed that the Colorado was what's called an "antecedent" river, which has always followed its modern course, and simply remained in place as the plateau rose around it. A more subtle refinement describes a process of "superposition," suggesting that the river previously ran atop new, even layers of sediment that had smothered the hills and uplifts we see today, and that when the plateau rose, it wore away those upper layers to reveal the hills, including the Kaibab Plateau, that we find so puzzling today. The trouble with both theories is that it can be proved that the Colorado does not predate the recent uplift, nor the canyon; they have all grown up together.

All the hypotheses currently in favor argue for some form of **"stream piracy,"** in which the Colorado River originally followed some other course, but was later "captured" by another river and began to flow in that direction instead. Such a capture might have occurred when a powerful stream, at the head of its own canyon, eventually cut so far back that it breached the stone barrier that separated it from the Colorado. The Colorado would then rush through, abandoning its own course and usurping this alternative channel.

While it has been shown that until five million years ago, the ancestral Colorado River did indeed skirt the Kaibab Plateau, it's not known quite where it went. Suggestions that it used to flow down the gorge of the Little Colorado to meet the Rio Grande have largely been discounted due to lack of evidence, as has the idea that all northern Arizona's rivers may once have flowed in the opposite direction. It's now thought most likely that the Colorado circled the southern edge of the Kaibab and then continued northwest. As ground levels to the southwest subsided, in tandem with the uplift of the Colorado Plateau, new rivers began to flow down to the Gulf of California. In some long-disappeared spot, one such river eventually captured, and thus became, the Colorado. The Grand Canyon was born.

THE GEOLOGY OF THE GRAND CANYON

Flora and fauna

onsidering that it measures almost three hundred miles in length, and ranges eight thousand feet in depth from the highest point on the North Rim down to the lowest elevation at Lake Mead, it's hardly surprising that the Grand Canyon is home to a tremendous assortment of plant and animal life. Naturally, all share one basic fact in common: they're adapted to survive in a **desert**, where the low rainfall, of around fifteen inches per year on the South Rim and twice that on the North, ensures that the soil cover is poor where it exists at all. Within those parameters, however, the range of life forms and environments is breathtaking, with such treats in store for visitors as the spectacle of an amazing **Californian condor** soaring above the rim, and the lush hidden oases that punctuate the cactus-studded plateaus of the inner canyon.

It was at the Grand Canyon, with its clearly stratified layers, that scientists first realized that just as different groups of plants and animals are to be encountered between the equator and the poles, so too are different collections of species found at the various levels of a mountainside or canyon. The crucial factor is, of course, **temperature**. In the canyon, altitude substitutes for latitude; the higher the elevation, the cooler the temperature.

The first scientist to describe and name the distinct "**life zones**" was Clinton Merriam of the US Biological Survey. After visiting the Grand Canyon in 1889, he announced that its range of habitats corresponded to that experienced in a trip from the deserts of Mexico to the forests of the Canadian mountains. His work remains the basis for accounts of the canyon's wildlife to this day, though, as he pointed out, much more than just elevation determines what will survive where. The temperature at any one spot also varies according to how much direct **sunlight** it receives, which itself depends on the angle of the slope and the direction in which it faces; localized **moisture**, from springs or streams; and how exposed it is to the currents of hot and cold air that rise and fall within the canyon.

Early explorers imagined that miraculous creatures might lurk in the canyon's recesses. Sadly, twentieth-century expeditions disproved tales of tiny horses, finding only some rather stunted and very thirsty ones, and of "Lost Worlds" atop such lone, isolated summits as Shiva Temple. The canyon does, however, offer some fascinating cases of **divergent evolution**, such as the distinct species of squirrel to be found on the North and South rims.

The North Rim

At between eight and nine thousand feet above sea level, the highest portions of Grand Canyon National Park, along and just back from the **North Rim**, belong to the **Boreal Zone**. As in the forests of Canada, the tree population here consists largely of **aspen**, **spruce** and **fir**, though higher elevations also hold **Douglas fir** – which is not a true fir but is capable of growing 130 feet tall – while **ponderosa pines** appear closer to the rim. Relatively high precipitation has resulted in richer soil, and the dense woodlands of the plateau are interspersed with Alpine **meadows**. These support wildflowers such as asters and sunflowers, and also hold burrowing creatures like weasels and voles, which in turn attract their own predators.

In the hundred years since Roosevelt first protected it within a national monument, the ecology of the North Rim has been particularly affected by park-service attempts at management. The long-standing policy of suppressing **wildfires** has had an adverse effect on the ponderosas. Without the natural fires that should sweep through regularly to eliminate needles and brush from the forest floor, debris accumulates to levels where it can fuel a major conflagration that burns long enough to kill the pines. In recent years, the park has moved toward allowing natural fires to blaze away – even though the charred landscape spoils the look of the place for visitors – and setting its own "controlled burns."

A notorious example of early techniques of **wildlife** management centers on the **mule deer** of the North Rim. Roosevelt's priority in "protecting" the deer was to preserve them for the sport of hunters such as himself. Natural predators like mountain lions, wolves and coyotes were therefore to be eliminated; a single warden, James Owens, shot 532 lions in twelve years. History has long recorded that the deer population then mushroomed from four thousand to a hundred thousand, and stripped the Kaibab Plateau bare before starving to death en masse during the winter of 1924–25. Although those figures are now being questioned, with scientists suggesting that such boom-and-bust cycles may be a normal feature of wild deer herds, the park service has abandoned the idea of culling predators, and hunting is no longer permitted. The wolves never returned – as yet, there's been no move to reintroduce them, as at Yellowstone – but there are now thought to be around a hundred lions on the North Rim, as well as plentiful coyote.

The South Rim

A thousand feet lower than the North Rim, the **South Rim** is in what's called the **Transitional Zone**. Here spruce and fir give way to **ponderosa pines**, interspersed with such species as **Gambel oak**, the only tree to lose its leaves in winter amid all the canyon's evergreens.

The largest inhabitants of the ponderosa forest are **elk**, for which, for example, the only pure ponderosa stand on the South Rim itself, near Grandview Point, is a favored haunt. Among smaller species, which include skunks, chipmunks, rabbits and porcupines, perhaps the most ubiquitous is the **Abert squirrel**, which exists in mutual dependence with the ponderosa, eating its bark, pollen and seeds; by failing to find all the seeds it buries, the squirrel unwittingly plants new generations of trees. In the best-known instance of how distinct species have evolved on opposite sides of the canyon, the corresponding **Kaibab squirrel** is only found on the North Rim. Once the two populations were separated by the river, no further interbreeding could take place. Both species have tasseled ears, but the Abert squirrel also has a reddish back and a dark tail with a white underside, while the Kaibab squirrel is dark gray with a white bushy tail.

Below the ponderosas comes the stunted "**pigmy forest**" of **pinyon** (also spelled pinon) pine and Utah **juniper** that's characteristic of the **Upper Sonoran** zone, which starts above the rim on the South Rim, but beneath it on the North Rim. Each of these gnarled, desiccated trees, which grow to a maximum of between twenty and thirty feet and live for hundreds of years, depends for survival on its own attendant **bird** species. The pinyon jay harvests and buries nuts from the pinyon, while Townsend's solitaire eats juniper berries and then excretes the seeds they contain.

Just to illustrate that the demarcation lines between these various zones seldom strictly follow the contours on the map, small groups of Douglas firs, normally found at much higher elevations, can be seen in north-facing alcoves below the South Rim, while if you hike down from the North Rim, you'll find that ponderosa reappear at cooler spots below the pinyon-juniper level.

The inner canyon

The pinyon-juniper forest thrives between elevations of approximately 7500 feet down to 4000 feet, which means it extends far below the rim on both sides of the canyon. While the plant and animal life of the inner canyon remains within the broad category of the Upper Sonoran zone as far down as the Tonto Platform, as conditions become hotter the pinyon and juniper are progressively replaced by even drier species.

First come the **prickly-pear** cactuses so noticeable on the Bright Angel Trail, and flowering shrubs such as cliffrose and Apache plume. Soon the landscape is dominated by desert scrub, and especially **blackbrush**, so named because its stems turn a deep black when wet. The Tonto Platform is also scattered with agave, yucca, and mesquite. Small **mammals** like mice and shrews are abundant, though as most are nocturnal they're rarely seen by visitors. Snakes, too, come out at night, most notably the pink-hued and poisonous **Grand Canyon rattlesnake**, which is unique to the inner canyon. (Two distinct but related species are to be found along either rim, the Hopi rattlesnake atop the South Rim and the Great Basin rattlesnake on the north side.)

Around five hundred **desert bighorn** sheep, which grow up to six feet in length, inhabit remote side canyons. Because no domestic sheep have ever been introduced into the region, this remains a remarkably pristine population, free from the imported diseases that have decimated bighorn numbers elsewhere in the West. For many years, they shared their range with wild descendants of the

donkeys released by prospectors around 1900, but very few donkeys now remain. To protect grazing for the bighorn, the park service killed thousands of burros, and eventually, after protests from wildlife campaigners, airlifted the rest out by helicopter in 1980.

Wherever **water** is present in the inner canyon, the picture becomes very different. Majestic **willows** and **cottonwoods** stand beside natural springs and tributary streams such as Bright Angel Creek; **hummingbirds** and **canyon wrens** dart through the air; mosses and maidenhair ferns cling to damp crevices; and there are even **treefrogs**, preyed upon by skunks and racoons.

The **Lower Sonoran** zone, which starts below the Tonto Platform, is home to the very hardiest of desert survivors. Hikers along the central Corridor Trails experience little of this world, as where the sheer walls of the Inner Gorge are breached at all, it's usually by water courses that have their own microenvironments. Toward the western end of the canyon, however, where elevations are lower and broad, dry side canyons reach right to the river, the flora and fauna are significantly different. Sadly, you won't encounter anything as distinctive as the multi-armed saguaro cactuses found in the Sonoran Desert of southern Arizona, but many characteristic species are present, including **kangaroo rats**, so finely adapted to the desert that they never need to drink at all, **scorpions**, the large brown lizards known as **chuckwallas**, and **kingsnakes**.

The Colorado River

The banks of the Colorado form a **riparian** environment of the kind described above, lined with rich vegetation, alive with insects and amphibians, and a magnet for whole echelons of predators. However, the river is now the least natural part of the canyon; nowhere in the Grand Canyon has the human impact had a more dramatic effect.

The Colorado today is a very different creature to the river that flowed through the Grand Canyon before the completion of the **Glen Canyon Dam** in 1963. It used to range in temperature from close to freezing in winter up to as much as 80°F (27°C) in summer. Now it remains a chilly, unvarying 48°F (9°C) year-round. What's more, where formerly the river was charged with colossal quantities of silt, and subject to massive floods, it now runs almost crystal-clear at flow rates that fluctuate within a much more limited spectrum, according to the demand for electricity from the dam.

The effect of those changes has been to eliminate four of the canyon's eight native **fish** species, including the six-foot **squawfish**, and leave the remainder barely clinging to life. The once ubiquitous **humpback chub** can now only find the murky waters it requires for spawning by swimming up the Little Colorado River. It has been supplanted, and often literally eaten, by species introduced for sport, such as **rainbow trout**, **carp**, and **striped bass**. **Crayfish** too, introduced as food for the trout, are now thriving, while **bald eagles** have turned up to prey on the trout in turn.

Before the dam went up, regular flooding ensured that the banks of the Colorado were unable to sustain growth below the highwater mark. Now they've become lined by coyote willow trees, and almost taken over by alien **tamarisk**. Many riverside beaches have disappeared altogether, as any sand that's swept away by the river can't be replaced by the silt that now settles instead to the bottom of Lake Powell. A much-publicized **artificial flood** in 1996, engineered by simply turning up the valves at the dam for a few days, briefly regenerated several beaches, but they were soon washed away again. The park service is constantly putting forward proposals for more such floods, more carefully designed to produce positive results within the canyon, while vigorous political campaigns are aimed at tearing down the dam altogether (see p.275).

Books

The following is a selection of books that proved useful, interesting or entertaining during the writing of this guide. A large proportion are only available in the US, and most of those you'd be lucky to find in bookstores anywhere outside the immediate vicinity of the Grand Canyon.

Bruce Babbitt (ed) *Grand Canyon – An Anthology* (Northland Press, o/p). A collection of classic canyon writing, put together in 1978, that includes firsthand exploration accounts from centuries gone by and some entertaining, seldom-seen pieces by the likes of Theodore Roosevelt and J B Priestley. Well worth seeking out.

Pedro de Castañeda *The Journey of Coronado* (Dover). An invaluable historic document; the eye-witness journals of a Spaniard who accompanied Coronado into the Southwest in 1540, including the first written report of the Grand Canyon.

Christopher M Coder *An Introduction to Grand Canyon Prehistory*; **Rose Houk** *An Introduction to Grand Canyon Ecology*; **L Greer Price** *An Introduction to Grand Canyon Geology* (All Grand Canyon Association). These three slim, very readable and beautifully illustrated volumes, sold individually or as a discounted set in the national-park bookstores, jointly form an ideal introduction to the canyon.

Edward Dolnick *Down The Great Unknown* (Harper Collins). Deft retelling of the saga of John Wesley Powell's first canyon voyage that takes great pains to make it all intelligible to modern readers, with a thick and fast flow of analogies.

Colin Fletcher *The Man Who Walked Through Time* (Vintage Books). Enjoyable account by the first man to hike the full length of the Grand Canyon.

Philip L Fradkin *A River No More* (University of California Press). The definitive account of the intricate and shadowy political maneuvrings that went into the ultimate taming of the Colorado River, from John Wesley Powell to the water-management issues of today.

Michael P Ghiglieri *Canyon* (University of Arizona Press). A highly experienced river guide reveals the lore of the Colorado River, mile by mile; an enjoyable read, even if he tells a bit more about his own personal life than many might prefer.

Michael P Ghiglieri and Thomas M Myers *Over The Edge: Death in Grand Canyon* (Puma Press). In their bid to account for the demise of every single person known to have died within the Grand Canyon, the authors transcend the merely morbid to throw fascinating light on every aspect of the canyon's history, and provide masses of useful advice on how to avoid becoming another fatality. The morbid stuff's good too.

J Donald Hughes *In The House of Stone and Light* (Grand Canyon Natural History Association). A comprehensive human history of the Grand Canyon in words and pictures, filled with fascinating yarns about the early days of tourism.

Robert H Keller and Michael F Turek *American Indians and National Parks* (University of Arizona Press). What happens when the federal park system appropriates land from its former indigenous inhabitants; the Grand Canyon and Pipe Spring National Monument are among examples considered in great detail.

John D Lee *Mormonism Unveiled* (Fierra Blanca

Publications). In his "Life and Confession," John Lee, of Lees Ferry fame, doesn't quite tell all he knows – like where he buried the gold – but there's a lot of eye-opening material in here.

Russell Martin *A Story That Stands Like A Dam* (Henry Holt). Meticulously chronicled indictment of the West's last great dam, which inundated Glen Canyon in the 1960s.

Lisa Michaels *Grand Ambition* (W W Norton, US; Hodder & Stoughton, UK). Gripping novelistic reconstruction of a true-life romantic mystery: just what did happen to honeymooners Glen and Bessie Hyde in the winter of 1928, when they tried to become the first couple to row down the Grand Canyon?

Barbara J Morehouse *A Place Called Grand Canyon* (University of Arizona Press). Fascinating academic analysis of how the Grand Canyon has been defined and exploited.

Stephen Plog *Ancient Peoples of the Southwest* (Thames and Hudson). Probably the best single-volume history of the pre-Hispanic Southwest, packed with diagrams and color photographs.

John Wesley Powell *The Exploration of the Colorado River and Its Canyons* (Dover). Powell certainly embellished his original journals in adapting the details of his first epic journey down the Colorado for public consumption, but they still make exhilarating reading.

Stephen J Pyne *How The Canyon Became Grand* (Penguin). Historical analysis of how the canyon has been perceived over the centuries, with especial reference to the artists of the late Victorian era. Some of the ideas are intriguing, even if the prose style isn't.

Marc Reisner *Cadillac Desert* (Penguin). The damning saga of the twentieth-century damming of the West.

Jeremy Schmidt *Grand Canyon National Park – A Natural History Guide* (Houghton Mifflin). A superb single-volume account of the canyon's environment, ecology, and geological origins.

Stephen Trimble *The People* (SAR Press). Excellent introduction to all the Native American groups of the Southwest, bringing the history up to date with contemporary interviews.

Stewart L Udall *Majestic Journey* (Museum of New Mexico Press). Lively, well-illustrated chronicle of Francisco Coronado's 1540–42 *entrada* into the Southwest, written by a former US Secretary of the Interior.

John C Van Dyke *The Grand Canyon of the Colorado* (University of Utah Press). First published in 1920, Van Dyke's work represents a determined attempt to apply academic rigor to developing a new aesthetic for appreciating the Grand Canyon; it's more interesting than it sounds.

Ted J Warner (ed) *The Domínguez-Escalante Journal* (University of Utah Press). The extraordinary diary of the two Franciscan friars who crossed Utah in 1776 in search of a new route to California, and came back via the Grand Canyon (see p.120).

Richard White *It's Your Misfortune and None of My Own* (University of Oklahoma Press). Dense, authoritative and all-embracing history of the American West that debunks the notion of the rugged pioneer by stressing the role of the federal government.

INDEX

D

E

F

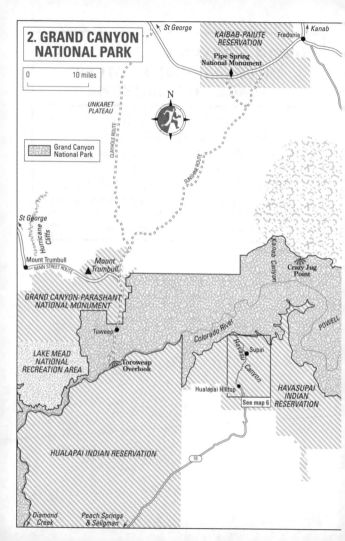

2. GRAND CANYON NATIONAL PARK

0   10 miles

Grand Canyon National Park

St George

Kanab

KAIBAB-PAIUTE RESERVATION

Fredonia

Pipe Spring National Monument

UNKARET PLATEAU

N

CLAYHOLE ROUTE

SUNSHINE ROUTE

St George

Hurricane Cliffs

Mount Trumbull

MAIN STREET ROUTE

Mount Trumbull

GRAND CANYON-PARASHANT NATIONAL MONUMENT

Kanab Canyon

Crazy Jug Point

POWELL

Tuweep

Colorado River

Havasu Canyon

Supai

LAKE MEAD NATIONAL RECREATION AREA

Toroweap Overlook

Hualapai Hilltop

See map 6

HAVASUPAI INDIAN RESERVATION

HUALAPAI INDIAN RESERVATION

18

Diamond Creek

Peach Springs & Seligman

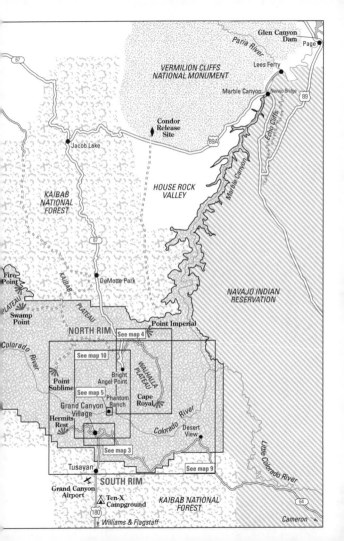

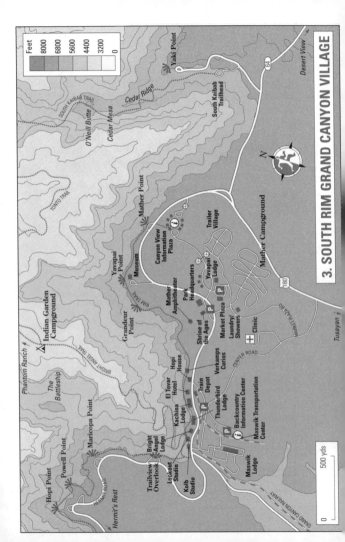

3. SOUTH RIM GRAND CANYON VILLAGE

Feet	
8000	
6800	
5600	
4400	
3200	
0	

Yaki Point

South Kaibab Trailhead

SOUTH KAIBAB TRAIL

Cedar Ridge

O'Neill Butte

Cedar Mesa

Desert View

64

Mather Point

TONTO TRAIL

N

Yavapai Point

Museum

Canyon View Information Plaza

Trailer Village

Mather Campground

Indian Garden Campground

Grandeur Point

RIM TRAIL

Mather Amphitheater

Park Headquarters

Shrine of the Ages

Yavapai Lodge

P

Market Plaza

Laundry/ Showers

Clinic

180

MARKET PLAZA RD

Tusayan

Phantom Ranch

The Battleship

BRIGHT ANGEL TRAIL

Hopi House

Verkamps Curios

El Tovar Hotel

CENTER ROAD

Maricopa Point

Powell Point

Hopi Point

Train Depot

Kachina Lodge

Thunderbird Lodge

Backcountry Information Center

Maswik Transportation Center

Bright Angel Lodge

Trailview Overlook

Lookout Studio

Kolb Studio

P

P

Maswik Lodge

Hermit's Rest

HERMIT ROAD

GRAND CANYON RAILWAY

0   500 yds

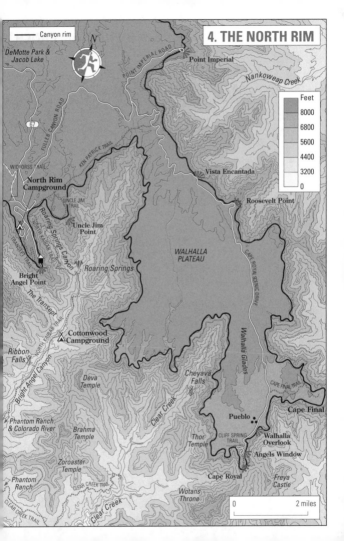

4. THE NORTH RIM

Canyon rim

Feet
8000
6800
5600
4400
3200
0

DeMotte Park & Jacob Lake

Point Imperial

Nankoweap Creek

POINT IMPERIAL ROAD

FULLER CANYON ROAD

KEN PATRICK TRAIL

67

WIDFORSS TRAIL

Vista Encantada

North Rim Campground

Roosevelt Point

UNCLE JIM TRAIL

NORTH KAIBAB TRAIL

Uncle Jim Point

Roaring Springs Canyon

WALHALLA PLATEAU

CAPE ROYAL SCENIC DRIVE

TRANSEPT TRAIL

Bright Angel Point

Roaring Springs

The Transept

Cottonwood Campground

Walhalla Glades

Ribbon Falls

Bright Angel Canyon

Deva Temple

Cheyava Falls

CAPE FINAL TRAIL

Phantom Ranch & Colorado River

Brahma Temple

Clear Creek

Pueblo

Cape Final

CLIFF SPRING TRAIL

Walhalla Overlook

Zoroaster Temple

Thor Temple

Angels Window

Phantom Ranch

CLEAR CREEK TRAIL

Cape Royal

Freya Castle

Wotans Throne

Clear Creek

0   2 miles

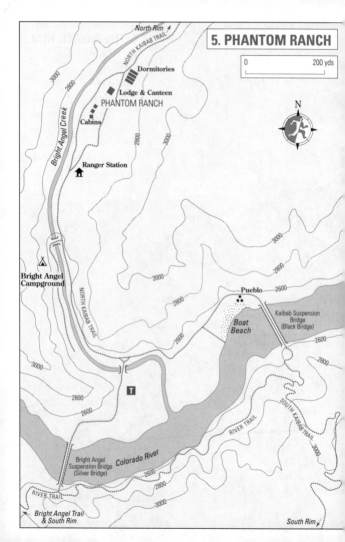

5. PHANTOM RANCH

0   200 yds

North Rim ↗

NORTH KAIBAB TRAIL

Dormitories
Lodge & Canteen
PHANTOM RANCH
Cabins

Bright Angel Creek

Ranger Station

N

NORTH KAIBAB TRAIL

Bright Angel
Campground

3000
2800
3000
2600
2800

Pueblo

Boat
Beach

Kaibab Suspension
Bridge (Black Bridge)

2600

2800

T

RIVER TRAIL

SOUTH KAIBAB TRAIL

3000

Bright Angel
Suspension Bridge
(Silver Bridge)

Colorado River

2600
2800
3000

RIVER TRAIL

Bright Angel Trail
& South Rim ↙

South Rim ↘

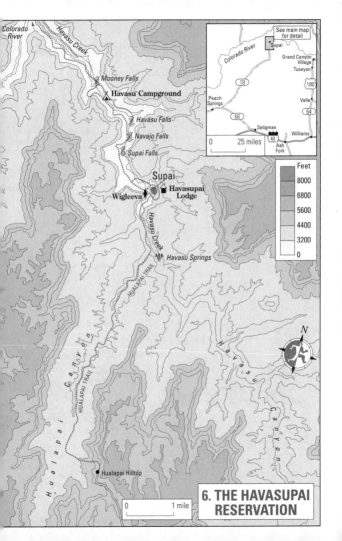

Colorado River

Havasu Creek

Mooney Falls

Havasu Campground

Havasu Falls

Navajo Falls

Supai Falls

Supai

Wigleeva

Havasupai Lodge

Havasu Creek

Havasu Springs

HUALAPAI TRAIL

Hualapai Canyon

HUALAPAI TRAIL

Havasu Canyon

N

Hualapai Hilltop

0   1 mile

6. THE HAVASUPAI RESERVATION

See main map for detail

Supai

Colorado River

Grand Canyon Village

Tusayan

18

Peach Springs

180

Valle

66

64

Seligman

40

Williams

Ash Fork

0   25 miles

Feet

8000

6800

5600

4400

3200

0

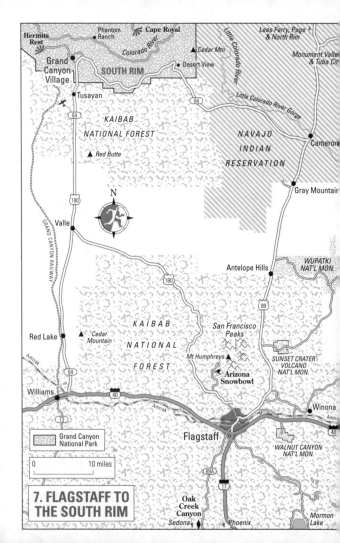

Hermits
Rest

Phantom
Ranch

Cape Royal

Colorado River

Lees Ferry, Page
& North Rim

Monument Valley
& Tuba Cit

Grand
Canyon
Village

SOUTH RIM

▲ Cedar Mtn

Little Colorado River

● Desert View

Little Colorado River Gorge

● Tusayan

(64)

Cameron ●

KAIBAB

NATIONAL FOREST

NAVAJO

INDIAN

RESERVATION

▲ Red Butte

180

Gray Mountain ●

N

Valle ●

180

Antelope Hills ●

89

WUPATKI
NAT'L MON.

GRAND CANYON RAILWAY

Red Lake ●

▲ Cedar
Mountain

KAIBAB

NATIONAL

FOREST

San Francisco
Peaks

Mt Humphreys ▲

Arizona
Snowbowl

SUNSET CRATER
VOLCANO
NAT'L MON.

Amtrak

64

Williams ●

40

Amtrak

Winona ●

Amtr

40

73

Flagstaff

WALNUT CANYON
NAT'L MON.

Grand Canyon
National Park

0   10 miles

89A

17

**7. FLAGSTAFF TO
THE SOUTH RIM**

Oak
Creek
Canyon

Sedona ▲

Phoenix

Mormon
Lake

8. DOWNTOWN FLAGSTAFF

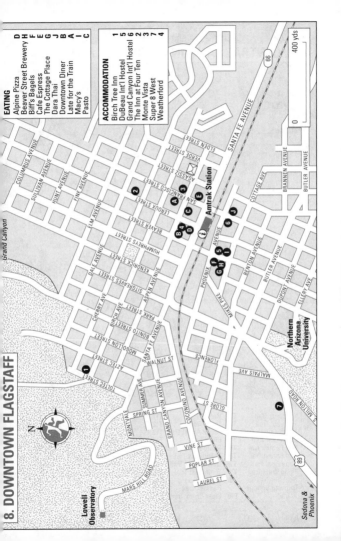

EATING

Alpine Pizza	D
Beaver Street Brewery	H
Biff's Bagels	F
Cafe Espress	E
The Cottage Place	G
Dara Thai	J
Downtown Diner	B
Late for the Train	A
Macy's	I
Pasto	C

ACCOMMODATION

Birch Tree Inn	1
DuBeau Int'l Hostel	5
Grand Canyon Int'l Hostel	6
The Inn at Four Ten	2
Monte Vista	3
Super 8 West	7
Weatherford	4

Grand Canyon

Lowell Observatory

MARS HILL ROAD

Northern Arizona University

Amtrak Station

Sedona & Phoenix

0   400 yds

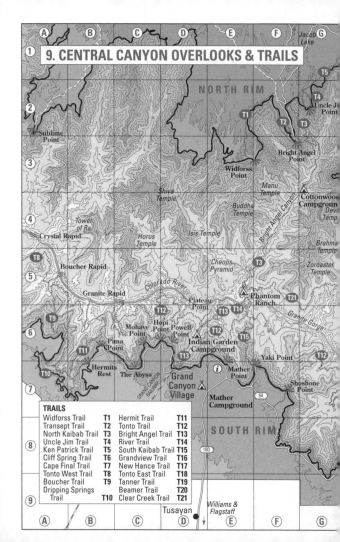

9. CENTRAL CANYON OVERLOOKS & TRAILS

A	B	C	D	E	F	G

NORTH RIM

Jacob Lake

T5

T4
Uncle Ji
Point

T1

T2 T3

Bright Angel
Point

Sublime
Point

Widforss Point

Manu
Temple

Shiva
Temple

Cottonwoo
Campgroun

Buddha
Temple

Deva
Temp

Tower
of Ra

Crystal Rapid

Horus
Temple

Isis Temple

Bright Angel Canyon

Brahma
Temple

T8

Boucher Rapid

Cheops
Pyramid

Zoroaster
Temple

Colorado River

Granite Rapid

T3

Plateau
Point

Phantom
Ranch

T21

Granite Gorge

T9

T12

T13 T14

Mohave
Point

Hopi
Point

Powell
Point

T12

T15

Indian Garden
Campground

T11

Pima
Point

T13

Yaki Point

T12

T10

Hermits
Rest

The Abyss

Grand
Canyon
Village

GRAND CANYON RAILWAY

Mather
Point

Shoshone
Point

Mather
Campground

64

TRAILS

Widforss Trail	T1	Hermit Trail	T11
Transept Trail	T2	Tonto Trail	T12
North Kaibab Trail	T3	Bright Angel Trail	T13
Uncle Jim Trail	T4	River Trail	T14
Ken Patrick Trail	T5	South Kaibab Trail	T15
Cliff Spring Trail	T6	Grandview Trail	T16
Cape Final Trail	T7	New Hance Trail	T17
Tonto West Trail	T8	Tonto East Trail	T18
Boucher Trail	T9	Tanner Trail	T19
Dripping Springs		Beamer Trail	T20
Trail	T10	Clear Creek Trail	T21

SOUTH RIM

180

Williams &
Flagstaff

Tusayan

A	B	C	D	E	F	G

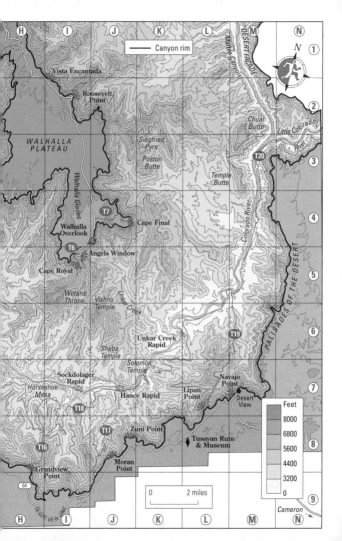

Canyon rim

N

WALHALLA PLATEAU

Vista Encantada

Roosevelt Point

Siegfried Pyre

Poston Butte

Chuar Butte

Little Colorado

Marble Canyon

DESERT FACADE

Temple Butte

T20

Colorado River

Walhalla Glades

T7

Cape Final

Walhalla Overlook

T6

Angels Window

Cape Royal

Wotans Throne

Vishnu Temple

Unkar Creek

PALISADES OF THE DESERT

Sheba Temple

Unkar Creek Rapid

Solomon Temple

T19

Sockdolager Rapid

Horseshoe Mesa

Hance Rapid

Navajo Point

Lipan Point

Desert View

T18

T17

Zuni Point

Tusayan Ruin & Museum

T16

Grandview Point

Moran Point

64

DESERT VIEW DRIVE

0   2 miles

Feet
8000
6800
5600
4400
3200
0

Cameron

H   I   J   K   L   M   N

10. THE CORRIDOR TRAILS

TRAILS

Widforss Trail	T1
Transept Trail	T2
North Kaibab Trail	T3
Uncle Jim Trail	T4
Ken Patrick Trail	T5
Clear Creek Trail	T6
Tonto Trail	T7
Bright Angel Trail	T8
River Trail	T9
South Kaibab Trail	T10
Tonto East Trail	T11

—— Canyon rim

Feet
8000
6400
5600
4400
3200
0

NORTH RIM

Roaring Springs Canyon

Uncle Jim Point

The Transept

Bright Angel Point

Roaring Springs

Widforss Point

Manu Temple

Ribbon Falls

Cottonwood Campground

Buddha Temple

Deva Temple

Isis Temple

Bright Angel Canyon

Brahma Temple

N

Cheops Pyramid

The Box

Zoroaster Temple

Colorado River

Phantom Ranch

Black Bridge

Clear Creek Trail

Plateau Point

Silver Bridge

The Tipoff

Pipe Creek

Colorado River

Hopi Point

Powell Point

Maricopa Point

Indian Garden

Skeleton Point

O'Neill Butte

Mohave Point

Grandeur Point

Yavapai Point

Cedar Ridge

Yaki Point

SOUTH RIM

Grand Canyon Village

Mather Point

Shoshone Point

Mather Campground

0   2 miles